EXCHANGE RATES AND
CORPORATE PERFORMANCE

EXCHANGE RATES AND CORPORATE PERFORMANCE

Edited by

Yakov Amihud
and
Richard M. Levich

NEW YORK UNIVERSITY SALOMON CENTER
Leonard N. Stern School of Business

IRWIN
Professional Publishing

Burr Ridge, IL 60521
New York, NY 10001

Senior sponsoring editor: Amy Hollands Gaber
Project editor: Beth Yates
Production manager: Jon Christopher
Typeface: Times Roman
Printer: Arcata Graphics/Kingsport

Library of Congress Cataloging-in-Publication Data

Exchange rates and corporate performance / edited by Yakov Amihud and
   Richard M. Levich.
      p.   cm.
      "Proceedings of a conference ... sponsored by the New York
   University Salomon Center at the Leonard N. Stern School of Business
   of New York University, and held at NYU on May 1st, 1992"—Foreword.
      ISBN 1–55623–596–8
      1. Foreign exchange rates—Congresses.   2. Corporations—Finance—
   Congresses.   I. Amihud, Yakov, 1947–   .   II. Levich, Richard M.
   III. New York University. Salomon Center.   IV. Leonard N. Stern
   School of Business.
   HG3851.E935   1994
   332.4'56—dc20   93–40725

Printed in the United States of America

1 2 3 4 5 6 7 8 9 0 AGK 0 9 8 7 6 5 4 3

FOREWORD

This book contains the proceedings of a conference on exchange rates effects on corporations, sponsored by the New York University Salomon Center at the Leonard N. Stern School of Business of New York University, and held at NYU on May 1st, 1992. The idea for this conference arose out of the feeling that exchange rate volatility was a powerful force in the 1980s that dominated the environment within which international firms operated. During the first half of the decade, the U.S. dollar exchange rate nearly doubled (on an effective basis against major trading partners) and then fell by about half before the end of the decade. These changes in exchange rates affected companies in many fundamental ways. Firms were forced to consider altering their input sources and the markets in which they sell their products. Some firms were induced to relocate production to other countries. And at all firms, financial policies were tuned to acknowledge changes in exchange rates. The conference provided a stage for scholars and practitioners to present and discuss these issues.

We thank Ingo Walter, the Director of the NYU Salomon Center, who greatly contributed to the planning for the conference, and we acknowledge with gratitude the Center for its financial support. We also thank Mary Jaffier for her efficient handling of the administrative arrangements for the conference. Finally, we thank the authors of the papers and the discussants for contributing their research and ideas to this collection of papers.

LIST OF CONTRIBUTORS

Michael Adler, Columbia University

Yakov Amihud, New York University

John F. O. Bilson, The Chicago Corporation

James N. Bodurtha, Jr., University of Michigan

Stephen J. Brown, New York University

Robert E. Cumby, New York University

Rudiger Dornbusch, MIT

Kenneth A. Froot, Harvard University

Brian C. Gendreau, J. P. Morgan

Ian Giddy, New York University

Philippe Jorion, Columbia University

Michael M. Knetter, Dartmouth College

Maurice D. Levi, University of British Columbia

Richard M. Levich, New York University

Robert N. McCauley, Federal Reserve Bank of New York

Toshiyuki Otsuki, International University of Japan

Marcia B. Whitaker, General Electric Company

Steven A. Zimmer, J. P. Morgan Asset Management

CONTENTS

PART THREE

EXCHANGE RATES AND CORPORATE STRATEGIC MANAGEMENT

CHAPTER 1

EXCHANGE RATES AND CORPORATE PERFORMANCE: INTRODUCTION AND OVERVIEW

Yakov Amihud
Richard M. Levich

INTRODUCTION

In the final years of the Bretton Woods system, debate centered on the effects of moving to a regime of floating exchange rates. Of particular concern was whether the adoption of floating exchange rates would be followed by a substantial increase in exchange rate volatility, and if so, whether this would impose substantial costs on international business activity. Since the breakup of the Bretton Woods system in 1973, exchange rate volatility has increased dramatically, whether measured day-to-day or over longer intervals. And over the same period, we have also experienced exchange rate misalignments (as measured by deviations from Purchasing Power Parity and other long-term equilibrium measures) that were both significant and prolonged.

While exchange rate misalignments and greater volatility of nominal and real exchange rates are stylized empirical regularities of the post-Bretton Woods period, the impact of exchange rates on international business activity has been more elusive to determine. First, consider the impact of *changes in the level* of the exchange rate—simple appreciation or depreciation of a

1

currency's value. The appreciation of the U.S. dollar by nearly 50 percent in real terms over the 1980–1985 period coincided with an increase in the U.S. merchandise trade deficit to nearly $160 billion in 1987. Some U.S. exporters were hit heavily by this period of dollar appreciation, losing market share and profitability to foreign competitors. Caterpillar Tractor, in its battle with Komatsu, is a textbook example. Foreign firms with domestic currency revenues and dollar-denominated costs were also hard hit in this period. Laker Airways, with fuel costs and aircraft financing set in U.S. dollars, wound up in bankruptcy in the early 1980s. On the other hand, some U.S. import competing firms could not use the dollar's sharp depreciation over the 1985–1987 period to gain market share and profits at the expense of foreign firms. For example, U.S. auto companies appeared to allow their prices to rise parallel to Japanese prices during this period.[1]

Second, consider the impact of *greater volatility* in exchange rate changes (relative to expectations). Exchange rate volatility raises the risks in international business, which could raise the cost of entry for importing and exporting firms. Unlike simple exchange rate changes that shift relative prices in favor of some firms and against others, increases in volatility raise costs for both foreign and domestic firms. With reference to the tight bid-ask spreads that usually prevail in the foreign exchange market, it is often argued that the cost of hedging exchange risk in financial transactions is relatively small. But simple option pricing models tell us that hedging costs rise with volatility. Furthermore, in response to volatile *real* exchange rates, firms could spread their production and sourcing activities worldwide. This strategy adds considerably to fixed capital costs and coordination costs, and firms incur setup costs when switching operations between countries in response to changes in exchange rates.[2] In addition, exchange rate volatility makes it more difficult for investors to monitor the firm's performance because it makes the information released by the firm noisy. Optimal resource allocation in the economy is thus hurt, and it is more difficult for firms to attract capital for investment. Finally, exchange rate fluctuations affect not only the cash flows from operations but also the required cost of capital by investors.

Thus, the risk to firms is not simply that exchange rates might rise (or fall) by some amount and remain stuck at this new level, leading to problems as the firm adjusts to the new rate. Rather, the risk is that exchange rates might perpetually be rising (or falling) by indeterminate amounts and for indeterminate periods, leading to ongoing problems of resource allocation, business strategy, and risk management.

While it seems clear that exchange rates ought to affect the performance of firms, the channels through which these effects are felt are numerous and complex. For example, an American firm using imported oil (priced in U.S. dollars) would not notice any cost change associated with a dollar appreciation. But in the same case, a German firm would immediately see an increase in their Deutsche Mark (DM) cost. If the German firm is producing for the local market, and local DM prices are sticky, then the stronger dollar leads to a decline in DM margins. However, if the German firm is producing for export to the United States, the stronger dollar may permit an increase in the DM price of its product or perhaps the product is already invoiced in U.S. dollars. If this pricing flexibility is present, the German firm will have a built-in hedge against the adverse effects of this exchange rate change.

In general, an exchange rate change could affect the market value of a firm through its impact on the basic costs and revenues of the firm (input prices and output prices as well as the quantities of output sold and inputs required) as well as the discount rate used to value these cash flows. To cause an impact on Firm A, the proximate effect of the exchange rate change need not be on Firm A—the effect could initiate with Firm A's competitor for a similar or substitutable product. Thus, even a domestic firm with no foreign input or sales, and no foreign currency assets or liabilities, could be at risk to exchange rate changes if the firm's competitive position is affected. The complexities of measuring a firm's exposure to exchange rate changes are well documented in the paper by Maurice Levi (in this volume).

Perhaps the difficulty in specifying the precise mechanisms by which exchange rate changes affect corporate performance have deterred research in this area. While many studies in macroeconomics examine how exchange rate changes affect the performance of the macroeconomy, there have been very few attempts to measure how the exchange rate changes affect individual firms.[3] The twentieth-century multinational firm may have operations in many countries, with many product lines, and with competitors in yet other countries. Unraveling the impact of an exchange rate change on such a firm is a daunting task.

Moreover, exchange rate changes themselves are not easily categorized. Day-to-day exchange rate volatility poses essentially tactical problems of international treasury management—a set of problems that are relatively well-understood and can be handled fairly easily and cheaply using broad and deep forward, futures, and options markets. Long-term exchange rate volatility suggests changes in real exchange rates that may reflect sustained changes in macroeconomic policies. These might include traditional monetary and fiscal policies, but go on to include regulatory, industrial, trade, and social policies as well as regional agreements (such as the European Community and the North American Free Trade Agreement). Long-term changes of this sort entail changes in location of markets, in the product-mix, and in the optimal location of production. Issues of this nature would typically be reflected in long-term strategic decisions as the evolution of these long-term trends becomes clear.

Medium-term changes in exchange rates may pose the most serious problems for firms. As exchange rates evolve, it may be unclear whether these movements are temporary or permanent. If temporary, management may view operational adjustments (such as changing the location of inputs or production) as too costly. Management may prefer to use financial hedging techniques to offset losses from adverse exchange rate movements. But if the exchange rate movements prove to be permanent *and* real, then operational changes may be required if a firm is to preserve its international competitive position. These medium-term exchange rate changes, where there is substantial uncertainty as to the magnitude and duration of the shock, may carry great impact on firms.

In the 1980s, the medium-term volatility of exchange rates increased along with the vulnerability of all firms to international competition. These factors suggest that the potential importance of exchange rates on the performance of the firm may be growing. This belief raises our desire for a fresh set of studies aimed at unraveling and measuring the link between exchange rates and corporate performance.

SUMMARY OF THE PAPERS AND COMMENTS

The research in this volume addresses the issues discussed above. The book contains three sections. Section I provides theoretical and empirical analysis of the macroeconomic environment and the microeconomic effects under exchange rates changes. Section II focuses on the effects of exchange rates on the firm's cost of capital and presents international comparisons. Section III deals with the policies of firms exposed to exchange rates fluctuations and the means employed by firms to deal with these fluctuations.

Rudiger Dornbusch (Chapter 2) provides a comprehensive survey of the impact of exchange rate changes on the economy. These changes affect domestic prices, interest rates, the demand for goods and services, and direct investment. In the standard textbook model, a depreciation of the domestic currency lowers the price of exported goods, while raising the price of imported goods and domestic import substitutes. These effects are reflected in the domestic consumer price index (CPI) and the wage level. Another link exists between expected changes in exchange rates and the relative (domestic to foreign) interest rates. This link is monotonic, but not necessarily 1:1, because of the path of adjustment of exchange rates to their long-run equilibrium and because of inter-country differences in risk premiums. The European experience (prior to September 1992) showed that pegging exchange rates may encourage a convergence of inflation rates and may narrow the interest rates differentials across countries. Exchange rate changes also directly affect the demand for goods and services by their effect on exports and imports. And finally, they affect direct investment because they affect the cost of production, mainly labor costs (adjusted for productivity).

Dornbusch then analyzes the interaction between exchange rates and macroeconomic variables, using a basic model which includes equilibrium in the money market and full employment equilibrium in the market for goods and services affected by the real exchange rate and interest rate, and an equilibrium relation of real interest rate differentials and the real exchange rate change. This model, though limited in scope, produces a rich set of predictions on the interaction between real exchange rate and macroeconomic variables. Dornbusch then considers the limitations of the model: it assumes perfect foresight or rational expectations and perfect asset substitution, which results in asset supplies being unimportant, it gives no role to the current account imbalance and assumes no limitation on the exchange rates (such as target zones). The consequences of these assumptions and their relaxation are discussed. In conclusion, Dornbusch discusses whether there should be a regime of fixed exchange rates among major industrialized countries, and whether the current dollar exchange rate is at the right level.

In Chapter 3, Maurice Levi analyzes the microeconomic effects of exchange rate changes, and in particular, their impact on the valuation of firms with foreign sales. The effect of exchange rate changes on value includes two components: (i) the total effect on the revenue from the countries where the firm sells (the effect may differ across countries), which depends on the revenue elasticity in each of the foreign countries, and (ii) the effect of the induced change in the total quantity sold by the firm in all countries on the production costs. The response of the firm's value to exchange rate changes (which Levi defines as the firm's exposure), is the sum of the two effects. Levi stresses that exchange rate exposure may vary over time and as a function of the variables involved. This variability makes it difficult to estimate exposure to exchange risk over time.

The final paper in Part I is by Yakov Amihud (Chapter 4), who presents empirical evidence on the effect of exchange rate changes on the equity values of 32 U.S. companies which were large exporters. The model estimates the relationship between these companies' stock returns (1979–1988) and changes in the real exchange rate of the U.S. dollar measured against its 15 largest trading partners, conditional on the overall stock market, using both monthly and quarterly intervals. The results show no significant contemporaneous relationship between exchange rate changes and equity returns for these 32 firms. The model is then extended to estimate the effect of lagged changes in exchange rates, and given that the firms' exposure may vary over time (see Levi), the model allows the coefficients to change over subperiods. Though there is some evidence, weakly significant, of a lagged effect for high exporters, the results on the whole still show no significant relationship between exchange rate changes and the returns on exporting companies' stocks. This may be evidence of the skill with which these companies are managing their foreign exchange exposure.

Robert Cumby discusses the papers in this section and offers some explanations for the weak relationship between exchange rate changes and the stock prices of exporting companies. Cumby suggests that the empirical evidence could reflect foreign sourcing by corporations, the fact that the relationship between companies' equity values and exchange rates varies over time, or hedging in the financial markets. Taken together, the evidence suggests that firms are successful in eliminating their foreign exchange exposure, which raises the question of why they make such a choice.

In addition to their effect on corporate cash flows, exchange rates affect the corporate cost of capital. Exchange rates changes constitute one of the macroeconomic factors which investors price in the market—that is, there may be a risk premium to compensate the holders of securities whose value is affected by exchange rate changes for the risk associated with this factor. Consequently, the exchange rate volatility affects the firm's cost of capital and the valuation of their cash flows. This effect may differ across countries and thus may result in differences in the cost of capital between countries. The question of whether exchange rates affect the corporate cost of capital is analyzed empirically in the three papers in Part II.

Stephen Brown and Toshiyuki Otsuki (Chapter 5) present a comprehensive multicountry and multiperiod Arbitrage Pricing Theory model to examine whether exchange rate changes are priced. The authors employ a system estimation approach that simultaneously estimates the factor structure with the innovation process. In the Brown and Otsuki model, the risk premium is allowed to vary over time as a function of a set of instrumental variables: the yield spread in the United States and in Japan, the U.S. inflation rate, and U.S. dividend yield. The global equity risk factors in their study are the Japanese currency return, the U.S. small firms' index, the treasury rate in the United Kingdom, and the residual U.S. market return. The Japanese currency return—measured with respect to U.S. dollars—plays an important role in the global capital market, but its effect differs across countries. It is priced in most of the 21 countries, but in the United States its effect is marginal. The implication is that in general, exchange rate volatility does affect the equity cost of capital in most countries, but in the United States this effect is mute.

The relationship between exchange rates and the corporate cost of debt is analyzed by Philippe Jorion (Chapter 6). Jorion measures the cost of debt in the United States, Germany, and Japan in the same currency: the U.S. dollar. This is relevant, for example, to a U.S. corporation which can borrow in any of the three currencies. Then, the relevant cost of borrowing depends both on the nominal rate of interest in any currency and on the rate of change of the exchange rate of that currency with respect to the U.S. dollar. This international comparison of the cost of debt contrasts with other measures in which the real cost of debt is taken as each country's nominal interest rate deflated by that country's inflation rate. The two measures would be the same if exchange rates *always* (i.e., in the short-run and in the long-run) conformed to Purchasing Power Parity (PPP), which is clearly not the case.

The comparison employed by Jorion is then more relevant for corporations in a world with cross-country capital mobility. The results show that the cost of borrowing in foreign currencies was often higher than the dollar nominal cost of borrowing, and that over the long run there was little difference between them. Also, the real (CPI-deflated) cost of debt in the three countries were, on average, the same over the long term. These results are consistent with the fact that PPP holds over the long run. In sum, Jorion's results suggest that U.S. borrowers of U.S. dollars were not disadvantaged over the long run.

Both the cost of debt and the cost of equity determine the cost of capital which is relevant for the discount of cash flows. In Chapter 7, Robert

McCauley and Steven Zimmer present evidence on the corporate cost of capital, after tax, in four major countries: the United States, Japan, Germany, and the United Kingdom for the years 1977–1991. Their calculations of the cost of capital employ the weighted average formula, with the cost of equity being calculated as the ratio of economic earnings (properly adjusted to make them internationally comparable) to the respective market capitalization. Differences in the cost of capital result from differences in the debt/equity ratios across countries, in the real interest rates, in risk premiums, and in tax rates. The evidence they present shows that the real after-tax cost of capital was higher in the United States and the United Kingdom compared to Japan and Germany, though the differences have narrowed considerably in 1992. In particular, the real after-tax cost of capital in the United States declined sharply to be about 1 percent above that of Japan and Germany, compared to a gap of 4–6 percent in the early and mid-1980s. The narrowing of the gap is partly due to the convergence in the components' real cost of capital and partly due to the decline in the debt/equity ratios in Japan and Germany—though this ratio is still higher there than in the United States and the United Kingdom. Underscoring the latter point is the fact that the debt-to-assets ratio of U.S. affiliates of foreign companies was higher through the 1980s than that ratio for American companies. The authors further show that there was a strong positive correlation in the last decade between the excess of the U.S. cost of capital over Japan's and the net direct foreign investment flow from Japan to the United States. The shrinking of the cost of capital gap in 1992 was associated with the elimination of this investment flow. However, McCauley and Zimmer caution that cross-country comparisons of the real cost of capital implicitly assume that PPP holds, which is not necessarily the case, though there is evidence that exchange rates tend towards PPP. In general, differences in the real cost of capital among countries may induce changes in the exchange rate. This should be taken into account when investors in one country are using another country's domestic cost of capital to evaluate cash flows in that country.

The effect of exchange rate fluctuations on companies' performance might seem to suggest that companies would better serve their shareholders if they hedged their currency risks, and were thus rewarded by having a lower cost of capital. In his comments, Ian Giddy claims that companies which hedge exchange rates may be doing their shareholders a disservice. In the Modigliani-Miller framework, hedging cannot increase the company value if shareholders can conduct the same hedging transactions on their own. If hedging is costly, the company may engage in costly hedging that does not reward shareholders, because shareholders' currency preferences vary relative to the mix chosen for them by the company. Giddy argues that investors do not buy a company's stock because they want to link their investment to any currency (this can be done with other means), but because they are interested in the particular business activities of the company. Thus, hedging by the company may duplicate costs and create uncertainties that will increase, rather than decrease, the company's cost of capital.

However, exchange rate volatility may raise the risks of bankruptcy for any given capital structure. As a result of the deadweight costs associated with bankruptcy, there will be an increase in the cost of debt. This in turn affects the corporate cost of capital, and provides a rationale for the company to apply hedging policies that reduce their exposure to exchange rate volatility.

The papers in Part III deal with the business decisions made by companies whose values may be affected by exchange rate changes. The techniques available to companies with exchange rate exposure include hedging in the financial markets, adjusting their pricing policies, changing the location of their production facilities, and switching between markets for their inputs and for their final products. Each of the papers in this section focuses on another aspect of the strategic decisions made by firms with foreign exchange exposure.

The paper by Michael Adler (Chapter 8) proposes that hedging in the forward markets against exchange rate changes cannot completely insulate firms from the effects of these changes on their revenues. Changes in exchange rates induce firms to change both the prices they charge in foreign markets and the quantities they sell. Altogether, the foreign currency revenues are random, whereas financial hedging can be made against a given quantity of foreign currency. Thus, Adler contends, the exchange rate exposure of a firm that operates in foreign markets cannot be completely hedged.

Another source of foreign exchange-induced uncertainty is the reaction of the firm's competitors in foreign markets. The competitors' effect on the firm's revenue depend on the exchange rate between their home currency and the currency in the country where the firm operates. This source of uncertainty also needs to be hedged, but again, it cannot be completely hedged because quantities of foreign currencies cannot be hedged, only their prices. Similarly, a firm that operates solely in the domestic market may need to hedge foreign currency risks if it is affected by foreign competitors (or suppliers), and again, this risk cannot be fully hedged for the above reason.

Adler suggests that if there were contracts designed to hedge against quantity changes, the problem would apparently be resolved; however, quantity (as opposed to foreign currency's price) contracts raise the problem of moral hazard, and are thus difficult to implement. The conclusion from Adler's analysis is that financial hedging cannot completely insulate a firm from the consequences of foreign exchange changes, and a more complex strategic hedging that involves the firm's real decision is necessary.

Exporting companies can respond to exchange rate fluctuations by implementing proper pricing strategies in markets with imperfect competition, in addition to adjusting the quantities they sell. Michael Knetter (Chapter 9) presents theory and evidence on the policy of "pricing to market" (PTM) by which firms change the markup of price over cost in response to exchange rate changes. This policy determines the "pass-through" of changes in exchange rates from exporters to importers. The extent of the pass-through depends on the market structure, the market power of the exporting company, segmentation of markets, and the strategy of competitors. Knetter examines the nature of PTM by exporters in two countries: Germany and the United States. He estimates the destination-specific export price as a function of the exchange rate in the destination country, controlling for factors unique to the destination country, including income, and time-varying factors. His results show that for the United States, there is usually no PTM in export industries, meaning that there is a complete pass-through of prices: the dollar price of the export product is unaffected, ceteris paribus, by exchange rate changes in the destination countries. This would indeed be expected in an environment with little friction between destination markets which enforce one price across them. In Germany there is greater evidence of PTM, implying a greater ability of German exporters to discriminate between markets.

John Bilson (Chapter 10) develops a practical approach for financial hedging in the case of American Airlines (AMR). The company's value is affected by exchange rate changes because part of its revenues is in foreign currency—the Deutsche Mark in this case. But more important, because the propensity of U.S. travelers to fly to Europe depends on the exchange rate between the U.S. dollar and the DM, the value of AMR should be negatively related to exchange rate changes. Bilson estimates that this exposure constitutes between 45 percent and 77 percent, depending on the method of estimation. To eliminate this source of risk AMR could hedge by taking a very large position in DM, but this could bankrupt AMR if economic conditions changed unexpectedly. Given the risk of hedging based on taking a fixed position in a foreign currency, Bilson then suggests an alternative hedging policy, based on discretionary trading which dynamically changes the hedge position in response to business conditions. This policy is based on a dynamic allocation of assets based on forecasting of currency returns, and would require the allocation of a smaller amount of assets to hedging. He demonstrates that a policy based on a combination of static and dynamic hedging would bring about a substantial reduction of the foreign exchange exposure and the resulting risk. A simulation of this policy using past data for AMR resulted in a higher average return and a lower standard deviation of returns.

Marcia Whitaker (in Chapter 11) describes the nature of foreign exchange risk management at General Electric Company (GE). As Whitaker makes clear, the responsibility for understanding and dealing with the impact of multiple currencies and variable exchange rates rests with project managers. Each business activity at GE, whether in appliances, medical services, or jet engines is expected to generate dollar profits for the firm. Managers are closest to these activities and have the strongest incentives to understand how exchange rate changes (along with other macroeconomic risks) will affect the profitability of a project. As Whitaker explains, often times the solutions to exchange rate variability have been fairly straightforward—netting arrangements across European operations, invoicing in terms of dollars or ECU, and using forward contracts. Nevertheless, Whitaker argues that these simple strategies have proved effective.

In his discussion of the papers in Part III, Kenneth Froot raises a fundamental question: Why should firms hedge their foreign exchange risk? Froot suggests that hedging can be valuable if it does not constitute a drain on their cash flows, when cash is in greater demand by firms because of greater investment opportunities. However, if hedging siphons off cash during exchange rate depreciation, when an exporting firm may need it most for investments, then Froot concludes that it would not be in the firm's interest to hedge. This analysis, it should be noted, implicitly assumes imperfect capital markets, problems of asymmetry in information between borrowers and lenders, or agency problems that make it costly to raise outside funds. In an expansionary period, the firm ought to be able to raise capital for its activities even though it has hedging losses. And in a period of declining or depressed real activity, a firm (and its shareholders) ought to welcome the cash generated through hedging.

As is often the case, a collection of research papers raises as many questions as they answer. Even so, we hope that the research presented in this volume will contribute to a better understanding of the numerous and complex ways by which exchange rates affect corporate values and the policies companies employ to deal with these changes.

NOTES

1. See "Did U.S. Car Makers Err by Raising Prices When the Yen Rose?" *Wall Street Journal*, April 18, 1988.
2. Tests of the impact of nominal and real exchange rate volatility on international trade volume have not found a significant systematic relationship. See Cushman (1983).
3. An early study by Giddy (1974) examined how share prices responded to discrete exchange rate changes during the Bretton Woods period of pegged exchange rates. A more recent paper by Jorion (1990) analyzes the share price response of large American multinational firms.

REFERENCES

Cushman, D. O. (1983). "The Effects of Real Exchange Rate Risk on International Trade." *Journal of International Economics*. August 15, pp. 45–63.

Giddy, I. H. *(1974). Devaluations, Revaluations and Stock Market Prices*. Ph.D. diss., University of Michigan.

Jorion, P. (1990). "The Exchange -Rate Exposure of U.S. Multinationals." *Journal of Business*. 63, no. 3, pp. 331–45.

PART ONE

EXCHANGE RATES, THE MACROECONOMIC ENVIRONMENT, AND THE FIRM

CHAPTER 2

EXCHANGE RATES AND THE ECONOMY

Rudiger Dornbusch

A cynic once observed "...we may have the exchange rates we deserve, even though they are not the exchange rates we want." [1] Floating exchange rates got a bad name in the interwar period and they never really quite recovered. They move too much, apparently, on occasion in the wrong direction, and almost always where you and your theory would not have thought they might go. Not surprisingly, floating exchange rates have made few friends, at least not lasting ones. When it became known that they are really asset prices that help anticipate reduced predictability and raise expectations of volatility, this made them welcome in the casino but offered little help to their social standing. Now that it is known that floating exchange rates are neither guided by rational forecasts nor firmly tied to fundamentals, they might as well be locked up altogether.

This chapter offers an essay-survey—no attempt to be either balanced or comprehensive—of the issues and the evidence. [2]

LINKAGES

Exchange rates play a role in each of the key linkages of an economy to the rest of the world. The linkages are in prices, interest rate, the demand for goods and services, the direction of direct investment, and in policy.

Prices   Prices in the United States are directly affected by movements in the exchange rate. A depreciation of the exchange rate will raise the prices of imports and may affect prices of import competing goods.[3] On the export side prices also will be affected. There is a clear difference between auction prices and customer prices. The prices of auction goods—homogeneous commodities traded in international markets—substantially follow the law of one price. A rise in the price of foreign currency will raise dollar prices of these goods and lower the prices in foreign currency.[4]

For customer goods—manufactures, more so, the more they represent differentiated products traded in oligopolistic markets with geographic segmentation—the law of one price does not hold. Still, exchange rate movements will have some impact on these prices. Foreign firms supplying the domestic market will not typically absorb, in profits or cost-cutting, the full extent of a dollar depreciation. If foreign firms pass on at least part of a dollar depreciation, domestic competitors will have some response in terms of matching price increase. A typical story might be that with a 10 percent dollar depreciation, import prices for a particular product rise by 5 percent and prices of domestic competing goods by 3 percent.

Since import prices and export prices show *some* responsiveness to exchange rate changes, there will be some impact on economy-wide prices.[5] (See, for example, Figure 2–1) To the extent that the prices of intermediate goods are affected by exchange rate changes, this will represent cost increases which will be passed on. If the impacted goods are final, then their higher prices will directly raise economy-wide price indices. These economy-wide price increases, say in the CPI, will then translate into wage increases directly via indexation or else in negotiations. The rule of thumb for the impact of exchange rates on the price level used to be 1:5—a 10 percent depreciation would raise prices by 2 percent. That was before the 1980s exchange rate shocks; no new estimate seems to command consensus.

Exchange rates may also play an important role in determining the path of prices. This is specifically possible when the nominal exchange rate is used as a nominal anchor for the economy. In the 1980s, Europe used this approach in the context of the European Monetary System (EMS): firm exchange rate commitments were used increasingly as an anchor on the drift in prices (relative to Germany), and as a result, inflation rates converged.

Interest Rates   Assets of different countries will be typically denominated in different currencies and be governed by different jurisdictions. If asset holders are risk-neutral (or if asset returns in a common currency are perfectly correlated) and if political risk can be neglected, expected ex-

FIGURE 2–1
Domestic and Import Prices (Consumer Goods, Index 1987 = 1)

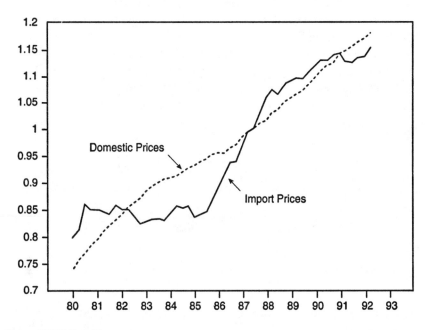

Source: DRI/McGraw-III

change rate depreciation will be reflected in nominal yield differentials.

With i and i^* the domestic and foreign interest rate and d the expected rate of depreciation, we have:

$$i = i^* + d \tag{2.1}$$

Of course, the equation cannot be expected to hold exactly. Some depreciation is anticipated, much represents "news." Let d^e be the anticipated depreciation and then we have:

$$i - i^* = d^e + \text{"news"} \tag{2.1a}$$

The international interest relationship highlights the role of exchange rate expectations. Other things equal, smaller rates of expected depreciation narrow the nominal interest differential. In the EMS context, the commitments to increasingly fixed rates (increasingly narrowing bands) with increasing credibility derived both from the accumulated performance and from the convergence of inflation rates has, in fact, visibly narrowed nominal interest differentials. A case in point is the Belgium–Germany differential shown in Figure 2–2 .

The interest relationship is also helpful in telling us about possible relations between the level of the exchange rate (relative to fundamentals) and the interest differential. Suppose a currency is overvalued and that the anticipated depreciation is a function of the overvaluation, $d = \phi\,(e' - e)$:

$$i = i^* + \phi\,(e' - e) \tag{2.2}$$

where e' is the long-run equilibrium exchange rate. The equation tells us that the more overvalued the rate, the larger the interest differential required to sustain the overvaluation—until further notice. Turning the equation around,

$$e = e' - (i - i^*)/\phi \tag{2.2a}$$

the exchange rate will be more overvalued, the higher is the domestic interest differential.

So far we have assumed perfect substitution. Risk aversion adds to the relationship by bringing in a risk premium that will depend on the variability of return differentials (measured in a common currency), risk aversion, and the relative supply of assets. When real exchange rates are not constant, and they patently are not, this risk premium comes potentially into prominence. In fact, however, as Frankel (1982) has argued persuasively, CAPM-based risk premia are negligibly small.

Demand for Goods and Services   The third linkage into which exchange rates enter is in the demand for goods and services—"goods" for short. Foreign demand for our goods will depend on their relative price and so does our demand for imports. But competitiveness is potentially affected by movements in the nominal exchange rate. If so, a nominal depreciation of the dollar will make U.S. goods more competitive both in home markets and in foreign markets. Conversely, a dollar appreciation will make U.S. goods less competitive.

There is pervasive evidence of a positive correlation between the nominal and the real exchange rate. In fact, nominal exchange rates changes translate substantially—not quite 1:1, but substantially so—into

FIGURE 2–2
Belgium-Germany Three Months' Differential (Euro Deposits, Percent Per Year)

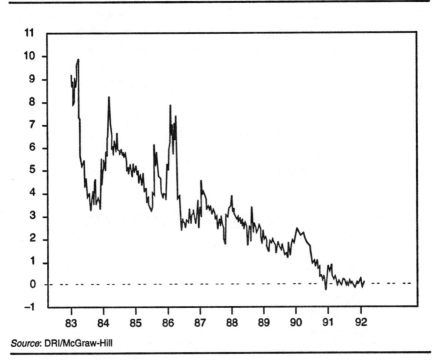

Source: DRI/McGraw-Hill

real exchange rates. There is also substantial evidence that demand responds to competitiveness. Specifically, a 10 percent gain in U.S. competitiveness will reduce real imports by 14 percent and raise export volume by 13 percent.[6] There are lags in the response, and the nominal trade balance in the short run may react perversely. But in a period of not much more than a year, real trade flows and the nominal trade balance will improve in the aftermath of a real depreciation.

The response of trade flows to exchange rates involves possibly important dynamic complications. One arises from hysteresis effects: a period of overvaluation de-industrializes a country. Going back to the initial exchange rate will not typically be enough to restore the initial trade flows. Firms will have disappeared or have given up their customers and markets. To restore the initial condition, an over-depreciation is required that creates enough excess profits to make it attractive to incur the fixed costs associated with rebuilding the trade capacity.

A further impact on the current account stems from the valuation of the income from net external assets. Dollar depreciation will tend to raise net investment income in dollars.

Direct Investment   Regions that enjoy low wages (relative to productivity) and large markets will naturally attract direct inward investment. By contrast, high wage regions are not attractive places to produce, unless they correspond to closed economies or else offer dynamic advantages connected with research and development. The adjustment of wages by productivity is, of course, central. Without it all goods would be produced in China, India, or Russia.

Labor costs in 1990, in manufacturing, are shown in Table 2–1. Judging the required productivity adjustment is hard. Comparisons of the *levels* of manufacturing productivity are very difficult to find; even when done for all of GDP they are precarious.

TABLE 2–1
Hourly Compensation in Manufacturing (U.S. $ per hour in 1990, Index U.S. = 100)

United States	100	Mexico	12
Germany	146	Korea	26
Japan	86	Taiwan	27
U.K.	84		

Source: U.S. Dept. of Labor

Policy   Exchange rates play a role in the coordination of monetary and fiscal policy within a country and between countries. In domestic policy, masking exchange rates has arisen because both monetary and fiscal policy affect the exchange rate; indeed, especially in small countries exchange rates may be a principal channel of operation for monetary and fiscal policy. In international policy, coordination exchange rates come up because they divide the world aggregate demand among countries, and they impact inflation. In the 1930s competitive depreciation was an instrument, along with commercial policy, to implement beggar-thy-neighbor policies.

In the 1980s large dollar movements led to coordinated policies to affect exchange rates. It is believed that since 1985 some form of exchange rate agreement has been in place among major central banks to limit fluctuations, and possibly trends, in the exchange rates among major currencies.

With this background we will now look briefly at the macroeconomic modeling of exchange rates.

THEORIES

Most models of the exchange rate combine three elements:
- Differential inflation trends among economies.
- A role for relative price levels (measured in a common currency) to shift over time in response to divergent experiences in the production or demand side across countries.
- Some role for capital flows motivated by the real exchange rate. These capital flows might be motivated by political factors or other considerations.
- Moreover, to complicate matters, the entire future path of these three factors exerts influence on current exchange rates as to expectations about the authorities' disposition or determination to defend certain levels of exchange rates, by intervention or changes in monetary policy.[7] No surprise that there is a proliferation of models and that none has performed well for very long. Those that are highly specific in the range of influences they admit do well, while their key variable is at the center of the stage, but they do not last. Those that give room to a very broad range of factors have no empirical counterparts and, as a result, never get to be tested.

PPP   The strongest hypothesis is PPP. A weaker version is that real exchange rates are constant, and an even stronger version is that prices are equalized (except for tariffs and transport costs). This hypothesis became fashionable under the auspices of Cassel and Keynes, in the face of high inflation in Europe in the aftermath of World War II. Cassel noted that exchange depreciation matched differentials in inflation rates reasonably well. Thus, at least when monetary disturbances dominate, real exchange rates were thought to be relatively constant, and nominal rates would move to preserve PPP.

PPP has not done well in empirical terms.[8] Only in the longest time series can a tendency to constancy be asserted in some meaningful way. And even here, allowing for some shift in the equilibrium level of the real exchange rate often helps.[9] (See Figures 2–3 to 2–5). But even so, PPP keeps being used as at least one of the reference points in evaluating whether exchange rates are where they belong. Thus Ohno (1990) presents estimates of the yen/$ and mark/$ PPP rates using alternative benchmarks.

Using these data (carried forward without much change to 1992), the dollar seems *under*valued at current exchange rates. Moreover, the

FIGURE 2–3
U.S.–Japan Real Exchange Rate (Index 1980 = 100)

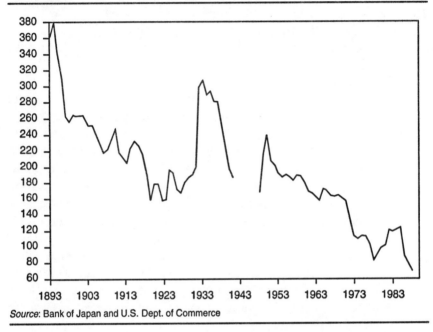

Source: Bank of Japan and U.S. Dept. of Commerce

interest differentials at best allow for a very moderate nominal dollar depreciation. Thus, either PPP is not right or the long-term rates are not. Moreover, some might argue that the dollar, far from being undervalued, is in fact *over*valued. That view would certainly not square with the PPP estimates in Table 2–2.

A Basic Model   Just to be specific, here is a simple model that lends itself to a discussion of the interaction between macroeconomic policies and the exchange rate. It also serves to highlight how various omitted factors

TABLE 2–2
Estimates of PPP (Using PPIs, 1990:I)

	Yen/$	Mark/$
Long-Run Averages		
75:I-90:I	175	2.03
80:I-90:I	172	2.14
Morrison-Hale Method	200	2.33
Ohno Method	170	2.04

Source: Ohno (1990), Table 1

FIGURE 2–4
**U.S.–Germany: Relative CPI Levels (Common Currency Basis,
Index 1985 = 100)**

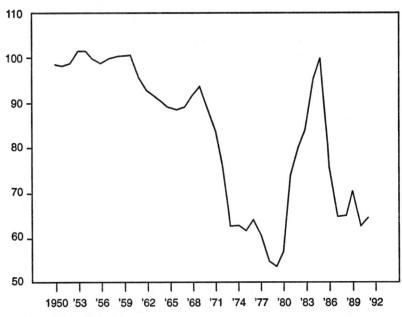

Source: International Monetary Fund

would enter. The model, in the tradition of Mundell, highlights goods and assets markets. Monetary equilibrium involves the equality of the real money stock and real money demand, the latter depending on the domestic nominal interest rate:

$$m - p = ky - \lambda i \qquad (2.3)$$

where p and y denote prices and output. Assets denominated in different currency denominations are assumed to be perfect substitutes on a currency depreciation-adjusted basis:

$$i = i^* + d \qquad (2.2)$$

where d is the expected rate of depreciation. This equation can be rewritten in terms of real interest differentials and the rate of change of the real exchange rate, $q = e - p$.

FIGURE 2–5
France–Germany: Relative CPIs (Common Currency Basis, Index 1985 = 100)

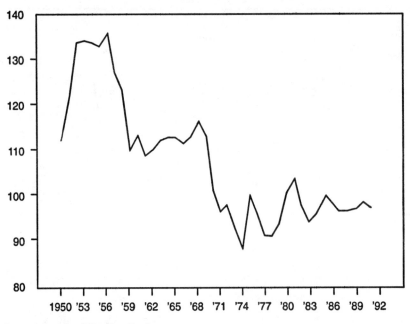

Source: International Monetary Fund

$$r = r^* + q \tag{2.4}$$

Because of perfect substitution, the model asserts that real interest rates are equated across countries except when the real exchange rate is changing. Countries undergoing real depreciation have higher real interest rates than countries whose currency is appreciating in real terms.

Equilibrium in the market for the country's output involves real interest rates and real exchange rates such that demand equals the full employment supply:

$$y = \alpha(e - p) - \beta(i - \pi) + u \tag{2.5}$$

where π denotes the rate of inflation and u is a shift variable that stands for the level of foreign demand or for domestic fiscal policy.

In the simplest of worlds, prices are fully flexible, output is always at the full employment level, the real exchange rate is constant, and real interest rates are equated. Two exercises can be offered:

- A sustained fiscal expansion, or a gain in export markets, leads to an immediate real appreciation. In this full employment economy, increased real demand must be crowded out. Since the real interest rate is set in world markets, real appreciation serves to bring demand for domestic goods in line with full employment output.
- A sustained increase in the growth rate of nominal money will immediately raise the interest rate, lead to a jump in the price level and an offsetting depreciation in the nominal exchange rate. The real exchange rate and the real interest rate remain unchanged and the nominal exchange rate depreciates in a manner that sustains purchasing power parity (PPP).

This model can be taken in two directions. One possibility is to pursue the implications of a richer structure involving intertemporal saving and investment aspects, and imperfect substitutability between assets. This inquiry would lead one to conclude that a fiscal expansion, to the extent that it involves current account imbalances, has implications for external debt and hence for the equilibrium real exchange rate over time. A fiscal expansion then would lead to a short-term real appreciation, while it lasts, but ultimately to a real depreciation when the country turns to serving and amortizing the accumulated debt. Portfolio considerations can add complications.

The alternative is to give more room to the short-run macroeconomic dynamics in an economy where wages and prices are not fully flexible. In such a setting nominal money changes represent, at least for a while, changes in real money, which induce changes in interest rates and economic activity. In the long run this economy would still show price flexibility and a tendency toward full employment. But the assumed stickiness of wages and prices adds the dynamics. A convenient way to close the model is to assume an inflation rate that depends on the divergence between real aggregate demand and full employment output,

$$p = \sigma\left[\alpha(e-p) - \beta(i-\pi) + u - y\right] \qquad (2.6)$$

where y denotes full employment output.

It is readily shown—Mundell (1986), Dornbusch (1976) and Mussa (1982)—that this model will generate the following implications:

- A sustained increase in the nominal money stock will lead to an immediate depreciation of the exchange rate, in excess of the long run depreciation. In the subsequent adjustment process the real depreciation creates demand and thereby induces inflation. Over time the real exchange rate returns to its initial equilibrium, the nominal rate appreciates, and prices rise. Thus, in the transition, clearly PPP does not hold. But across long-run equilibria it does.

- A sustained fiscal expansion leads to immediate real appreciation that crowds out the increase in demand.
- Anticipation of a future monetary expansion will lead to an immediate depreciation, a depreciating rate until the increase does occur, and at that time a turn toward appreciation. Prices will be rising throughout.
- Anticipated fiscal expansion leads to some initial appreciation followed by a period of deflation and appreciation, until the time where fiscal expansion does occur. At that point the exchange rate further appreciates while inflation helps restore the initial price level.

Further complications involve transitory fiscal expansions, current or future. The model already goes some way in explaining a macroeconomic place for the real exchange rate, including the fact that real exchange rates can move during the adjustment prices as well as permanently, if real factors have changed on a lasting basis.

Extensions   The model can be faulted either for the basic assumption of price stickiness and/or neglect of full, explicit and rigorous intertemporal optimization. I will not pursue that direction since it is unlikely to offer interesting findings. More compelling are the following three limitations:

First, the model (1986) assumes perfect foresight or rational expectations.[10] The problem is that tests of the rational expectations assumption (always joint tests with some specific model of asset demand) fail systematically. It is not obvious how to do better. Chartism is now in vogue, especially for the short run.

Frankel and Froot (1988, 1990) were the first to make the leap. They argued, based on not finding evidence to support the assumption of rationality, that asset markets use a combination of chartism and fundamentalism, with changing weights. Further evidence by Ito (1990), Froot and Frankel (1989), Taylor and Allen (1992) and Takagi (1992) rounds out the picture of some role, especially in the short run, for market factors rather than fundamentals.[11] Striking evidence for this comes, for example, from expectations of foreign exchange participants in the Tokyo market. Figure 2–6 from Takagi, first shown by Ito (1990), makes the point that short-run expectations are extrapolative, but that a reversal is expected in the longer term.

Second, the model assumes perfect asset substitution and hence makes no room for the relative supplies of assets to affect the risk premium. In models of portfolio diversification based on risk aversion, the relative supplies of outside assets matter. The higher the relative supply of an asset, other things equal, the higher the required rate of return. If asset supplies do matter, then the financing of budget deficits, which does not even appear in this formulation, clearly assumes importance.

The asset market modeling may also be flawed in that it assumes away the entire range of issues raised by the economics of credit rationing. The link from money to spending, including interest rates and exchange rates, may have an extra leg involving credit rationing by banks or other financial intermediaries. Indeed, this may be the basis for the finding by Feldstein–Horioka that changes in the national saving rate have a systematic and sizable impact on the rate of investment.

Third, there is no room for current account balances to affect spending and wealth. The omission is important since, as it stands, the model assumes that deficits can go on forever. Yet, as we have learned from Herb Stein, something that cannot go on forever must ultimately stop. Indeed, Krugman (1985, 1992) based his argument of an unsustainable dollar precisely on the accumulated debt burdens that would arise if the real exchange rate (extrapolated by long term interest rates) were to persist indefinitely.

Adding net external assets (or wealth) would enrich the dynamics of the story. In the short run sticky prices would give money a prominent role, and in the long run the net external asset dynamics would force a balanced current account. A fiscal experiment in the augmented model would still lead to an initial real appreciation. In the long run, however, the long-run real exchange rate would depreciate below the original level to generate full employment and external balance.[12]

A fourth limitation of the model is to assume "open" floating rather than target zones. If exchange rates have implicit or explicit target bands there will be an impact on expectations. The closer the exchange rate is to the band, the more likely is depreciation. Conversely, at the lower band, appreciation must be expected. These expectations in turn affect the level of asset demands and hence the equilibrium level of the exchange rate.[13]

FIGURE 2–6
The Yen–Dollar Rate: Actual and Expected

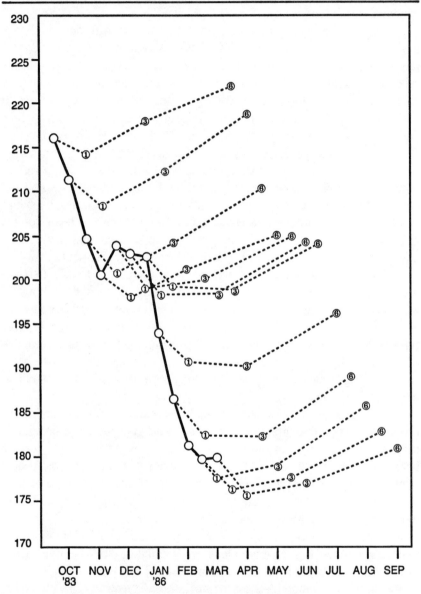

NOTE: Semimonthly time series of the spot and one-month, three-month, and six-month exchange rates of the Japanese yen against the U.S. dollar. The expected exchange rates are dated according to the future periods for which the expectations are formed.

Source: Takagi (1992)

EMPIRICAL EXCHANGE RATE MODELS: LIMITED SUCCESS

Results from two decades of empirical testing of exchange rate models are mixed, if not disappointing. Research by Meese and Rogoff (1983) dealt a vast blow to accepted Mundell–Fleming models and, indeed, to any kind of model of the exchange rate. They concluded that a random walk would outperform accepted exchange rate models.

There is no surprise in the poor performance of exchange rate models. We know three basic facts: first, that forward looking expectations place a great role on future variables and innovations rather than current actual variables. Accordingly, the right regressors are surely not current monetary and fiscal variables. Second, with substantial financial deregulation we cannot expect a stable money demand and hence a predictable effect of actual money growth on exchange rates. In fact, monetary policy was as much geared to offsetting the impact of deregulation as it was to achieve particular macroeconomic outcomes. Third, a major regime change occurred in the late 1970s and the early 1980s. An appropriate model of the exchange rate would include some learning process about the shift in the U.S. to a low-inflation monetary policy. Much of this agenda remains to be included in the testing of exchange rate models.

But even without these refinements, a host of new research has weakened the Meese–Rogoff conclusion substantially.[14] While there is no great success for long sample periods or for all sample periods, the random walk is no longer the winner. The interesting question today is already the relative role of fundamentals and technical factors.

RESULTS FROM POLICY MODELS

In the 1970s, in the transition to flexible exchange rates, macroeconomic modeling of the economy had to adapt to the increasing openness of the economy and to the prevalence of external shocks. The absence of good—in the sense of empirically robust—exchange rate models did not help. But there is now a variety of models available, notably the Federal Reserve Board model and the IMF model which are routinely used to simulate policy experiments in the open economy.[15]

Table 2–3 shows simulation results using the IMF's MULTIMOD

TABLE 2–3
Multimod Simulations (Impact and 2-Year Effect)

	GDP [a]		Exchange Rate [b]		Current Account [c]	
U.S. Fiscal Expansion[d]						
U.S.	3.7	–0.5	5.0	4.6	–3.9	–6.3
Japan	0.5	0.2	–2.5	–2.4	0.4	0.4
Germany	0.6	0.4	–1.0	–0.9	0.5	0.7
U.S. Money Supply Increase[e]						
U.S.	4.5	5.0	–12.6	–6.7	–0.7	0.6
Japan	–0.3	–1.0	6.7	3.2	0.1	–0.4
Germany	–0.3	–1.2	3.0	1.5	–0.1	–0.8
Japanese Fiscal Expansion[f]						
U.S.	0.1	–0.1	–1.4	–1.4	0.1	0.1
Japan	3.2	–0.3	8.5	7.5	–0.9	–0.7
Germany	0.2	–0.0	–1.0	–0.9	0.2	0.1

[a] Real GDP, percent change relative to base line.
[b] Nominal Effective exchange rate. Percentage change relative to base line.
[c] As a percent of GNP compared to baseline.
[d] A 5 percent of GNP increase in U.S. government spending.
[f] An increase of 10 percent in the U.S. money supply target.
[e] Fiscal expansion of 5 percent of GDP.

Source: Masson et al. (1990), tables 9 and 10.

model. This model has the virtue of imposing a fair amount of rationality as well as intertemporal budget constraints. It disaggregates trade flows substantially and it insists on integrating the main industrial countries and their policy responses to disturbances in world capital markets and exchange rates. The table shows the responses of output, the nominal effective exchange rate and the current account (as a percent of GDP) to a fiscal and monetary expansion respectively. The results are shown for the year of a policy change and the second year following the change.

Note that even a large fiscal expansion in Japan—5 percent of GDP—has very little impact on U.S. real GDP, the trade weighted dollar, or the current account.

The model retains the key properties of the Mundell–Fleming model: a monetary expansion raises output as does a fiscal expansion.

But the 2-year effects are already different. Easy money sustains a longer expansion, while fiscal expansion via increased interest rates and appreciation shows substantial offsets. The current account shows a lasting deterioration in response to fiscal expansion because of appreciation. Monetary expansion, by contrast, deteriorates the current account in the short run (the J-curve) but then brings about an improvement as a result of depreciation.

The results from simulations of the world econometric models clearly support two conclusions. First, that the exchange rate regime—fixed versus flexible—has a major incidence on *how* monetary and fiscal policy work themselves out. In a closed economy of the old textbooks monetary policy worked chiefly via the cost of capital; in the actual economy with flexible rates the external sector is a key channel of transmission.

Second, and closely connected, the extent to which foreign countries accommodate or offset the exchange rate movements that accompany our monetary and fiscal policies has a critical impact on the size and direction of adjustments. If they pursue exchange rate-oriented monetary policies they will tend to follow our monetary lead, and if they target money supplies they will cause exchange rates to do more of the adjustment.

CONCLUSION: TWO QUESTIONS

In concluding this essay we raise two questions for discussion. Should we return to fixed rates among major industrialized countries? And, is the dollar in the right place for the early 1990s?

A return to fixed rates is attractive if we believe that exchange rate volatility is an inevitable byproduct of a flexible rate *and*, that it is very undesirable and, that under fixed rates, there would not be an even worse volatility or other outlet for disturbances or policy shocks.

The case for a return to more fixed rates in the form of reasonably firm target zones with a set of rules for exchange rate policy has been made by Williamson and Miller (1987).[16] The rules of the game envisage monetary and fiscal policy to be internationally coordinated with well-specified responses to domestic and foreign shocks. The concept is fine, but the implementation could not be further off. Europe is grappling with the most extreme difficulty with the idea of a common money. Even the notion of a rigidly fixed exchange rate is not yet accepted; a common money is thought to be as much a threat in Italy as in Germany. And all that after a decade of "convergence" achieved by pegging to the Deutsche Mark. And if the continent is having trouble, Britain has even more.

Monetary integration between the United States and Germany, not to speak of Europe, is nowhere to be seen across the North Atlantic. The U.S. Congress is certainly not disposed to exercise an exchange rate-oriented fiscal policy and the Fed would be poorly advised to conduct monetary policy with a view to pegging the Deutsche Mark. The recent trouble in Europe highlights only too well that the exchange rate remains an excellent tool to isolate an economy that experiences idiosyncratic disturbances.

The second question concerns the dollar in the 1990s. Krugman (1985) concluded rightly, it turns out, that the overvalued dollar could not last. (see Figure 2–7) Since then it has declined and we are back to the level of the early 1980s. But is that level sustainable once the U.S.

FIGURE 2–7
United States: The Real Exchange Rate (Index 1980–1982 = 100)

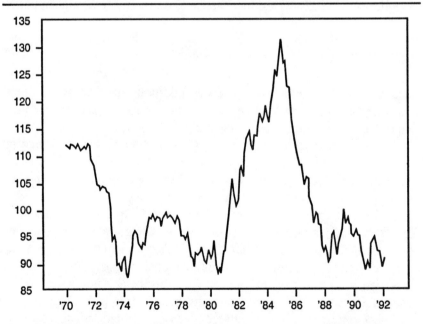

Source: Morgan Guaranty

undergoes fiscal contraction, as we surely will some day? The accumulating external net indebtedness of the 1980s, structural change that hurts, or trade performance at unchanging levels of relative prices and the prospect of fiscal restraint all suggest that the dollar is overvalued relative to where it will be five years from now.[17]

The interesting question is to know what currencies are on the other side of the dollar overvaluation. Germany already looks expensive with labor costs that exceed those in the United States by almost 50 percent and those in Japan by 70 percent. How about Japan? To judge from Japan's current ills and aches, dollar depreciation would appear like the last nail in the coffin. Yet, major yen appreciation is probably the most likely course of adjustment in the 1990s. Why should the secular trend not continue? (See Figure 2–8.)

Increasingly the dollar/DM, and the dollar/yen rate have less than dramatic effects in the real effective exchange rates of any of the three countries and therefore larger nominal rate movements among the key

FIGURE 2–8
Japan: The Real Exchange Rate (Index 1980–1982 = 100)

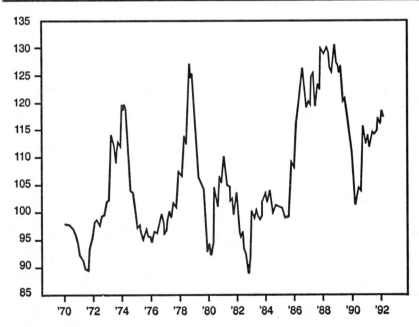

Source: Morgan Guaranty

countries are altogether plausible. But to get there we have to experience first persistent, large real-interest differentials and then give up the belief that there are implicit or explicit target zones still "louvreing" around.

NOTES

1. See Levich (1985).
2. For excellent, complete surveys see Takagi (1991) and MacDonald and Taylor (1992).
3. Implicitly the discussion assumes an exogenous asset, market-driven exchange-rate shock.
4. In oil markets contract prices are set in dollars. Thus foreign currency cost of contract oil responds one for one to the exchange rate.
5. See Mussa (1979,1986).
6. See Hickok and Hung (1991) as well as Bryant et al. (1988).
7. See Mussa (1985) for a model of intervention and Dobson (1991) for a review of the experience in the 1980s.
8. See, however, Ohno (1990) for a review and new findings.
9. See Kravis(1986) and Marston (1989).
10. Strictly, it makes a difference between forward-looking assets markets and sticky pricing of goods.
11. See too the review of anomalies in Froot and Thaler (1990).
12. See Sachs and Wyplosz (1984).
13. A first account of exchange rate economics with target zones is presented in Krugman and Miller (1992).
14. See MacDonald and Taylor (1992) and Meese (1990).
15. A major study led by Ralph Bryant (1988) evaluates the comparative predictions of alternative econometric models in response to a precisely specified disturbance.
16. For an argument supporting an even tighter return to fixed rates, see McKinnon (1984). Frenkel, Goldstein and Masson (1991) offer a broad perspective on what a good system has to and can deliver.
17. Hickok and Hung (1991) show the deterioration of the U.S. external balance.

REFERENCES

Bryant, R. et al. (1988). *Empirical Macroeconomics for Interdependent Economies.* Washington, DC: Brookings Institution.

Dobson, W. (1991). *Economic Policy Coordination: Requiem or Prologue.* Policy Analyses No. 30. Washington, DC: Institute for International Economics.

Dornbusch, R. (1976). "Expectations and Exchange Rate Dynamics." *Journal of Political Economy.* December.

Dornbusch, R. (1987). "Purchasing Power Parity." *The New Palgrave.* London:

Macmillan.

Frankel, J. (1982). "In Search of the Exchange Risk Premium: A Six-Currency Test Assuming Mean Variance Optimization." *Journal of International Money and Finance*. 1, December, pp. 255–74.

Frankel, J., and K. Froot. (1990). "Using Survey Data to Test Propositions Regarding Exchange Rate Expectations." *American Economic Review*. 77, pp. 133–53.

Frankel, J., and K. Froot. (1986). "Understanding the Dollar in the 1980s: The Expectations of Chartists and Fundamentalists." *Economic Record* (Supplement). pp. 24–368.

Frenkel, J., M. Goldstein, and P. Masson. (1991). *Characteristics of a Successful Exchange Rate System!*. IMF Occasional Paper no. 82.

Froot, K., and J. Frankel. (1989). "Forward Discount Bias: Is it an Exchange Risk Premium?" *Quarterly Journal of Economics*. 104, no. 2, pp. 139–62.

Froot, K., and R. Thaler. (1990). "Anomalies: Foreign Exchange." *Journal of Economic Perspectives*. Summer.

Hickok, S., and J. Hung. (1991). "Explaining the Persistence of the U.S. Trade Deficit in the late 1980s." *Federal Reserve Bank of New York Quarterly Review*. Winter, pp. 29–44.

Ito, T. (1990). "Foreign Exchange Rate Expectations.: Micro Survey Data." *American Economic Review*. 80, no. 3, June, pp. 434–49.

Kravis, I. (1986). " The Three Faces of the International Comparison Project." *World Bank Research Observer*. January.

Krugman, P. (1985). "Is the Strong Dollar Sustainable?" *The U.S. Dollar: Recent Developments, Prospects and Policy Options*. Federal Reserve Bank of Kansas City.

Krugman, P. (1989). *Exchange Rate Instability*. Cambridge: MIT Press.

Krugman, P., and M. Miller, eds. (1992). *Exchange Rate Targets and Currency Bands*. Cambridge: Cambridge University Press.

League of Nations (Nurkse). (1944). *International Currency Experience: Lessons of the Interwar Period*. Princeton University Press, ch. 5.

Levich, R. (1985). "Gauging the Evidence on Recent Movements in the Value of the Dollar." *The U.S. Dollar—Recent Developments, Outlook and Policy Options*. Federal Reserve Bank of Kansas City.

MacDonald, D., and M. Taylor. (1992). "Exchange Rate Economics: A Survey." *IMF Staff Papers*. March.

Marston, R. (1989). "Real Exchange Rates and Productivity Growth in the United States and Japan." S. Arndt and D. Richardson, eds., *Real-Financial Linkages Among Open Economies*. Cambridge: MIT Press.

Masson, P., et al. (1990). *Multimod Mark II: A Revised and Extended Model*. International Monetary Fund. Occasional Paper no. 71.

Masson, P., and M. Taylor. (1992). "Common Currency Areas and Currency

Unions: An Analysis of the Issues." CEPR Discussion Paper no. 617.

McKinnon, R. (1984). *An International Standard for Monetary Stabilization.* Policy Analyses no. 8. Washington, DC: Institute for International Economics.

Meese, R. (1990). "Currency Fluctuations in the Post Bretton Woods Era." *Journal of Economic Perspectives.* Winter.

Meese, R., and K. Rogoff. (1983). "Empirical Exchange Rate Models of the Seventies: Do They Fit Out of Sample." *Journal of International Economics.* February, pp. 3–24.

Merrill Lynch. (1992). *Currency Forecasting. Theory and Practice.* New York.

Mundell, R. (1968). *International Economics.* New York: Macmillan.

Mundell, R. (1991). "Do Exchange Rates Work? Another View." IMF Working Paper 91/37.

Mussa, M. (1986). "Nominal Exchange Rate Regimes and the Behavior of Real Exchange Rates: Evidence and Implications." Carnegie Rochester Conference Series. Autumn.

Mussa, M. (1979). "Empirical Regularities in the Behavior of Exchange Rates and Theories of the Foreign Exchange Market." Carnegie Rochester Conference Series.

Mussa, M. (1982). "A Model of Exchange Rate Dynamics." *Journal of Political Economy.* February.

Mussa, M. (1985). "Official Intervention and Exchange Rate Dynamics." J. Bhandari, ed., *Exchange Rate Management Under Uncertainty.* Cambridge: MIT Press.

Ohno, K. (1990). "Estimating Yen/Dollar and Mark Dollar Purchasing Power Parities." *IMF Staff Papers* no. 3, September, pp. 700–07.

Sachs, J., and C. Wyplosz. (1984). "Real Exchange Rate Effects of Fiscal Policy." NBER Working Paper no. 1256.

Takagi, S. (1991). "Exchange Rate Expectations." *IMF Staff Papers.* March, pp. 156–83.

Taylor, M., and H. Allen. (1992). "The Use of Technical Analysis in the Foreign Exchange Market." *Journal of International Money and Finance.*

Williamson, J., and M. Miller. (1987). *Targets and Indicators: A Blueprint for the International Coordination of Economic Policy.* Policy Analysis no. 22. Washington DC: Institute for International Economics.

CHAPTER 3

EXCHANGE RATES AND THE VALUATION OF FIRMS

Maurice D. Levi

INTRODUCTION

If exchange rates are to affect the value of a firm they must influence operating income, corporate taxes, or the rate at which future after-tax operating incomes translate into current market values. This paper explores these channels of influence in order to relate the foreign exchange exposure that a firm faces to the nature of the market in which the firm operates, and to the financial characteristics of the firm. The purpose is to obtain a checklist of the factors that are behind exposure, and to explain why it is that estimation of exposure has proven to be so difficult. The focus is on the value of exporting and importing firms, although the approach taken could apply to any exposed firm such as an import-competing firm, or a firm that is exposed only via its balance sheet.

While there have been several previous studies of exchange rates on the value of firms, these have been cast in terms of the traditional paradigms of corporate finance. In contrast, this paper presents the analog using the standard analytical approach of microeconomics.[1] Furthermore, this paper directly relates the microeconomics of exchange rates to empirical efforts to measure exposure. This helps explain why researchers have faced substantial difficulties in obtaining stable measures of exposure. In particular, the microeconomics of exchange rates identifies several factors which influence the size of exposure and which are likely to vary considerably over time. For example, an exporter's exposure to a particular currency is shown to depend on the profitability of sales in the country which uses that currency, as well as on the foreign market's elasticity of demand. With profitability as well as other pertinent factors varying over time, the low statistical significance of exposure coefficients and the other disappointments in empirical research should come as little surprise.

The paper is organized as follows. The first section considers the case of an exporting firm which maximizes profit in each foreign market, and produces all of its product at home without imported inputs. The second section considers the antithetical situation of an importing firm which buys a homogenous product in different foreign markets, and sells the product at home. The third sections relates the microeconomics of exchange rate effects on the firm to the estimation of exposure. The final section offers some concluding remarks concerning the implications of the causes of the difficulty of measuring exposure for future research and for the management of foreign exchange exposure.

EXCHANGE RATES AND THE EXPORTER

We can write the value of an exporting firm as

$$V = \frac{TR - TC}{\rho}(1 - \tau) + \sum_{i=0}^{k} \pi_i X_i \tag{3.1}$$

where

$$TR = \sum_{i=0}^{k} \pi_i p_i q_i \tag{3.2}$$

and

$$TC = c \sum_{i=0}^{k} q_i \tag{3.3}$$

In this statement of value

V = market value of firm.

TR = total revenue.

TC = total cost.

ρ = risk-adjusted shareholder opportunity cost of capital.

τ = tax rate.

π_i = exchange rate, in units of home currency per unit of currency i.

X_i = net monetary asset/liability position in currency i, (negative for liabilities).

p_i = product price in country i.

q_i = quantity sold in country i.

c = marginal cost of production at home, assumed constant.[2]

The value of the exporter is written in its standard form, namely as the present value of the after-tax profit stream, with this assumed to be a perpetuity. The rate of return required by shareholders is adjusted for systematic risk. Total revenue comes from sales in k countries, with all revenues converted into the home currency.[3] Total cost is calculated on the assumption of constant marginal cost, and where all of the cost is incurred at home. The final term gives the home currency value of all foreign assets and liabilities. In the event of foreign currency denominated liabilities in currency i, the value of X_i is negative. The term X_i reflects all foreign currency assets or debts as well as futures and forward contracts. These might or might not be related to the firm's hedging activities.

The response of the value of the firm to a change in the exchange rate vis-à-vis currency j is

$$\frac{\partial V}{\partial \pi_j}.$$

If we assume a change in π_j is real and permanent, we can write $\partial V / \partial \pi_j$ as:[4]

$$\frac{\partial V}{\partial \pi_j} = \{ p_j q_j + \pi_j p_j \frac{dq_j}{dp_j} \frac{dp_j}{d\pi_j} + \pi_j q_j \frac{dp_j}{d\pi_j} - c \frac{dq_j}{dp_j} \frac{dp_j}{d\pi_j} \} \frac{(1-\tau)}{\rho} + X_j . \quad (3.4)$$

In this statement of $\partial V / \partial \pi_j$ we assume that the corporate tax **rate** is not affected by the exchange rate, which would be reasonable if corporate taxes are paid to the home government which cares about profit, not where or how the profit was earned. We also assume the required shareholder rate of return is invariant to the exchange rate.

The expression for $\partial V / \partial \pi_j$ in (3.4) can be simplified by noting that for a profit-maximizing firm $dTR/dq_j = dTC/dq_j$. Therefore, from (3.2) and (3.3) and the eminently reasonable assumption that the firm's output does not affect the exchange rate:

$$\pi_j p_j + \pi_j q_j \frac{dp_j}{dq_j} = c$$

or

$$p_j = \frac{c}{\pi_j \left(1 - \frac{1}{\eta}\right)}, \qquad (3.5)$$

where

$$\eta_j = -\frac{p_j \, dq_j}{q_j \, dp_j}$$

is the elasticity of demand in country j. The statement of prices in (3.5) assumes the firm can effectively price discriminate between markets. This requires that it is not possible to arbitrage the firm's goods between markets when prices differ.[5] That is, the home-currency equivalent of the price in country j is

$$\pi_j p_j = \frac{c}{\left(1 - \frac{1}{\eta}\right)}.$$

so that the more elastic the demand in j, the lower the price. (Since the firm is a profit-maximizer, we know $\eta_j > 1$, as no firm sells where demand is inelastic, ensuring a positive price.)

From (3.5) we have

$$\frac{dp_j}{d\pi_j} = -\frac{p_j}{\pi_j}.$$

Using this and the definition of η_j in (3.2) gives:

$$\frac{\partial V}{\partial p_j} = \{ p_j q_j - p_j q_j (1 - \eta_j) + c \frac{dq_j}{dp_j} \frac{p_j}{\pi_j} \} \frac{(1 - \tau)}{\rho} + X_j$$

That is:

$$\frac{\partial V}{\partial p_j} = \eta_j \, q_j \, (p_j - \frac{c}{\pi_j}) \frac{(1-\tau)}{\rho} + X_j \, .$$ (3.6)

This can be stated in terms of elasticity of firm value vis-à-vis the exchange rate, namely

$$\frac{\pi_j}{V} \frac{\partial V}{\partial \pi_j} = \eta_j \frac{\pi_j q_j \, (p_j - \frac{c}{\pi_j})(1-\tau)/\rho}{V} + \frac{\pi_j X_j}{V} \, .$$ (3.7)

Equation (3.7) tells us that the sensitivity of the value of the firm vis-à-vis the exchange rate of currency j depends directly on the elasticity of demand for the product in country j, η_j. It also depends on the profit generated in country j which is the per unit mark-up, $(p_j - c/\pi_j)$, times the amount sold, q_j.[6] The profit is seen to be converted into home currency by premultiplication by π_j. We can see that if market j is profitable, so that the first term in (3.7) is positive, then the value of the firm increases more after a depreciation/devaluation of the home currency the more elastic is demand; recall that π_j increases with depreciation, so the exporting firm's value goes up with home currency depreciation. The impact of exchange rates also varies inversely with the tax rate and the opportunity cost of capital.

The financial position of the firm, specifically the home currency value of the net position in currency j, also impacts on the value of the firm. Indeed, if

$$X_j = -\eta_j q_j (p_j - \frac{c}{\pi_j})(1-\tau)/\rho$$ (3.8)

there is no impact at all. This is the exporter's "delta" hedge, suggesting the firm take on foreign currency-denominated liabilities or a short forward position in the foreign currency equal to the present value of the after-tax foreign currency profit in market j, times j's demand elasticity. Clearly, there are several factors in (3.7), or (3.8), that can change over time, thereby affecting the sensitivity of the firm's value to changes in exchange rates from period to period.

Exchange Rates and the Importer

As with the exporter, we can write the value of an importing firm as in (3.1), namely

$$V = \frac{TR - TC}{\rho}(1 - \tau) + \sum_{i=0}^{k} \pi_i X_i$$

but where

$$TR = \sum_{i=0}^{k} q_i \tag{3.9}$$

$$TC = \sum_{i=0}^{k} \pi_i c_i q_i \tag{3.10}$$

and where, in this case, p is the price of the product in the home market and home currency, and c_i is the marginal cost in the source country/ currency, assumed constant. The importer is assumed to face a downward-sloping demand for the imported product which is assumed homogeneous, and to be able to buy all that it wants at price c_i.

From (3.1) using (3.9) and (3.10) and the reasonable assumption that $dc_j / d\pi_i = 0$, we can write $\partial V / \partial / \pi_i$ as

$$\frac{\partial V}{\partial \pi_j} = \{p \frac{dq_j}{dp} \frac{dp}{d\pi_j} + q_j \frac{dp}{d\pi_j} - c_j q_j - \pi_j c_j \frac{dq_j}{dp} \frac{dp_j}{d\pi_j}\} \frac{(1 - \tau)}{\rho} + X_j. \tag{3.11}$$

Assuming the importer is a profit-maximizing firm so that sourcing from each market is where $dTR / dq_j = dTC / dq_j$, we can simplify (3.11) by noting that

$$p + q_j \frac{dp}{dq_j} = \pi_j c_j$$

i.e.,

$$p = \frac{\pi_j c_j}{(1 - \frac{1}{\eta})} \tag{3.12}$$

where because the import is homogeneous, all demand elasticities are the same, η.

From (3.12) we have that

$$\frac{dp}{d\pi_j} = \frac{p}{\pi_j}.$$

(3.13)

Using this in (3.11) gives

$$\frac{\partial V}{\partial \pi_j} = \{-\frac{pq_j}{\pi_j}\eta + \frac{pq_j}{\pi_j} - c_j q_j + c_j q_j \eta\}\frac{(1-\tau)}{\rho} + X_j$$

(3.14)

$$= (1-\eta) q_j (\frac{p}{\pi_j} - c_j)\frac{(1-\tau)}{\rho} + X_j.$$

Alternatively, in terms of elasticities

$$\frac{\pi_j}{V} \frac{\partial V}{\partial \pi_j} = (1-\eta) q_j (p - \frac{c}{\pi_j})\frac{(1-\tau)}{V} + \frac{\pi_j X_j}{V}$$

(3.15)

First, we note that because $\eta > 1$ (implying that all firms that can set their price operate where demand is elastic), then if importing firms make a profit, (3.15) is negative, and losses are made from depreciations and gains from appreciations. Further, the higher the elasticity is, the greater are the losses or gains. Similarly, the sensitivity of the firm's value is affected by the profitability, $q_j (p - c_j/\pi_j)$, where this is measured in the importer's currency. Again, the higher is the tax rate or shareholder's required rate of return, the lower is the sensitivity of value to exchange rates. As in the case of an exporter, if the firm selects its balance sheet position such that, in this case:

$$X_j = (1-\eta) q_j (\frac{p}{\pi_j} - c_j)(1-\tau)/\rho$$

(3.16)

there is no exchange rate sensitivity. Of course, it is clear from (3.15) or (3.16) that there are many factors that can vary and affect the impact of exchange rates on the importing firm during any period.

DIFFICULTIES IN EMPIRICALLY ESTIMATING EXPOSURE

In their seminal article defining foreign exchange risk and exposure, Adler and Dumas (1984) defined exposure in terms of the sensitivity of the value of a firm—or a portfolio of firms—to unanticipated changes in (real) exchange rates. That is, the expressions in (3.6) and (3.14) *are* foreign exchange exposure, provided we correctly interpret π_j. Alternatively, as explained in Adler and Simon (1986), we can think of exposure in elasticity terms, in which case it is defined by (3.7) or (3.15). That is, when we use, for example, a regression such as

$$\Delta V_t = \sum_{i=0}^{k} \beta_i \Delta \pi_{it} + u_t \tag{3.17}$$

to measure exposure from the estimated β's, these β's are directly related to (3.7) or (3.15) according to whether the firm exports or imports.[7]

Inspection of (3.7) and (3.15) reveals many factors which can change over time, introducing variability in the regression coefficients measuring exposure. First, the elasticity of demand, η, might not be constant. Second, the profitability of operations, given by the terms $q_j (p_j - c/\pi_j)$ and $q_j(p - c_j/\pi_j)$ in (3.7) and (3.15), can be expected to change substantially over the business cycle. Third, *effective* tax rates and required shareholder returns are likely to vary from period to period. Finally and perhaps most importantly, X_j is not only likely to change but, indeed, is an endogenous variable that the firm adjusts to influence exposure. In the limit, if X_j were maintained as in (3.8) or (3.16), exposure would always be zero. This is, of course, as it should be, but if X_j varies over time, exposure will be unstable. Indeed, given that the hedging X_j depends on much that the firm does not know and is also influenced by financial market changes and other factors, it is hard to believe that exposure would be anything but variable.

If exposure was the dependent variable in a regressive equation, it would be a straightforward matter to add explanatory variable in (3.17) to account for variability in profits, effective tax rates, rates of return, and the firm's position in financial assets, liabilities, and forward contracts. Unfortunately, however, exposure is measured from regression coefficients. This means that other than by explicitly modeling the variability of coefficients by special variable-coefficients econometric techniques, the volatility of exposure will force the coefficients toward statistical insignificance. This would lead us to erroneously conclude that the firm has little exposure, and to infer either that the firm's foreign exchange management is brilliant or the market is stupid.

CONCLUSIONS

The microeconomics of the effects of exchange rates on the value of a firm suggests that a lot of factors influence exposure. Indeed, as we have suggested, it is difficult to distinguish between magnificent exposure management and markets which cannot identify the real thing when they see it. Both would result in no significant sensitivity in the value of the firm with respect to exchange rate changes. So what are we to learn from the difficulty of determining exposure, something readily apparent to anybody who has tried? Fortunately, all is not lost.

While regression coefficients themselves, which are almost invariably insignificant, tell us very little—maybe profits have varied, exposure management has varied or been successful, and so on—the standard errors of the estimate and associated R^2's tell us quite a lot.[8] In regressions of exchange rates against firm values when no other regressors are involved, the R^2 tells us how important exchange rates are in the overall scheme of what is affecting a firm's value. When very little of the variability of firm value is attributable to changes in exchange rates, the firm can devote an appropriately small portion of its marginal, managerial resources to managing exchange rate risk and exposure. More specifically, it can devote no more than it has been devoting. The alternative is to proceed as others have suggested, and simulate the effects of different actions under alternative managerial scenarios. Indeed, the intrinsic variability in a firm's exposure as described in this paper suggests that simulation is probably the best route to follow.

NOTES

1. The previous studies include those of Dumas (1978), Heckerman (1972), Hekman (1983), Hodder (1982), and Shapiro (1975).
2. Clearly, one factor that could influence the effect of changes in exchange rates is the presence of imported inputs, which we exclude. The introduction of imported inputs makes profit-maximizing output dependent on more than one exchange rate and thereby complicates the analysis.
3. We assume that current values of p_i, q_i, and also of π_i are expected to continue. It is possible to allow for inflation by building this into ρ, c, and p_i, but this does not affect

the conclusions reached.

4. The assumptions, which may not hold in practice—for example, *real* rate changes may very well eventually be reversed—are discussed later.

5. The evidence from Isard (1977) and Kalter (1978) supports the view that exporters can indeed discriminate.

6. The outcome of differentiation shows marginal cost to be divided by π_j which means the domestic currency cost is converted into units of currency j, the same units of measurement as p_j. The term $(p_j - \frac{c}{\pi_j})$ is hence the per-unit profit measured in currency j.

7. If the firm both exports and imports, the β is a combination of the two.

8. The difficulty obtaining significant exposure coefficients is evident in the work of Amihud (1992), presented in this conference volume and in work by this author that is summarized in the appendix. As the appendix show, it is difficult to observe exposure, even in a specific context where exposure, at least in the absence of hedging, is likely to be found.

REFERENCES

Adler, M., and B. Dumas. (1984). "Exposure to Currency Risk: Definition and Measurement." *Financial Management*. Summer, pp. 41–50.

Adler, M., B. Dumas and D. Simon. (1986). "Exchange Risk Surprises in International Portfolios." *Journal of Portfolio Management*. Winter, pp. 44–53.

Amihud, Y. (1992). "Exchange Rates and the Valuation of Equity Shares." Chapter 4, this volume.

Dumas, B. (1978). "The Theory of the Trading Firm Revisited." *Journal of Finance*. 33, June, pp. 1019–29.

Heckerman, D. (1972). "The Exchange Risk of Foreign Operations." *Journal of Business*. 45, January, pp. 42–48.

Hekman, C. (1983). "The Real Effects of Foreign Exchange Rate Changes on a Competitive, Profit-Maximizing Firm." Unpublished.

Hodder, J. (1982). "Exposure to Exchange-Rate Movements." *Journal of International Economics*. 13, November, pp. 375–86.

Isard, P. (1977). "How Far Can We Push the 'Law of One Price'?" *American Economic Review*. December, pp. 942–48.

Kalter, E. (1988). "The Effect of Exchange Rate Changes upon International Price Discrimination." Washington, DC: Board of Governors of the Federal Reserve International Finance Discussion Paper no. 122.

Shapiro, A. (1975). "Exchange Rate Changes and the Value of the Multinational Corporation." *Journal of Finance*. 30, May, pp. 485–502.

APPENDIX A TO CHAPTER 3

In Canada, where almost 35 percent of output is exported, 80 percent of which goes to the United States, we have a fertile area for estimating exporting firms' exposures. A particularly good candidate for examination is the forest product industry since, for example, in 1984, approximately 70 percent of paper and over 80 percent of lumber was exported.

Table A–1 shows exposure against real changes in exchange rates, where real rate changes are actual changes minus relevant differences in inflation. The dependent variable is the percent change in the Toronto Stock Exchange index for paper and forest products, measured over the period January 1970 to August 1985. The interest rate is added to reduce serial correlation, where this is the three-month Canadian treasury bill rate, although this variable itself is insignificant. The table shows that exposure to the U.S. dollar is totally insignificant. Exposure to the U.K. pound works in the "wrong" direction: a depreciation of the Canadian dollar vis-à-vis the pound is associated with a decline in the forest product index, although this is not quite significant at the 5 percent level. Only exposure against the Japanese yen is significant and of the expected sign. Since hedging against the yen does not occur whereas it is common to hedge against the U.S. dollar via U.S. denominated debt, this might suggest good hedging ability is the cause of poor exposure coefficient estimates.

Table A–2 includes the overall market index in case the effect of exchange rates is obscured by indirect effect of exchange rates working on the market index. However, this is seen to have no noticeable effect on the ability to detect exposure.

Of not in Table A–1 is the low R^2, even when the interest rate is included. It would appear that a major part of the variation in the value of forest product companies is attributable to factors not associated with exchange rates.

TABLE A–1
Exposure of the Canadian Forest Products Industry

Period	Constant	Interest rate	Exchange Rate (C$/US$)	(C$/£)	(C$/¥)	R^2	D-W
1980–85	0.0170 (0.7065)	−0.0015 (−0.0118)	−0.0063 (−0.0118)	−0.4147 (−1.8671)	0.3502 (1.4981)	0.07	1.73
1975–85	−0.0062 (−0.4407)	−0.0003 (0.2341)	0.1094 (0.3104)	−0.2570 (−1.7421)	0.5589[a] (3.6703)	0.11	1.72
1973–85	0.0041 (0.3375)	−0.0005 (−0.4252)	0.0697 (0.1994)	−0.2701 (−1.8673)	0.5956[a] (4.1820)	0.12	1.84
1970–85	−0.0039 (−0.4412)	0.0001 (0.1550)	0.2459 (0.7370)	−0.2727 −1.9323	0.5841[a] (4.2365)	0.11	1.83

[a] Significant at the 1 percent level.

TABLE A–2
Exposure of the Canadian Forest Products Industry: Overall Market Effect Included

			Exchange Rate				
Period	Constant	Market return	(C$/US$)	(C$/£)	(C$/¥)	R^2	D-W
1980–85	0.1131 (0.4358)	1.0727[a] (9.1433)	−0.0011 (−0.5617)	−0.4329 (−1.9161)	0.3639 (1.5433)	0.65	1.77
1975–85	−0.0093 (−0.6352)	1.0675[a] (13.812)	0.0005 (0.3888)	−0.2806 (−1.8690)	0.5662[a] (3.7089)	0.64	1.76
1973–85	0.0035 (0.2848)	1.0332[a] (14.603)	−0.0005 (−0.3916)	−0.2811 (−1.9136)	0.5957[a] (4.1716)	0.63	1.85
1970–85	−0.0052 (−0.5980)	1.1051[a] (17.080)	0.0002 (0.2337)	−0.3081[b] (−2.1670)	0.5820[a] (4.2365)	0.64	1.87

[a] Significant at the 1 percent level.
[b] Significant at the 5 percent level.

CHAPTER 4

EXCHANGE RATES AND THE
VALUATION OF EQUITY SHARES

Yakov Amihud

"Computer stocks were on the comeback trail Wednesday...Helping the stocks, analysts said, was the weakening dollar, which makes it easier for those companies to sell overseas."

USA Today, March 28, 1985.

The common wisdom is that a decline of the exchange rate of foreign currencies against the U.S. dollar is beneficial to U.S. exporting companies, and an appreciation of the exchange rate hurts these companies. If the exporting company maintains its revenue in foreign currency, its revenue in domestic currency will increase. If the company changes its prices abroad, the final effect on revenue depends on the demand elasticities of the companies' products in foreign and domestic markets.[1] Additional factors that affect the results are the demand elasticity of the exporting company to imported inputs, and the weight of exports in the companies' sales relative to the weight of imports in their inputs. Exchange rate changes also affect interest rates, prices, and national income, which in turn affect companies' values. Companies in the import-substituting industries are also affected by exchange rate changes. All these other effects are often unobserved; for example, there is no publicly available information on the weight of imports in companies'

The author thanks Rudi Dornbusch, Richard Levich, and Ingo Walter for helpful suggestions and J.P. Morgan for providing the exchange rates data. Research assistance was provided by W. Lui.

inputs or on the hedging positions of companies, including their hedging through financial contracts. In addition, the effects of all these factors may be varying over time (Levi, this volume), and the firms may respond dynamically to changes in exchange rates in a way that may offset or change their effect over time.

In general, the hypothesis can be stated as the following: *changes in the exchange rate of foreign currencies against the U.S. dollar affect negatively the values of U.S. exporting companies.* The final result depends on the factors mentioned above.

There are some earlier tests of this hypothesis. Giddy (1974) studied the effect of the large change in the exchange rates regime during the early 1970s and the subsequent devaluation of the U.S. dollar on stock prices using the event-study methodology. While the market as a whole showed a positive reaction to the devaluation, the results for specific industries were mixed. Mann (1986) examined the behavior of product prices and profit margins of U.S. companies in some export industries relative to the U.S. dollar exchange rates during 1977–1985. She found that on average, both profit margins and product prices in dollars were insensitive to exchange rates, adversely affecting the price competitiveness of U.S. exporters. This leaves open the question of the effect of the exchange rate changes on the profitability and values of exporting companies. Recently, Jorion (1990) examined the cross-sectional relationship between the exchange-rate exposure of companies and the weight of exports in their sales. He found a relationship which is consistent with the theory: the greater the weight of exports in sales, the greater the response of companies' stock prices to exchange rate changes. However, almost all companies in his sample showed no relationship between exchange rates changes and companies' equity values, and the number of companies with significant such relationship did not differ from what could be obtained by random sampling of companies (regardless of their exporting intensity). Here, I examine this issue in a different way by looking not only at the contemporaneous effect of exchange rates changes on companies' values but also on their lagged effects. I also use data on *real* exchange rates—that take into account the differential rate of inflation between the U.S. and its trading partners.

To test the hypothesis, I first estimated the contemporaneous effect of the relative (percentage) changes in the exchange rate index of 15 industrial-country currencies against the U.S. dollar, DXk_t, on the return (equally-weighted) of a portfolio of U.S. exporting companies, RP_t, controlling for the return on the market portfolio (equally-weighted) 1, RM_t (data are monthly).[2]

$$RP_t = \alpha + \beta \cdot RM_t + \delta k \cdot DXk_t + \epsilon_t \qquad (4.1)$$

where k denotes *real* $k = r$ or *nominal* $k = n$ exchange rate.[3] The hypothesis on the effect of exchange rate changes on companies' values implies $\delta k < 0$.

The sample of exporting companies consists of 32 companies that appeared in *all* annual lists of "50 Leading Exporters" in *Fortune* between 1982 and 1988. The returns data were obtained from the University of Chicago CRSP monthly file. The exchange rate indices were provided by Morgan Guaranty Trust Company of New York (a subsidiary of J.P. Morgan & Co.). They are "effective," trade-weighted, both nominal and real indices, the latter reflecting differences in inflation between the U.S. and its trading partners.[4] The sample period is January 1979–December 1988, during which there was a large rise and then a fall in the exchange rate index.

The estimation results of model (1) were as follows:

For *real* exchange rates: $\delta r = -0.049$ ($t = 0.42$).

For *nominal* exchange rates: $\delta n = -0.054$ ($t = 0.48$).

Also, $\beta = 0.99$ ($t = 25.16$) DW $= 2.25$ (indicating autocorrelated residuals). The coefficients δk are insignificantly different from zero. This suggests that exchange rate changes have no contemporaneous effect on the values of exporting companies (relative to the market).[5]

The 32 companies in the sample were the largest exporters in dollar terms but not necessarily the largest in terms of exports-to-sales ratio. On average, export sales constituted 13.9 percent of the total sales of the sampled companies over the period 1982–1988. I therefore tested next the relationship between the exchange rate effect and the weight of exports in the companies' sales. Companies were ranked by their average exports/sales ratios during 1982–1988 and divided into two groups of 16 companies with the highest and lowest average ratios, denoted H16 and L16 (respectively). The average exports/sales ratio for the group H16 was 19.3 percent, and for L16 it was 8.55 percent. I also constructed a portfolio H8 of the 8 companies whose exports/sales ratios were the highest, averaging 24 percent.[6] The effect of exchange rate should be the strongest for these companies.

The estimation results of model (1) for the three portfolios are as follows (results are presented for real exchange rates):

High 8 exporters: $\delta r = -0.122$ ($t = 0.70$).

High 16 exporters: $\delta r = -0.042$ ($t = 0.30$).

Low 16 exporters: $\delta r = -0.056$ ($t = 0.47$).

The coefficient of the H8 portfolio is the most negative, as expected, but all coefficients are insignificantly different from zero. These results are consistent with those of Jorion (1990), who found that changes in nominal exchange rates do not have a significant effect on the contemporaneous stock returns of individual companies, while cross-sectionally, the effect is more pronounced for companies with high export/sales ratios. The results are also consistent with those presented in Levi (this volume).

The relationship between exchange rates changes and companies' values may change over time, as analyzed by Levi (this volume). I divided the sample into two equal subperiods of 60 months each, and estimated model 1 for each separately. The results are presented here for the portfolio of the highest eight exporting companies, where the relationship is expected to be the strongest:

First period, 1979-1984: $\delta r = 0.221$ ($t = 0.78$).
Second period, 1985-1988: $\delta r = -0.256$ ($t = 1.12$).

This is, however, a *joint* test of the exchange rate effect and of the market efficiency hypothesis. Model (1) assumes that the publicly available information on exchange rates is immediately and fully incorporated in stock prices. Departing from the market-efficiency paradigm, I estimated a model that allows for *lagged* effects of exchange rate changes and for a lagged effect of the companies' returns:

$$RP_t = constant + 0.98RM_t - 0.088RP_{t-1} + 0.064DXr_t - 0.226DXr_{t-1}$$
$$(25.62)\qquad(2.43)\qquad\quad(0.53)\qquad\quad(1.77)$$

$$(4.2)$$

$$+ 0.149DXr_{t-2} - 0.220DXr_{t-3} + 0.046DXr_{t-4} - 0.061DXr_{t-5} - 0.162DXr_{t-6} + \epsilon_t.$$
$$(1.18)\qquad\quad(1.76)\qquad\quad(0.37)\qquad\quad(0.49)\qquad\quad(1.36)$$

($DW = 2.02$). The results show a considerable cumulative negative effect of exchange rate changes on the values of exporting companies, but none of the coefficients of DXr_{t-i} ($i = 0, 1,\ldots, 6$) is significantly different from zero at the standard 5 percent level of significance. Also, a joint test of all coefficients being zero produced F = 1.31, insignificant. Thus, the hypothesis that exchange rate changes do not affect the values of exporting companies cannot be rejected. This could reflect the success of companies in hedging the foreign exchange effects. However, currency hedges are usually short-term and if the exchange rate changes are not transitory or short-lived,[7] their effect cannot be entirely eliminated. Short-term financial hedging could also bridge the time necessary to implement long-term response by companies (e.g., changing their production location, the sources of inputs, and the export markets). However, these changes are costly and relatively slow, and thus the exchange rate changes may still be expected to affect companies' values.

Because the alternative hypothesis to the null is that the coefficients of DXr_{t-1} are *negative*, a one-tail test applies and then the coefficients of lags 1 and 3 in model (2) are significantly different from zero at the 5 percent level. This suggests that if exchange rates affect at all the values of exporting companies, the effect comes with lags of one and three months. The results for the nominal exchange rates ($k = n$) were similar and are omitted hereafter for parsimony.

A possible explanation for the lagged reaction of stock prices to exchange rate changes is that the effect on profitability is observed when companies publish their financial reports, which occurs with a lag. Although exchange rate changes are public information, the extent of a company's short-term hedging against them is private (inside) information which is reported after the fact in the financial reports. (Long-term hedges such as foreign currency debt or foreign operations is public information.) However, rational investors should expect that when the changes in exchange rates occur, it cannot have a systematic effect on the results. There is an information lag in the real exchange rates, because the price indexes of the countries whose currencies comprise the index of the real trade-weighted exchange rate are known to investors with a lag of one month; however, similar lagged effects are observed for nominal exchange rates. In summary, while there are reasons to expect that part of the information on the effects of exchange rate changes on companies' values is reported to investors with a time lag, much of these effects should be anticipated and incorporated into stock prices at the time the changes take place, and should not have a systematic effect later.

The series DXr_t (and DXn_t) are autocorrelated,[8] implying that part of the exchange rate changes were anticipated and their effects were already partially incorporated in stock prices by the time they took place. To test the effects of *unanticipated* exchange rate changes on the values of exporting companies, I first estimated the model

$$DXr_t = f_0 + f_1 \cdot DXr_{t-1} + \epsilon DXr_t. \qquad (4.3)$$

The estimated slope coefficient was $f_1 = 0.309$ ($t = 3.63$), and $DW = 1.97$.

(Estimation period: July 1978–December 1988). Higher-order lags were insignificant, and so were the residuals autocorrelations (up to 6 lags). The residuals series ϵDXr_t, representing the *unanticipated* exchange rate changes, were then used to estimate the following model:

$$RP_t = constant + 0.983RM_t - 0.086RP_{t-1} + 0.062\epsilon DXr_{t-1} - 0.211\epsilon DXr_{t-1}$$
$$\qquad\qquad\quad (25.46) \qquad (2.35) \qquad\quad (0.51) \qquad\qquad (1.74)$$

$$+ 0.078\epsilon DXr_{t-2} - 0.204\epsilon DXr_{t-3} - 0.015\epsilon DXr_{t-4} - 0.063\epsilon DXr_{t-5} \qquad (4.4)$$
$$\quad (0.65) \qquad\quad (1.72) \qquad\qquad (0.13) \qquad\qquad (0.53)$$

$$- 0.143\epsilon DXr_{t-6} + \epsilon_t.$$
$$\quad (1.19)$$

($DW = 2.01$). The F-statistic testing the joint significance of the coefficients of ϵDXr_{t-i} ($i = 0, 1,...,6$) was 1.13, insignificant. The results for the residuals are similar to those in model (4.2), and in both models the strongest effect is after one and three months.

To test the stability of the results over time,[9] I estimated models (4.3) and (4.4) separately for two five-year subperiods, 1979–1983 and 1984–1988. The slope coefficients f_1 in model (4.3) were not significantly different in the two subperiods. Importantly, *none* of the coefficients of ϵDXr_{t-1}, ($i = 0, 1,..., 6$) were significantly different from zero in either subperiod.[10] The insignificance of the exchange rate effect during the second subperiod, 1984–1988, is particularly striking, given that period's sharp rise and fall in the exchange rate index which was then said to have affected the export industries.

I further adjusted the exchange-rate autoregression model (4.3) as follows:

$$DXr_t = f_0 + f_1 \cdot DXr_{t-1} + f_{0,1} \cdot \text{DUMMY} + f_{1,1} \cdot (\text{DUMMY} \cdot DXr_{t-1}) + \epsilon DXr_t,$$

where DUMMY = 1 for the first half of the period (July 1978–December 1983) and zero thereafter. The estimated values of the added coefficients were $f_{0,1} = 0.062$ ($t = 2.01$) and $f_{1,1} = -0.13$ ($t = 0.75$), implying that the slope coefficient was stable over the two subperiods. The residuals ϵDXr_t from this model were used to estimate model (4.4). Then, *none* of the coefficients of ϵDXr_{t-1} ($i = 0, 1,..., 6$) were significantly different from zero (at a one-tail test).

Model (4.4) was reestimated for each group of companies, using the residual exchange rate changes from model (3.3). Because only lags 1, 3 and 6 had marginal significance in model (4.4), I estimated the model with these lags only. The results are presented in Table 4–1.

As expected, the estimated coefficients of the (residual) exchange rate changes were the most negative for portfolio H8 (the eight companies with the highest exports/sales ratios).[11] However, the statistical significance of the results was low. Strictly, the effect of exchange rates changes on the equity values of the companies with the highest exports is nil.

Finally, I estimated a model where the data—returns and exchange rate changes—were all quarterly:

$$RP_t = \alpha + \beta \cdot RM_t + \gamma \cdot RP_{t-1} + \sum_{i=0}^{4} \delta_i \cdot DXr_{t-i} + \epsilon_t \qquad (4.5)$$

The results, presented in Table 4–2, show that exchange rate changes have a weakly significant effect on companies' values, but only with a lag of two quarters. Although the coefficient δ_2 is significant and with the correct

TABLE 4–1
The Effect of Exchange Rate Changes on Stock Prices, Monthly Data, 1979–1988

The model is

$$RP_t = \alpha + \beta \cdot RM_t + \gamma \cdot RP_{t-1} + \delta_1 \cdot \epsilon DXr_{t-1} + \delta_3 \cdot \epsilon DXr_{t-3} + \delta_6 \cdot \epsilon DXr_{t-6} + \epsilon_t$$

where RP_t is the portfolio return of exporting companies, RM_t is the return on the equally-weighted market portfolio, and ϵDXr_t are the residuals from first-order autoregression of changes in the real trade-weighted effective exchange rate. There are 3 portfolios: 16 companies with the highest exports/sales ratios, 16 companies with the lowest exports/sales ratios, and 8 companies with the highest exports/sales ratios. F is the statistics of the test $\delta_1 = \delta_3 = \delta_6 = 0$; t-values are in parentheses.

Portfolio	β	γ	δ_1	δ_3	δ_6	DW	F
16 High Exports	1.05 (22.9)	–0.048 (1.21)	–0.148 (1.03)	–0.204 (1.44)	–0.206 (1.42)	1.90	1.80
16 Low Exports	0.92 (24.0)	–0.127 (3.39)	–0.273 (2.27)	–0.190 (1.61)	–0.065 (0.55)	2.12	2.64
8 High Exports	1.08 (18.8)	–0.095 (2.09)	–0.302 (1.66)	–0.271 (1.52)	–0.232 (1.30)	1.77	2.45

TABLE 4–2
The Effect of Exchange Rate Changes on Stock Prices, Quarterly Data, 1979–1988

The model is

$$RP_t = \alpha + \beta \cdot RM_t + \gamma \cdot RP_{t-1} + \sum_{i=0}^{4} \delta_i \cdot DXr_{t-i} + \epsilon_t \qquad (4.5)$$

where RP_t is the portfolio return, RM_t is the return on the equally-weighted market portfolio, and DXr_t is the quarterly change in the trade-weighted effective real exchange rate. The estimation is for the all sampled 32 companies and for the portfolios of 16 and 8 companies ranked by their exports/sales ratios. t-values are in parentheses.

Portfolio	γ	δ_0	δ_1	δ_2	δ_3	δ_4	$\sum_{i=0}^{4} \delta_i$
All 32 Stocks	0.131 (2.00)	−0.033 (0.19)	0.005 (0.03)	−0.476 (2.57)	0.269 (1.41)	−0.057 (0.31)	−0.292
16 High Exports	0.128 (1.57)	−0.022 (0.09)	−0.081 (0.31)	−0.472 (1.82)	0.350 (1.31)	−0.091 (0.36)	−0.316
16 Low Exports	0.125 (2.05)	−0.042 (0.29)	−0.088 (0.56)	−0.483 (3.11)	0.182 (1.13)	−0.018 (0.11)	−0.449
8 High Exports	0.147 (1.57)	−0.182 (0.62)	−0.127 (0.40)	−0.431 (1.36)	0.522 (1.61)	−0.281 (0.90)	−0.499

sign for the entire sample, the joint effect of all coefficients (employing F-test) is not significant. The effect of the exchange rate changes is most negative for portfolio H8, as expected, but the coefficients are not significantly different from zero.

The quarterly series of exchange rate changes, DXr_t, were not significantly autocorrelated, and therefore I do not present the results employing the procedure used for the monthly data [models (4.3) and (4.4)]. The autoregressive coefficient for the quarterly real exchange rate changes, estimated by model (4.3), was 0.28 with $t = 1.89$ (the results are similar for nominal exchange rates). The estimation results of model (4.5) using the residuals ϵDXr_t from the autoregressive estimation in lieu of DXr_t are not qualitatively different from those presented in Table 4–2. The coefficient δ_2 became slightly more negative and had greater statistical significance,[12] indicating again a lagged effect of exchange rates. Model (4.5) was also estimated using nominal instead of real exchange rates, and the results were qualitatively similar to those reported for the real exchange rates. The estimated cumulative effect of nominal exchange rate changes was negative, as expected, and with a lag, but the statistical significance of the esimated coefficients was low, in fact lower than that found for the real exchange rates. Again, the hypothesis that the values of exporting companies are unaffected by exchange rate changes could not be rejected.

CONCLUSIONS

This chapter examined the hypothesis that the values of U.S. exporting companies are negatively related to changes in the exchange rates of foreign currencies against the U.S. dollar. The estimations show the following:

First, while the direction of the exchange-rate effect on is as expected, the statistical significance of the results is very low, implying that it could be that exchange rate changes have no effect on the values of exporting companies.

Second, the strongest effect of exchange rate changes on the values of exporting companies comes with a considerable lag of up to two quarters. This is puzzling because although it takes a while for changes in exchange rates to affect companies' cash flows and for the information on these effects to be reported to investors, their anticipated impact can be promptly incorporated in stock prices.

These results should be regarded cautiously because while the sampled companies were large exporters, there were no data on their imported inputs and on their total exchange-rate exposure (including the exposure in their financial contracts). It is also hard to estimate the exposure of companies to exchange rate changes, partly because it changes over time. Still, the results question the commonly-held belief that the depreciation of the U.S. dollar helps the U.S. export industry. They may also suggest that U.S. corporations are very efficient in hedging their foreign currency risks.

NOTES

1. See Knetter (this volume) on the transmission of exchange rate changes into export prices. He finds that in some U.S. industries, destination (foreign) export prices are insensitive to exchange rate changes against the U.S. dollar. Thus, a depreciation of

the U.S. dollar should increase the dollar revenues of the U.S.-based companies. For other industries he finds that the destination price is increasing with the destination exchange rate. In these cases, the dollar revenues depend on the demand elasticities.

2. The study is conducted on returns of stock portfolios which diversify idiosyncratic noise on the individual stocks.

3. Jorion (1990) used nominal exchange rates and also used individual stock returns. Clearly, the portfolio's β coefficient is the average of the individual stocks' β coefficients, because the variables on the right-hand side are the same.

4. The exchange rate indexes are described as follows: "A currency's nominal effective exchange rate is an index of its trade-weighted average value against the currencies of the corresponding country's principal trade partners. The real effective exchange rate, which adjusts the nominal index for relative price changes, gauges the effect on the international price competitiveness of the country's manufactures due to currency changes and differential inflation. The monthly...exchange rates used are averages of daily spot rates. The relative price changes are based on indices most closely measuring the prices of domestically-produced finished manufactured goods, excluding food and energy at the first state of manufacturing. The weight of the narrow indices (versus 15 industrial-country currencies) are proportional to the value of the bilateral exports plus imports of manufactures in 1980." *World Financial Markets*, April 17, 1989, p. 15.

5. Because the monthly exchange-rate index number is an average of the daily index numbers during the month, the calculated monthly relative change, *DXk*, lags slightly behind the monthly returns *RP* and *RM* which reflect changes in stock values from the beginning to the end of the month. On the other hand, the use of daily average for exchange rates may reduce the extent of noise in these data, which is helpful in estimation.

6. These companies were: Archer Daniel Midland, Boeing, Caterpillar, Digital, FMC Corp., Hewlett Packard, McDonnell Douglas, Weyerhaeuser. The median Exports/sales ratio was 21percent.

7. Changes in the real exchange rates could be expected to be reversed over the long run to reflect adjustments to purchasing power parity. Transitory changes in exchange rates imply negative serial correlation, which is not the case for the sample in this study. In addition, the results are the same for nominal exchange rates, for which reversals are not necessarily expected. Dornbusch (1976) showed that overshooting of exchange rates can occur if real economic activity adjusts slowly to shocks; however, short-term overshooting is not a necessary feature of the adjustment process if intrerest rates and prices react sufficiently. See also Dornbusch (this volume) on the effect of exchange rate changes on the economy.

8. Agmon and Amihud (1981) found no serial correlations in changes in the exchange rate of the U.S. dollar against individual currencies, but Amihud and Mendelson (1989) showed that portfolio (index) returns can be positively autocorrelated even if the underlying individual assets' returns are seemingly serially independent.

9. See Levi, this volume.

10. In the first subperiod, the coefficients for lag 3 had $t = 1.71$, significant at a one-tail test.

11. This is consistent with Jorion (1990). However, the return-exchange rate relationship

was not stronger for portfolio H16 than it was for L16, as could be expected.

12. When model (4.5) was estimated only with the lag of two quarters ϵDXr_{t-2} (eliminating other lags), the coefficient of this variable for portfolio H16 was -0.505 with $t = 2.12$, and the coefficient for portfolio H8 was -0.517 with $t = 1.74$, significant at one-tail test.

REFERENCES

Agmon, T., and Y. Amihud. (1981). "The Forward Exchange Rate and the Prediction of the Future Spot Rate." *Journal of Banking and Finance*. pp. 425–37.

Amihud, Y., and H. Mendelson. (1989). "Index and Index-Futures Returns." *Journal of Accounting, Auditing and Finance*. pp. 415–31.

Dornbusch, R. (1976). "Expectations and Exchange Rate Dynamics." *Journal of Political Economy*. pp. 1161–76.

Dornbusch, R. (1993). "Exchange Rates and the Economy." Chapter 2, this volume.

Giddy, I. (1974). *Devaluation, Revaluation and Stock Market Prices*. The University of Michigan Ph.D. dissertation.

Jorion, P. (1990). "The Exchange-Rate Exposure of U.S. Multinationals." *Journal of Business*. pp. 331–45.

Knetter, M. (1993). "Exchange Rates and Corporate Pricing Strategies." Chapter 9, this volume.

Levi, M. (1993). "Exchange Rates and the Valuation of Firms." Chapter 3, this volume.

Mann, C. (1986). "Prices, Profit Margins and Exchange Rates." *Federal Reserve Bulletin*. June, pp. 366–79.

DISCUSSION

_____

COMMENTS ON DORNBUSCH,
LEVI, AND AMIHUD

_____

Robert E. Cumby

_____

The three chapters in this part lead one nicely through how one might go about exploring the link between exchange rates and firm values. Rudi Dornbusch (Chapter 2) describes how exchange rates can have important and quantitatively substantial effects on the real side of the economy, particularly on traded goods industries. Maurice Levi (Chapter 3) adopts a microeconomic perspective and shows how, under specific assumptions, exchange rate changes might affect firm values and then shows how the magnitude of that affect depends of various parameters. Yakov Amihud (Chapter 4) does some regressions and finds that, in his sample, there is essentially no relationship between exchange rate changes and equity values. Finally, Maurice Levi, anticipating this result, uses the results that he derives to suggest that the regression coefficients Amihud obtains might not be constant over time.

In my comments I would like to do two things. First, I will look at Amihud's results with an eye toward asking what they tell us, and then make some suggestions about what else might be done. Second, I will turn to a discussion of why we might not be surprised by the failure to find any significant relationship between exchange rate changes and equity returns.

The key result in Amihud's paper is that there is essentially no relationship between the monthly returns on an equally weighted portfolio of equities of 32 of the largest U.S. exporters and monthly changes in the J. P.

Morgan real effective exchange rate, holding constant the return on an equally weighted market index. Interestingly, while he finds the point estimates of the exposure coefficients for firms with high and low exports to sales ratios differ, the difference is not statistically significant. This is contrary to the earlier results of Jorion (1990) who found that, while it was difficult in his sample (which differs from Amihud's) to measure the exposure coefficients sufficiently precisely to distinguish them individually from zero, there was statistically significant evidence of cross-sectional variation based on export to sales ratios.

Amihud also suggests that lags of real effective exchange rate changes might help predict the returns on the equally weighted portfolio of these equity returns, and that this indicates a "delayed reaction of stock prices to exchange rate changes" that he states is inconsistent with market efficiency and/or rational expectations. I am not convinced that the evidence warrants such strong conclusions. First, the coefficients on lagged changes in real effective exchange rates are not jointly significant at standard significance levels. While the coefficients on one or more lag are marginally significant, there is often substantial covariance between individual point estimates in an unconstrained distributed lag. As a result one should not place too much importance on one marginally significant coefficient.

Even if one does interpret the estimates as suggesting that lagged real effective exchange rate changes predict the returns on this equally weighted portfolio of equities, the predictability of returns may or may not be consistent with equilibrium in an efficient market. Before we can make any such judgments, we need to determine whether the behavior of the predictable component is consistent with the predictions of equilibrium models of asset returns. Even then, all tests are necessarily joint tests of market efficiency and a particular model of equilibrium returns.

I have a suggestion for additional regressions that might be run on Amihud's data set, although I suspect that similar results will arise. As we see in Levi's paper, under the assumptions he adopts, the elasticity of firm value with respect to the exchange rate should depend on the elasticity of demand for the firm's output in the foreign market, the per unit profits of the firm in the foreign market, the volume of firm sales in the foreign market, as well as the firm's tax rate and opportunity cost of capital. Levi points out that these need not be constant over time. They do not need to be constant across firms either. It might be interesting to estimate the effect of changes in real effective exchange rates on the share values of the individual firms in the sample and to test whether the coefficients are jointly zero. This would allow cross-sectional differences in the "exposure" coefficients that might be masked by aggregation. Of course, doing so would not deal with the potential problems of temporal instability in these coefficients that Levi raises. Jorion (1990) has done this and in his data set finds that, while it is difficult to measure exposure coefficients sufficiently precisely to distinguish them individually from zero, the hypothesis that they are jointly zero can be rejected at standard significance levels.

I suspect that the reason that Amihud fails to find statistically significant evidence of any effects of exchange rate changes on equity returns in his sample is not due to his aggregation of the firms. I will briefly describe four possible reasons for the absence of any statistically significant relationship in his data that go beyond those made explicitly in Levi's paper. Several of these are either explicit or implicit in the papers by Levi and Dornbusch.

The first reason why we might not expect to find any significant relationship between equity returns and real effective exchange rate changes is suggested by Dornbusch. Difficulties in relating either exchange rates or equity prices to the present value of expected future fundamentals has lead some to suggest that both exchange rates and equity prices might be thought of as the outcome of the workings of a casino. If equity prices and exchange rates are the outcomes of the roulette wheels of two casinos, why should we expect there to be any relationship between the two? This explanation, however, is not particularly satisfying, since it leaves little or no room for further inquiry.

The second reason why we might not expect to find much a relationship between the two is that exchange rates and equity prices are jointly endogenous variables. Often the discussion of exposure loses sight of this. While it may be useful to assume that exchange rates are exogenous when analyzing some aspects of the microeconomic behavior of firms, it can be potentially misleading when we examine regressions such as the ones Amihud presents. Dornbusch's paper takes us through a fairly standard model that shows that shocks of different origin can have very different effects on exchange rates and the rest of the economy. For example, an appreciation of the currency that results from a demand shock such as an investment boom or an export boom might have a different effect on equity values than does an appreciation that results from a monetary contraction. Dornbusch also reminds us that the affect of shocks can differ according to whether the shocks are anticipated or unanticipated. Thus the exposure coefficient is some sort of a statistical description of the average covariability of these two jointly endogenous variables. It may not be surprising that as the nature of the shocks that are dominant at any point in time changes, the exposure coefficient will change. The average covariability might not be measured with any precision at all in these circumstances.

Third, the 32 large exporters are likely to be multinational firms with sizable operations and sourcing abroad. The value of these overseas operations might change in ways that offset changes in the values of the domestic export-oriented operations. In fact, as is examined elsewhere in this volume, one purpose of these foreign operations and foreign sourcing is to insulate cash flows and firm values from the effects of exchange rate changes.

Fourth, in addition to foreign sourcing and foreign operations, financial markets present firms with opportunities for taking financial positions that insulate cash flows from exchange rate changes. As the discussion above suggests, the extent of exposure is essentially a choice variable for firms. Absent a model of the choice of exposure, it is difficult to determine why one should expect any particular value for this coefficient. As a starting point, we might expect such a model to predict that exposure is indeterminate for reasons similar to those that Modigliani and Miller advance to predict that capital structure is indeterminate. In this light, it is not at all surprising that little evidence is found linking real effective exchange rate changes to changes in the return on the equally weighted portfolio of equities of these 32 large U.S. exporters. Smith and Stulz (1985) explore hedging decisions further and raise some issues that have parallels in the capital structure literature (cost of bankruptcy and financial distress and taxes, for example) as well as other considerations such as risk aversion on the part of managers that influence a firm's hedging decision. Stulz (1990) extends the analysis of hedging when bankruptcy is costly. Froot, Scharfstein, and Stein (1992) also examine the hedging decision by firms in a way that is parallel to capital structure literature and provide a fairly general treatment of optimal corporate risk management. They point out that when it is costly for firms to resort to external finance, a firm's optimal hedging policy will depend on the investment opportunities available and its ability to raise external funds.

Taken in this light, Amihud's results might be interpreted as evidence that these firms have been successful in insulating cash flows from the effects of exchange rate changes. The results seem to imply that over this sample period and taken as a whole, the firms in his sample have chosen an exposure that is not significantly different from zero on average. The natural next questions might be: "is this result as robust across firms and over time?" and, "if it is robust, why is this the choice that is made by the firms?"

REFERENCES

Froot, K., D. Scharfstein, and J. Stein. (1992). "Risk Management: Coordinating Corporate Investment and Financing Policies." NBER Working Paper no. 4084.

Jorion, P. (1990). "The Exchange Rate Exposure of U.S. Multinationals." *Journal of Business.* 63, pp. 331–45.

Stulz, R. (1990). "Managerial Discretion and Optimal Financial Policies." *Journal of Financial Economics.* 26, pp. 3–27.

Smith, C., and R. Stulz. (1985). "The Determinants of Firms' Hedging Policies." *Journal of Financial and Quantitative Analysis.* 19, pp. 127–40.

DISCUSSION

COMMENTS ON EXCHANGE RATES, THE MACROECONOMIC ENVIRONMENT, AND THE FIRM

Brian Gendreau

At the outset I should issue a disclaimer. This conference was designed to present the views of academics and practitioners, and my affiliation might suggest that I am an active market participant. I am not. I am an economist, and though I work with practitioners my views remain principally those of a researcher rather than a trader or corporate treasurer.

I am going to discuss the three papers out of order, beginning with Maurice Levi's chapter, "Exchange Rates and the Valuation of Firms."

In an era in which the treatment of the firm's foreign exchange exposure has come to be dominated by the tools of corporate finance, Professor Levi uses instead the traditional tools of the classic microeconomic model of the firm. This is a refreshing change, if only because it promises to focus on the concrete—on behavior, goals, costs, and market structures—the messy stuff of which corporate foreign exchange decisions are made, rather than on the safer, cleaner tests of arbitrage conditions and portfolio optimization.

The chapter's central result is that the sensitivity of the value of an exporting or importing firm depends, unavoidably, on a number of factors, including (1) the elasticity of demand for the firm's product; (2) the firm's profitability ; (3) the tax rate; and (4) the firm's opportunity cost of capital. Because virtually all of these factors can be expected to change over time, the sensitivity of the firm's value to exchange rate fluctuations should also change over time. We should, therefore, expect temporal parameter instability in regressions of firm value on exchange rates, and the regression coefficients should be biased toward zero.

A good analogy, in my view, is the parameter instability that should be expected in regression tests of the determinants of default premiums on corporate bonds. Suppose the underlying relationship between the default premiums and measures of risk such as asset volatilities and debt-to-asset ratios is governed by an option pricing model, which is highly nonlinear, has no fixed coefficients, and has first-order conditions whose values vary systematically with the values of the model's independent variables. Then there would be no reason to expect to recover stable estimates of the sensitivity of changes in default premiums to changes in asset volatility and debt-to-asset ratios in a linear regression.

Professor Levi's chapter has presented strong results with empirical implications from a fairly simple and compact model—a highly desirable outcome. It is worth pausing, though, and asking whether the model is really as simple as it seems.

First, firms in this model practice price discrimination across markets. They set prices and take quantities. Consequently, if these firms want to hedge their foreign exchange exposures they have to have a good idea of the magnitude of their demand elasticity, cost of capital, and operating costs, all of which are difficult to measure. No firm would want to take this approach in determining what its hedge should be (and I am sure that Professor Levi is not recommending it as a hedging strategy).

Second, it appears that in Professor Levi's model the firm's net monetary asset–liability position is independent of its revenues and costs. It appears in the equation describing the value of the firm as a simple additive term. I am not persuaded that firms' foreign currency holdings are independent of their business operations. To the contrary, it is reasonable to expect that a firm's net foreign currency exposure is related to specific projects, outputs, and inputs. For example, some inputs may have to be imported, and firms may have an overseas sales force whose salaries and expenses are in local currencies, all of which may give use to cash balances and off-balance sheet positions in foreign exchange. Taking into account any interdependence between a firm's revenues, costs, and net foreign exchange position would complicate the model greatly. I suspect the increased complexity would not be matched by an equally large increase in insight, and that Professor Levi may have been wise to take this simpler approach.

Yakov Amihud's chapter, "Evidence on Exchange Rates and the Valuation of Equity Shares," is a fitting companion to Professor Levi's paper in that it presents regressions of market returns on exchange rate changes, and those regressions feature both insignificant coefficients and some evidence of parameter instability. Professor Amihud regresses the return on a portfolio of American exporting companies on the market return and current and lagged changes in the J. P. Morgan nominal effective exchange rate index for 15 industrial countries against the dollar. He finds that exchange rate changes affect the stock returns of the exporting companies only with lags of up to two quarters; that the statistical significance of individual coefficients on the exchange rates is very low and jointly not different from zero; and that virtually no coefficient on an exchange rate is significant statistically when the sample is divided into two sub-periods, 1979–83 and 1984–88. The author concludes that the "hardly significant" results fail to support the widespread belief that the depreciation of the dollar helps American exporters.

Reading the Amihud chapter on the heels of the Levi chapter, it is difficult to agree that the weak results and parameter instability mean that exchange rate changes have no effect on exporters' stock returns. Professor Levi, after all, has shown precisely why the effect of exchange rate changes on firms' valuation may be hard to detect in statistical tests.

There are other reasons, moreover, to wonder whether the evidence on the impact of exchange rate changes on exporters presented in the paper is as weak as Professor Amihud believes. The empirical tests show that lagged exchange rates have a statistically significant impact on stock returns, with relatively large coefficients. The author, noting that the exchange rate coefficients are not jointly significant, downplays their significance (though he falls short of dismissing it altogether). These results are a bit odd: typically individual coefficients on variables lagged over several time periods fail to be significant statistically, yet are significant jointly according to an F-test. The reason for the significance of the individual coefficients but insignificance of the coefficients considered as a group, may be that the chosen lag length is suboptimal. Formal statistical tests—some of which rely on the significance of the F-statistic as the length of the lag structure is changed—are available to determine whether the lag length is optimal. None, however, is reported in the paper.

Professor Amihud, in addition, argues that the lagged impact of exchange rate changes on stock returns is not credible because it is at odds with rational expectations. He notes that the lagged effect could be explained by the lack of information available to investors on exporters' foreign currency hedging activity: absent such information, investors have little choice but to wait until earnings are released. He then rules out hedging as an explanation, arguing that currency hedges are mostly short-term. But medium-term currency hedges are available to firms in the large, liquid, and growing market for currency swaps. Information on such swaps are not disclosed continuously to investors, so the hedging information problem identified by Professor Amihud may indeed explain the statistical significance of the lagged exchange rate changes.

Finally, I will offer a few comments on Rudiger Dornbusch's essay, "Exchange Rates and the Economy." Professor Dornbusch finds in essence that economic theory today is of relatively little help in explaining exchange rate movements. This is not a controversial conclusion, and other author's assessments have, if anything, been even more bleak. For example, a 1989 survey by Jane Marrinan of the Federal Reserve Bank of Boston found that:

> Neither the forecasts of market participants as revealed by the forward discount or survey data, nor simple time series models, nor theoretically sophisticated models based on market fundamentals appear able to appreciably and consistently out-predict a simple random walk model of exchange rates.

I cannot speak for other banks, but I know that the economic research department of J.P. Morgan uses *no* structural or reduced form econometric model to forecast exchange rates. On the other hand, J. P. Morgan does get input from chartists (technical analysts). Originally, the explanation was "markets trade on the advice of chartists so we might as well see what they're saying," or "clients want to see it," but I have seen reports prepared by technical analysts for internal distribution.

Now this is an embarrassing state of affairs. Economic models seem to have failed a market test, while charting has passed. How did we get to this point? I think a look at a U.S. dollar exchange rate chart for the 1980s provides a number of hints. I am confident that academic studies using monthly data during the 1980s would have found exchange rate movements difficult or impossible to predict statistically. Yet a chartist thinking that he or she was seeing a trend and recommending a dollar buy through early 1985 would have looked prescient (though I am not sure they would have fared so well after early 1985). Meanwhile, quite a few economists were saying that the dollar was overvalued. The problem was that many were predicting a decline in the early 1980s—too soon. This week's London

Economist, in an article on the IMF's forecasts, advises economists to "forecast a number or a date, but not both." Economists did not have this luxury. They were eventually right, but too late.

Nonetheless, it is worth pointing out that the practical value of economic theory in explaining exchange rate movements may be greater than is generally appreciated. First, as Professor Dornbusch notes, some recent research has found better empirical support for models based on fundamentals than research done in the early 1980s, both within and out-of-sample (which is a relief).

Second, while many economic models have not passed a market test, economists have. Risk-takers still eagerly solicit the advice of economists on questions such as: Is there a risk premium in forward rates? How is Chile going to manage its capital inflows? Under what conditions will Argentina devalue? When economists answer these questions they have in mind theoretical models, and these are not the kind of questions that technical analysis can answer.

PART TWO

EXCHANGE RATE VOLATILITY AND CAPITAL MARKETS

CHAPTER 5

EXCHANGE RATE VOLATILITY
AND EQUITY RETURNS

Stephen J. Brown
Toshiyuki Otsuki

INTRODUCTION

Evidence of the role of exchange rates on world equity markets is mixed. The consensus appears to be that there is little evidence of a significant average risk premium associated with currency risk exposure. However, there is also evidence that the premium changes through time in a predictable fashion.[1] Is the apparent predictability of premium changes due to an accident of the data, or is it a reflection of an equilibrium response to changes in international risk premia? The purpose of this chapter is to examine this issue in the context of a multiperiod Arbitrage Pricing Theory model of global asset markets.

Recent evidence has suggested that the relaxation of capital controls in Japan and elsewhere in the late 1970s has served to make the international capital markets more integrated than they were in previous years.[2] This integration suggests that a small number of common international factors might explain the variations of international asset returns.

These international factors affect returns in two ways. In the first place, the internationalization of the capital markets suggests that returns in the different markets are becoming more highly correlated as the markets are affected by similar factors around the world. Subsequent to the relaxation of capital controls in 1974, the evidence is generally consistent with the existence of nontrivial international factors in an Arbitrage Pricing Theory framework, factors that are highly related to equity returns and exchange rate changes.[3] The second way in which factors affect returns is through predictable variations in risk premia. The Arbitrage Pricing Theory applied on a global scale implies that risk premia should be similar across countries. In addition, the variations in risk premia should depend on similar factors.[4] There has been some work that has attempted to show that similar factors govern movements in expected returns across major markets.[5] To this point, there has been little work that has attempted to combine both insights in a unified asset pricing model framework.[6]

Of course, the challenge confronting any empirical application of the Arbitrage Pricing Theory is to identify the factors. In this paper we are most interested in the effect of exchange rate changes on asset returns. However, this factor alone will not suffice to explain differences in risk premia across equity markets. Korajczyk and Viallet (1989) use factors identified through the method of principal components. Recent work has suggested that this technique may not be able to reliably estimate more than the first factor.[7] The work of Gultekin, Gultekin and Penati (1989) relies on a few prespecified factors. In any empirical work of this kind, the choice of which variables to include as factors is bound to be somewhat arbitrary. The approach used in this paper is to prespecify a minimal set of macrofactors, and include a *residual market factor* orthogonal to the other factors. This allows for the possibility that an important priced factor has been excluded from the analysis. This approach was suggested by McElroy and Burmeister (1988). They point out that this not only gives one degree of freedom in specifying the factors, but also allows the empirical implementation of the capital asset pricing model to be considered a simple parametric restriction of the more general Arbitrage Pricing Theory. By considering the residual market factor a latent variable in the analysis, the model fits naturally into the multibeta framework of Shanken (1987).

The framework of McElroy and Burmeister (1988) also suggests that the asset pricing model be considered in a systems estimation context. It is possible to show that the use of iterated generalized least squares procedures provide robust estimates for the risk tolerances and risk premia factors specified in the model. The model we estimate in this paper differs from the McElroy and Burmeister approach in at least two important ways. In their model, the innovations that are used as proxies for risk factors are estimated outside the model using a state space approach. However, this approach neglects information from security returns that may be useful in estimating the innovations process. In our work we estimate the innovation process and the asset pricing model *simultaneously*. In the second departure from their approach, we allow the risk premia to be themselves functions of a vector of instruments, known as of the beginning of each month.

There are at least two major advantages of the systems estimation approach over related factor analytic or asymptotic principal components approaches and the widely used cross section regression approach.[8] As in the factor analysis and principal components procedure, data on rates of return are used to estimate the factors. However, by estimating the innovations process *simultaneously* with the factor structure, we increase the amount of information being used to estimated the factors. We also resolve the rotational indeterminacy of factor analysis and related procedures in an economically meaningful way. The second major advantage of the systems estimation approach is that if iterated seemingly unrelated procedures are used, the set of priced factors can be considered a strict subset of the set of factors that influence security returns. The other procedures, including the widely used cross-section regression approach introduced by Fama and MacBeth (1973), implicitly assume that the factors that influence security returns are limited to those factors that are priced. In other words, they assume the residual covariance matrix is diagonal.[9] This assumption is relaxed in the systems estimation approach.

In summary, our model specifies the risk factors as innovations from a first order vector autoregression of a set of macrovariables on their own past values and the values of a vector of instruments known as of the start of the month. Risk factors defined in this way are therefore orthogonal to the vector of instruments used to explain the variations in risk premia through time. Thus the model we consider is generically similar to one proposed by Ferson (1990) for the study of time variation in risk premia in the U.S. economy. The model differs from that of Ferson in the technique of estimation and the choice of variables. In particular, we consider the residual market factor an additional factor, given as that part of the return on a global market index orthogonal to the already specified factors and vector of instruments.

In the next section, we develop the model and present the system of equations we estimate. We then define the data used and, in the following section, give the results we obtained estimating the model using a maximum likelihood systems estimation approach.

THE MODEL

It is a simple matter to extend the equity asset pricing model to the study of global asset equity markets. An interesting feature of these markets is the fact that the expected equity risk premia differ across equity markets and change in predictable ways.

The equity asset pricing model we apply to the international equity markets is the intertemporal version of the Arbitrage Pricing Theory. In this model, the observed risk premium for a particular equity market is made up of two components: the expected risk premium and risk factors. The risk factors are further subdivided into macrofactor risk and country-specific components. The sensitivity to these sources of macrofactor risk (or β) determine the expected risk premium:

$$R_{ti} = \lambda_{t0} + \lambda_{t1} \beta_{Ii} + \ldots + \lambda_{tk} \beta_{ki} + f_{t1} \beta_{ki} + \upsilon_{ti} \qquad (5.1)$$

where f_{kt} is the kth source of macrofactor risk, and λ_{kt} is the expected risk premium in period t per unit of exposure to the kth source of macrofactor risk. The factors f_{it} are understood to have zero mean as of the start of period t. If we consider the rate of return on the ith country rate of return to be in excess of the return on some reference asset, the risk factors β are interpreted as in excess of the reference asset, and the λ_{t0} shall equal zero.[10] The intertemporal version of the asset pricing model implies that the risk premium elements will themselves depend on macroeconomic factors (or *instruments*) known at the beginning of period t. If these relationships are linear

$$\lambda_{tj} = \alpha_{1j} X_{t1} + \alpha_{2j} X_{t2} + \ldots + \alpha_{mj} X_{tm} \qquad (5.2)$$

then the relationship between equity returns and factors can be represented

$$R_{ti} = \rho_{1t} X_{t1} + \ldots + \rho_{mk} X_{tm} + f_{t1} \beta_{1i} + \ldots + f_{tk} \beta_{ki} + \upsilon_{ti} \qquad (5.3)$$

Equation (5.3) provides a very simple representation of the process generating security returns. The β_{ji} coefficients describe the exposure of equity index i to global macro factor risk j, and the ρ coefficients describe the way that expected returns vary systematically through time. Ordinary least squares provide efficient estimates of these parameters given a set of predefined factors f and vector of instruments X.

However, equation (5.3) is incomplete for at least two reasons. While expected returns may depend upon risk premia, they may depend on other country specific factors as well.[11] Furthermore, on a country by country basis, both risk premia and country-specific factors may vary through time in an arbitrary fashion. This would be inconsistent with global integration of capital markets, but would be implied by equation (5.3) were we to allow the constant term and slope coefficients ρ to incorporate country-specific factors.

In addition, a model such as equation (3) estimated on a country by country basis is difficult to validate, without introducing additional information. While there has been much empirical work done that documents the effect of observed factors on asset returns, there is no general agreement on the identity of the factors, and precisely which instruments to use. The asset pricing model implies that the r coefficients can be expressed in terms of the α and β parameters of equations (5.2) and (5.3). In addition, the implied constant term λ_{0t} should be the same for all countries. The importance of these constraints is that they help to validate the model and justify the particular choice of factors. In short, by imposing the asset pricing model constraints we obtain a useful test of how well specified the model is.[12] In addition these constraints potentially give us more efficient estimators of the relevant parameters.

To understand the nature of the asset pricing constraints, it is helpful to express equations (5.1) through (5.3) in a convenient matrix notation:

$$R_t = \lambda_{0t} + \lambda_t B + f_t B + v_i \tag{5.4}$$

$$\lambda_t = X_t \alpha \tag{5.5}$$

and

$$R_t = X_t \rho + f_t B + v_t \tag{5.6}$$

where we set λ_{t0} equal to zero. The asset pricing model implies

$$\rho = \alpha B \tag{5.7}$$

In addition, the factors f_t are not known but have to be estimated. Suppose we represent these factors as the innovations derived from a vector of macro variables y_t

$$f_t = y_t - Z_t \gamma \qquad (5.8)$$

where Z_t represents a vector of instruments known as of the start of period t.

The constraints of the asset pricing model, combined with the necessity to estimate the factors f implies the following nonlinear system of equations[13] obtained by substituting equations (5.7) and (5.8) into (5.6):

$$y_t = Z_t \gamma + f_t$$

$$\qquad (5.9)$$

$$R_t = [X_t \alpha + y_t - Z_t \gamma]B + v_t$$

This system of equations can be estimated using maximum likelihood assuming that the errors f_t and v_t are joint normally distributed. It is possible to relax this assumption and estimate the system of equations using Generalized Method of Moments, at some loss in the precision of the estimates obtained.

McElroy and Burmeister (1988) suggest incorporating as the 0th factor, a residual market factor f_0. This factor can be thought of as a residual factor not explained by the set of predefined macro variables. The existence of such a factor allows the Capital Asset Pricing Model and related Multibeta models to be consistent with the Arbitrage Pricing Model estimated using such a multi factor model. This factor can be defined by aggregating equation (5.6) using an appropriate set of market weights

$$f_{0t} = R_{mt} - [X_t \rho_m + f_t B_m] \qquad (5.10)$$

The inclusion of a residual market factor defines the equation system:

$$y_t = Z_t \gamma + f_t$$
$$R_{mt} = X_t \rho_m + [y_t - Z_t \gamma] B_m + f_{0t} \qquad (5.11)$$
$$R_t = X_t [\alpha B + \alpha_m \beta_0] = [y_t - Z_t \gamma]B + (R_{mt} - [y_t - Z_t \gamma] B_m) \beta_0 + v_t$$

This is the system of equations that we estimate. The first and second equations define the macro factors and residual market factors respectively. The third equation shows how equity returns relate to instrumental variables X_t and the various risk factors. The first term gives the risk premium as a function of the instrumental variables X. The second term shows how returns depend on the risk factors defined in the first equation. The third term gives the influence of the residual market factor on individual country returns.

DATA

Measures of returns, instruments and factors appearing in equation (5.11) are provided by monthly global data provided by Roger Ibbotson and Associates for the period February 1981 through the end of March 1991. The proxy for the global market is the FT–Actuaries World index, with returns measured in U.S.$ terms.[14] Rates of return for individual countries are given as the return on diversified equity portfolios calculated inclusive of dividend yield, from data originally provided by Financial Times–Actuaries. These rates of return are all measured in U.S.-dollar terms, in excess of the return on the reference asset, the U.S. Treasury Bill.

Extensive empirical research both in the United States and Japan has suggested that a small number of prespecified factors can explain the unexpected components of equity returns in those two countries.[15] Extensive empirical analysis based on the Ibbotson data reveals that a similar small set of factors are sufficient to explain global equity returns.[16] The exchange rate variable most highly correlated with equity returns in the United States, Germany, Japan and the United Kingdom for the period of data was the unexpected component of yen currency returns (in U.S. dollars). The remaining factors most highly correlated with equity returns in those four equity markets are the unexpected components of UK short term interest rates and of U.S. small stock equity return. These unexpected components are defined in terms of a vector autoregression (VAR) involving past values of these variables, and the vector of instruments defined below. A fourth factor is given as the residual market factor, defined as the total dollar return on the FT–Actuaries World index not explained by these unexpected components, or the vector of instruments known as of the start of the month.

Since we measure returns in U.S. dollars in excess of the U.S. Treasury Bill rate, the role of the first two macrofactors is not surprising. The Japanese exchange rate variable is highly correlated with other exchange rates, and the short interest rate variable might be interpreted as a spread between the U.S. Treasury Bill rate and short rates elsewhere. These variables are similar to ones used by Ferson and Harvey (1992) among others. The small firm equity return variable might be interpreted as a U.S. risk factor. However, as reported later, the results seem to indicate that sensitivity to this variable is associated with seasonal factors correlated with macroeconomic determinants of risk premia.

Indeed, there is increasing evidence that changes in expected equity returns have a predictable component. This work as it applies to the United States equity markets is summarized in Ferson and Harvey (1992). Work by Campbell and Hamao (1991) suggest that these findings apply to both the United States and Japanese equity markets. The consensus appears to be that the variables most significant in explaining expected returns are yield spreads on government paper, short term interest rates and dividend price ratios. If there is at least partial integration of international equity markets, these factors explaining expected returns should be similar across different equity markets. Four instruments that appear to be sufficient to explain observed time series behavior of global expected returns are given by previous month values of yield spreads in the United States and Japan, and U.S. inflation and dividend yields last month.

RESULTS

Table 5–1 summarizes these relationships. The residuals from the VAR given in Panel 1 define the macrofactors in Panel 2. The results reported in Panel 2 shows that these global macrofactors and risk premium factors explain a significant proportion of the variation of global equity returns. Since these factors are largely related to the U.S. economy, it is not surprising that the model works best for the U.S. equity market. However, the factors are significant for most of the other markets as well. This reflects not only the influence of the U.S. markets on equity markets worldwide, but also the important global effect that these factors have on their own account. The magnitude and direction of the effects are strikingly similar in equity markets worldwide. In terms of the global market index, the U.S. small firm equity returns and yen currency returns are the most significant risk factors. These factors, together with the residual market factor are also important in most of the regional markets, with the U.K. short bond return significant in the European equity markets. U.S. yield spreads and dividend yields appear to be the most significant explanators of the global equity risk premium. These risk premium effects are similar across the regional markets, but are stronger in some markets than in others. They are most pronounced in the United States.

TABLE 5-1
Global Risk Factors and Equity Premia—March 1981 to March 1991

This table reports results from regressing macrovariables y on a set of instruments

$$y_i = \gamma_{i0} + \sum_{j=1}^{7} \gamma_{ij} Z_j + f_i, \qquad i = 1, 2, 3 \qquad (5.12)$$

where y_i represents the macrovariables return on U.S. small stocks (y_1), U.K. short bond returns (y_2), and Japanese currency returns in U.S. dollars (y_3), and the γ_i refers to the instruments: the previous month U.S. yield spread (χ_{YSUS}), Japanese yield spread (χ_{YSJAP}), U.S. inflation rate (γ_{IUS}), U.S. dividend yield (γ_{DIV}), and Japanese currency return last month (χ_{XJAP}). The residuals from these regressions define a set of factos f_i which, together with a residual market factor (f_0) defined by the market regression:

$$R_m = \rho_{0m} + \sum_{j=1}^{4} \rho_{jm} X_j + \sum_{i=1}^{3} B_{im} f + f_0 \qquad (5.13)$$

are used to estimate the equity premia given in Panel 2:

$$R_k = \rho_{0k} + \sum_{j=1}^{4} \rho_{jk} X_j + \sum_{i=0}^{3} \beta_{ik} f + v_k, \qquad k = 1, \ldots, 12 \qquad (5.14)$$

where R_k represents equity return (measured in U.S. dollars) in excess of U.S. Treasury Bill return, and the X_j are the predetermined variables that explain the equity risk premia. The coefficients ρ_j relate to the previous month U.S. yield spread (ρ_{YSUS}), Japanese yield spread (ρ_{YSJAP}), U.S. inflation rate (ρ_{IUS}), and U.S. dividend yield (ρ_{DIV}). The coefficients β_i give sensitivities to the common factors: β_{MKT} to the residual market factor, β_{SML} to the U.S. small firm innovation, β_{TUK} to the innovation in U.K. short bond returns, and β_{XJAP} to innovations in Japanese exchange rates (t-values in parentheses).

Panel 1: Global Risk Factors

γ_0	γ_{YSUS}	γ_{YSJAP}	γ_{IUS}	γ_{DIV}	γ_{SML}	γ_{TUK}	γ_{XJAP}	R^2	DW
1. U.S. Small Stock Equity Return									
0.062	−2.011	−2.475	−1.109	63.222	0.028	−8.205	0.098	0.262	1.98
(1.51)	(−2.93)	(−2.87)	(−0.60)	(4.31)	(0.29)	(−2.58)	(0.72)		
2. U.K. Short Bond Return									
0.001	−0.001	−0.003	0.019	−0.029	−0.001	0.917	0.004	0.877	1.80
(1.85)	(−0.09)	(−0.31)	(0.83)	(−0.17)	(−0.91)	(23.89)	(2.20)		
3. Japanese Currency Returns in U.S. Dollars									
−0.041	0.166	−0.389	1.947	4.583	0.049	0.083	−0.028	0.050	1.98
(−1.38)	(0.33)	(−0.62)	(1.44)	(0.43)	(0.70)	(0.04)	(−0.28)		

TABLE 5–1, continued
Global Risk Factors and Equity Premia—March 1981 to March 1991

Panel 2: Equity Risk Premia and Risk Factors

ρ_0	ρ_{YSUS}	ρ_{YSJAP}	ρ_{IUS}	ρ_{DIV}	β_{MKT}	β_{SML}	β_{TUK}	β_{XJAP}	R^2	DW
0. Financial Times–Actuaries World Equity Index										
0.045 (2.92)	-1.188 (-3.54)	-0.753 (-1.74)	-4.164 (-4.55)	24.266 (3.61)		0.592 (11.59)	9.656 (2.30)	-0.563 (-8.06)	0.686	1.88
1. Austria										
0.063 (1.55)	-0.544 (-0.62)	-1.501 (-1.33)	-1.523 (-0.64)	2.282 (0.13)	0.436 (1.78)	0.233 (1.75)	10.927 (1.00)	-0.487 (-2.67)	0.159	1.67
2. Australia										
0.063 (1.51)	-1.657 (-1.83)	-2.747 (-2.35)	-5.366 (-2.17)	34.526 (1.90)	0.376 (1.48)	0.764 (5.54)	2.153 (0.19)	-0.285 (-2.04)	0.352	2.02
3. Belgium										
0.055 (1.86)	-1.020 (-1.61)	-0.671 (-0.82)	-3.869 (-2.24)	18.516 (1.46)	0.771 (4.35)	0.451 (4.68)	17.842 (2.26)	-0.670 (-5.08)	0.424	2.04
4. Canada										
0.054 (2.58)	-2.005 (-4.47)	-0.193 (-0.33)	-3.417 (-2.79)	40.406 (4.49)	0.512 (4.07)	0.791 (11.57)	2.842 (0.51)	-0.258 (-2.76)	0.633	2.31
5. France										
0.110 (2.17)	-0.280 (-0.26)	-2.334 (-1.66)	-9.873 (-3.31)	-8.055 (-0.37)	0.990 (3.23)	0.524 (3.15)	43.486 (3.18)	-0.819 (-3.59)	0.383	2.05
6. Germany										
0.010 (0.31)	-0.451 (-0.65)	-1.622 (-1.81)	-2.169 (-1.15)	15.151 (1.09)	0.880 (4.51)	0.371 (3.51)	17.910 (2.06)	-0.636 (-4.39)	0.359	1.95

7. Hong Kong										
0.064	−0.531	−3.657	−6.733	8.261	0.531	0.858	27.886	−0.229	0.310	1.86
(1.18)	(−0.45)	(−2.43)	(−2.11)	(0.35)	(1.62)	(4.83)	(1.91)	(−0.94)		
8. Ireland										
0.052	−1.254	−2.938	−0.753	24.896	0.910	0.721	12.008	−0.776	0.466	2.27
(1.48)	(−1.65)	(−2.99)	(−0.36)	(1.63)	(4.27)	(6.22)	(1.26)	(−4.89)		
9. Italy										
0.020	0.276	−3.389	−5.135	−1.933	0.770	0.380	24.504	−0.736	0.386	1.94
(0.53)	(0.34)	(−3.28)	(−2.35)	(−0.12)	(3.42)	(3.11)	(2.44)	(−4.40)		
10. Japan										
0.075	−1.121	0.320	−6.421	16.295	1.581	0.369	8.359	−1.283	0.813	2.15
(3.94)	(−2.73)	(0.60)	(−5.73)	(1.97)	(13.70)	(5.90)	(1.63)	(−14.9)		
11. Malaysia										
0.127	−2.756	0.186	−5.496	40.090	0.773	0.983	−1.681	−0.037	0.403	2.06
(2.90)	(−2.91)	(0.15)	(−2.13)	(2.11)	(2.91)	(6.81)	(−0.14)	(−0.19)		
12. Netherlands										
0.041	−0.962	−0.261	−4.890	21.275	0.575	0.561	17.336	−0.495	0.556	2.12
(1.89)	(−2.09)	(−0.44)	(−3.89)	(2.30)	(4.44)	(7.98)	(3.01)	(−5.15)		
13. New Zealand										
0.043	−1.542	−2.473	−5.208	35.854	0.118	0.585	12.970	−0.257	0.238	1.88
(0.94)	(−1.55)	(−1.92)	(−1.91)	(1.79)	(0.42)	(3.85)	(1.04)	(−1.24)		
14. Norway										
0.049	−0.648	−1.274	−2.185	8.438	0.746	0.637	29.360	−0.327	0.324	1.48
(1.28)	(−0.78)	(−1.19)	(−0.97)	(0.51)	(3.20)	(5.04)	(2.83)	(−1.89)		
15. South Africa										
0.148	−3.570	−1.322	−4.170	52.614	0.582	0.285	23.316	−0.323	0.221	2.06
(2.69)	(−3.01)	(−0.86)	(−1.29)	(2.21)	(1.75)	(1.58)	(1.57)	(−1.31)		

TABLE 5-1, continued

Panel 2, continued: Equity Risk Premia and Risk Factors

	ρ_o	ρ_{YSUS}	ρ_{YSJAP}	ρ_{IUS}	ρ_{DIV}	β_{MKT}	β_{SML}	β_{TUK}	β_{XJAP}	R^2	DW
16. Singapore	0.055	−2.781	−1.418	−0.410	62.111	1.343	0.732	6.578	−0.278	0.411	1.81
	(1.34)	(−3.16)	(−1.25)	(−0.17)	(3.51)	(5.43)	(5.45)	(0.60)	(−1.51)		
17. Spain	0.035	0.431	−2.738	−3.191	−10.86	0.810	0.582	8.255	−0.677	0.400	2.03
	(1.02)	(0.58)	(−2.85)	(−1.57)	(−0.73)	(3.88)	(5.14)	(0.89)	(−4.36)		
18. Sweden	0.056	−2.206	−1.177	−2.887	48.588	0.630	0.584	20.812	−0.698	0.456	2.15
	(1.78)	(−3.25)	(−1.34)	(−1.56)	(3.56)	(3.31)	(5.65)	(2.45)	(−4.93)		
19. Switzerland	0.032	−0.818	−0.767	−3.512	17.414	0.610	0.553	17.992	−0.632	0.519	1.83
	(1.34)	(−1.59)	(−1.16)	(−2.51)	(1.69)	(4.23)	(7.07)	(2.80)	(−5.90)		
20. United Kingdom	0.032	−0.995	−1.712	−2.231	23.098	0.895	0.680	25.874	−0.659	0.615	2.26
	(1.33)	(−1.91)	(−2.54)	(−1.57)	(2.20)	(6.11)	(8.55)	(3.96)	(−6.05)		
21. United States	0.011	−1.184	−1.242	−2.883	33.427	0.560	0.769	4.184	−0.051	0.844	2.24
	(1.00)	(−4.82)	(−3.92)	(−4.30)	(6.78)	(8.12)	(20.57)	(1.36)	(−1.00)		

The risk factors and instrumental variables which were defined using data for four important equity markets have explanatory power for equity markets worldwide.

While these results indicate that there are significant global risk factors, and that the risk premium varies systematically through time, it is clear that the ordinary least squares estimates do not give very precise estimates of the magnitude of these effects. International equity returns provide information on the effect of the global macro factors. A systems estimation approach provides information necessary to specify these effects. Such an approach also allows us to incorporate cross section constraints implied by the asset pricing relationships.

Table 5–2 provides a summary of the results obtained by estimating the system of equations equation (5.11) using the Iterated Nonlinear Seemingly Unrelated Regression procedure.[17] In the systems estimation context, equity returns themselves help explain the time variation in global macrofactors, as illustrated by the reduced statistical significance of the terms in the VAR given in Panel 1. However, the sensitivity to these macrofactors, particularly the residual market factor, has generally increased in statistical significance (Panel 3). The results in Panel 2 indicate that the sensitivity to these macrofactors is associated with significant and time varying risk premia. The residual market risk premium is chiefly associated with U.S. realized inflation, the U.S. small stock risk premium is influenced by U.S. inflationary tendencies which is also true of the Japanese currency risk premium, while the U.K. short bond risk premium depends on the Japanese yield spread. These results did not appear to be sensitive to the method of estimation, and the data do not appear to violate the asset pricing model constraints given as equation (5.7).[18] As can be observed in Panel 3, the asymptotic t values indicate a significant role for each of the risk factors in explaining global equity returns.

The single equation results reported in Table 5–1 indicate a significant role for dividend yield in explaining the systematic component of returns in the international equity markets. The instruments we use to explain risk premia display a reasonably high correlation (Table 5–3). In particular, for the February 1981 through February 1991 period, the correlation of the yield spread and dividend yield variables is .875. This raises the possibility that the results are sensitive to the choice of instruments.

Results reported in Table 5–4 begin to address this issue. In single equation results not reported here, the incidence of the month of January has little systematic effect on global equity returns given our choice of instru-

TABLE 5–2
Systems Estimation of Global Equity Premia and Risk Factors

In this table, we report results from estimating the system of equations given as equation (5.11) in the text for the period March 1981 to March 1991. The Iterated Nonlinear Seemingly Unrelated Regression (ITNLSUR) procedure was used. Other procedures, such as Nonlinear Seemingly Unrelated (NLSUR) and Nonlinear Ordinary Least Squares (NLOLS) yield results that differ only slightly in the precision with which the parameters are estimated. The t-values (in parentheses) were computed on the basis of the relevant asymptotic standard errors. Panels 1 and 3 correspond to Panels 1 and 2 of Table 5–1. Panel 2 shows how the risk premium factors depend on the instruments: previous month U.S. yield spread (α_{YSUS}), Japanese yield spread (α_{YSJAP}), U.S. inflation rate (α_{IUS}), and U.S. dividend yield (α_{DIV}).

Panel 1: Global Risk Factors

γ_0	γ_{YSUS}	γ_{USJAP}	γ_{IUS}	γ_{DIV}	γ_{SML}	γ_{TUK}	γ_{XJAP}
\multicolumn{8}{l}{1. U.S. Small Stock Equity Return}							
0.012	−2.204	−2.151	−2.185	65.147	−0.018	−1.531	0.102
(0.42)	(−3.92)	(−2.76)	(−1.40)	(5.67)	(−0.46)	(−1.13)	(1.80)
\multicolumn{8}{l}{2. U.K. Short Bond Return}							
0.001	0.000	−0.004	0.026	−0.052	-0.000	0.894	0.003
(2.52)	(0.05)	(−0.37)	(1.28)	(−0.33)	(−0.47)	(27.49)	(2.04)
\multicolumn{8}{l}{3. Japanese Currency Return in U.S. Dollars}							
−0.031	0.009	−0.451	2.474	6.852	0.092	−0.767	0.001
(−1.31)	(0.02)	(−0.78)	(2.06)	(0.75)	(2.07)	(−0.51)	(0.01)

Panel 2: Determinants of Time Varying Risk Premia

α_0	α_{YSUS}	α_{YSJAP}	α_{IUS}	α_{DIV}
\multicolumn{5}{l}{1. Residual Market Risk Premium}				
−0.124	0.606	−2.479	8.645	16.429
(−2.31)	(0.49)	(−1.03)	(2.58)	(0.72)
\multicolumn{5}{l}{2. U.S. Small Stock Risk Premium}				
0.100	−2.909	−0.416	−7.434	55.136
(2.43)	(−3.17)	(−0.26)	(−2.94)	(3.16)
\multicolumn{5}{l}{3. U.K. Shart Bond Risk Premium}				
−0.001	0.102	−0.216	−0.041	−1.942
(−0.65)	(2.12)	(−2.33)	(−0.31)	(−2.19)
\multicolumn{5}{l}{4. Japanese Currency Risk Premium}				
−0.192	1.855	−6.232	12.613	1.191
(−2.92)	(1.24)	(−2.18)	(3.08)	(0.04)

Panel 3a: Equity Risk Premia and Risk Factors—World Index

ρ_0	ρ_{YSIS}	ρ_{YSJAP}	ρ_{IUS}	ρ_{DIV}	β_{SML}	β_{TUK}	β_{XJAP}
0. Financial Times–Actuaries World Equity Index							
0.049	−1.283	−0.861	−4.273	26.701	0.575	9.885	−0.564
(2.15)	(−2.64)	(−1.30)	(−3.17)	(2.73)	(12.72)	(2.78)	(−9.14)

Panel 3b: Equity Risk Factors—Individual Country Indices

	β_{MKT}	β_{SML}	β_{TUK}	β_{XJAP}
1. Austria	0.702	0.288	13.673	−0.523
	(3.60)	(2.61)	(2.61)	(−3.69)
2. Australia	0.405	0.916	11.369	−0.164
	(1.96)	(8.13)	(1.90)	(−1.12)
3. Belgium	1.005	0.475	11.589	−0.717
	(7.17)	(5.48)	(2.44)	(−6.36)
4. Canada	0.335	0.706	0.108	−0.122
	(3.22)	(11.96)	(0.03)	(−1.59)
5. France	1.012	0.608	28.807	−1.061
	(3.92)	(4.16)	(3.32)	(−5.53)
6. Germany	1.040	0.403	12.743	−0.618
	(6.72)	(4.24)	(2.45)	(−5.00)
7. Hong Kong	0.402	0.831	19.397	−0.276
	(1.49)	(5.63)	(2.41)	(−1.44)
8. Ireland	1.131	0.688	16.065	−0.548
	(6.50)	(6.68)	(2.72)	(−4.07)
9. Italy	0.902	0.474	23.244	−0.657
	(4.76)	(4.39)	(3.53)	(−4.61)
10. Japan	1.509	0.419	17.565	−1.280
	(14.41)	(4.66)	(2.67)	(−10.56)
11. Malaysia	0.103	0.863	1.949	−0.139
	(0.46)	(7.01)	(0.31)	(−0.88)
12. Netherlands	0.797	0.519	7.432	−0.560
	(7.70)	(8.17)	(2.04)	(−6.74)
13. New Zealand	0.215	0.832	8.159	−0.032
	(0.95)	(6.78)	(1.33)	(−0.20)
14. Norway	0.663	0.443	10.684	−0.422
	(3.60)	(4.17)	(2.19)	(−3.10)
15. South Africa	0.028	0.825	8.426	−0.139
	(0.10)	(5.34)	(1.07)	(−0.70)
16. Singapore	1.215	0.947	4.029	−0.428
	(6.05)	(7.69)	(0.61)	(−2.68)
17. Spain	0.995	0.392	20.952	−0.683
	(5.73)	(3.89)	(3.45)	(−5.15)

TABLE 5–2, continued

Panel 3b, continued: Equity Risk Factors—Individual Country Indices

	β_{MKT}	β_{SML}	β_{TUK}	β_{XJAP}
18. Sweden	1.075	0.789	7.321	–0.542
	(7.08)	(8.95)	(1.48)	(–4.73)
19. Switzerland	0.714	0.442	9.154	–0.492
	(6.25)	(6.31)	(2.51)	(–5.45)
20. United Kingdom	1.065	0.573	12.442	–0.594
	(8.98)	(7.27)	(2.63)	(–5.74)
21. United States	0.496	0.698	2.288	–0.102
	(7.94)	(17.27)	(0.82)	(–1.89)

TABLE 5–3
Correlation of Variables Used as Instruments for Risk Premia—
February 1981–February 1991

This table reports correlations among variables used as instruments for risk premia. These include previous month values of the following variables: U.S. yield spread (YSUS), Japanese yield spread (YSJAP), U.S. inflation rate (IUS), and U.S. dividend yield (DIV). We also consider a dummy variable that indicates the incidence of the month of January (JAN). To judge the magnitude of these pairwise correlations, the reciprocal of the square root of the number of observations is .091.

	YSUS	YSJAP	IUS	DIV	JAN
U.S. Yield Spread (YSUS)	1.000				
Japanese Yield Spread (YSJAP)	0.528	1.000			
U.S. Inflation Rate (IUS)	0.249	0.280	1.000		
U.S. Dividend Yield (DIV)	0.875	0.425	0.160	1.000	
January Dummy (JAN)	–0.047	–0.230	–0.309	–0.012	1.000

TABLE 5–4
Systems Estimation Incorporating a January Instrument

In this table, we report results from estimating the system of equations given as equation (5.11), using the Iterated Nonlinear Seemingly Unrelated Regression (ITNLSUR) procedure for the period March 1981 to March 1991, allowing for a January instrument. The t-values (in parentheses) were computed using the relevant asymptotic standard errors. Panel 1 shows how the return on the world equity index depends on a January dummy variable (ρ_{JAN}). Panel 2 shows how the risk premium factors depend on the instruments: previous month U.S. yield spread (α_{YSUS}), Japanese yield spread (α_{YSJAP}), U.S. inflation rate (α_{IUS}), U.S. dividend yield (α_{DIV}), and the January dummy (α_{JAN}). The Chi-square values refer to a likelihood ratio test of the hypothesis that all elements in the corresponding rows and columns are equal to zero. Chi-square values corresponding to each row are asymptotically distributed as Chi square with 6 degrees of freedom, while values corresponding to the columns are distributed with four degrees of freedom. All are significant at the one percent level, with the exception of the Chi-square value corresponding to the constant term α_0, which is significant at the five percent level.

Panel 1: Equity Risk Premia and Risk Factors—World Index

ρ_0	ρ_{YSUS}	ρ_{YSJAP}	ρ_{IUS}	ρ_{DIV}	ρ_{JAN}	β_{SML}	β_{TUK}	β_{XJAP}
0.056	−1.275	−0.553	−4.778	24.418	0.003	0.567	9.236	−0.596
(2.70)	(−2.78)	(−0.88)	(−3.68)	(2.63)	(0.36)	(12.67)	(2.68)	(−8.69)

Panel 2: Determinants of Time Varying Risk Premia

	α_0	α_{YSUS}	α_{YSJAP}	α_{IUS}	α_{DIV}	α_{JAN}	Chi square
1. Residual Market Risk Premium							
	−0.095	0.465	−2.236	12.096	5.837	0.134	46.8
	(−1.72)	(0.35)	(−0.83)	(2.44)	(0.23)	(2.54)	
2. U.S. Small Stock Risk Premium							
	−2.849	−2.849	−0.331	−9.485	58.495	−0.074	58.0
	(2.26)	(−2.94)	(−0.18)	(−2.81)	(3.09)	(−2.26)	
3. U.K. Short Bond Risk Premium							
	−0.001	0.102	−0.226	0.024	−2.031	0.002	53.6
	(−0.65)	(1.96)	(−2.15)	(0.12)	(−2.01)	(0.79)	
4. Japanese Currency Risk Premium							
	−0.175	1.698	−6.552	18.947	−8.552	0.164	44.2
	(−2.20)	(0.89)	(−1.73)	(2.69)	(−0.23)	(2.24)	
Chi square							
	11.8	30.8	27.8	48.8	61.2	34.4	

ments and risk factors. This was also true for the systems estimation results reported in Table 5–4. The month of January is not a factor which explains the return on the global index. However, the incidence of the month of January has a significant impact on global risk premia. Furthermore, the month of January and other seasonal macrovariables have a significant impact on the U.S. small stock risk premium. This suggests that the small firm effect may proxy for a seasonal factor affecting global returns. The Chi square values show that all risk premia are statistically significant (at the one percent level) and are all significantly affected by the five instrumental variables (including the January seasonal component).

In particular, currency risk exposure implies a significant risk premium. It is largest for Japan, Singapore and all European countries in the sample. In addition, the currency risk premium also has a strong seasonal component, being most heavily influenced by the incidence of January and by the level of dividend yields.

CONCLUSION

We have proposed a simple approach to the analysis of asset pricing in global capital markets. This approach has the following attributes. It models the risk factors and premia due these factors simultaneously in an empirical framework consistent with Capital Asset Pricing Models, Arbitrage Pricing Theory, and Multibeta models. By using iterated, nonlinear, seemingly unrelated regression procedures, one obtains robust estimates of the relevant parameters. We have applied this approach to data for twenty one national equity markets for the period March 1981 through March 1991, and find that the asset pricing model restrictions are not violated in the data. The results further indicate that currency risk exposure commands a significant risk premium in equity markets around the world. However, this risk premium changes in a predictable fashion through time. These changes do not appear to be an accident of the particular data we use. The data suggest they represent an equilibrium response to changes in global risk preference.

NOTES

1. The evidence from the currency market data seems to suggest no significant currency risk premium (Hodrick, 1987). However, allowing the risk premium to vary through

time, strong evidence of risk premia are found (McCurdy and Morgan, 1992). Similar results are found in the equity markets. In their studies of the Japanese equity markets, Hamao (1988) and Brown and Otsuki (1990) find that the currency risk premium is small. However, allowing the risk premium to vary through time, both Dumas and Solnik (1991) and Ferson and Harvey (1992) find some evidence of an exchange rate premium.

2. See, for example Gultekin, Gultekin and Penati (1989).

3. See Korajczyk and Viallet (1989).

4. This point is made relative to the US market risk premium in Chan, Karolyi, and Stulz (1991).

5. J. Campbell and Y. Hamao (1991).

6. Notable exceptions to this are the work of Wheatley (1988), which applied a consumption-based asset pricing model to explain returns in 18 global equity markets, and Ferson and Harvey (1992), which uses similar data in a multibeta pricing model framework.

7. See Brown (1989).

8. For a discussion of these relationships between factor analysis and cross-section regression approaches, see Brown and Weinstein (1983). Connor and Uhlaner (1989) make a similar point and, moreover, observe that repeated application of the CSR approach will lead to a rotational indeterminacy similar to that of factor analysis.

9. Using Ordinary Least Squares in the cross-section regressions they report, Fama and MacBeth (1973) assume that the residuals are independent and identically distributed in the cross-section of securities. Litzenberger and Ramaswamy (1979) relax this assumption, and allow the residuals to have different variances. However, they still require residuals to be uncorrelated across securities. By not imposing any constraints on the covariance matrix of residuals, the systems estimation approach implicitly allows for an arbitrary number of nonpriced factors.

10. The U.S. Treasury Bill return, which we use as the reference asset in this study, is free of risk only in U.S. dollar terms. In general, this return will depend on the same risk premia and risk factors as other assets.

11. Differences in the degree of cross-listing, or restriction on foreign ownership might tend to explain differences in expected returns, and would be evidence of partial segmentation of these markets. See Hietala (1989).

12. This corresponds to the bilinear test proposed by Brown and Weinstein (1983) for studying the equivalence of asset prices across groups, where in this instance, each group corresponds to a particular national equity market. In a GMM framework, the mean restriction implied by the asset pricing model corresponds to a general "goodness of fit" test [see Hansen and Singleton (1982)].

13. This system of equations is similar to one provided by Ferson (1990). The one difference is that Ferson prefers the reduced form given as equation (5.6) and defined in terms of k reference assets, k being defined as the number of factors. This parameterization involves the inverse of a matrix of the reference asset coefficients. Numerical nonlinear least squares procedures (in a likelihood or GMM framework) require conditions to guarantee that the inverse matrix exists, and thus violate the standard convergence criteria. While formally identical, equation system equation (5.9) is simpler to estimate using standard numerical maximum likelihood or GMM

procedures.

14. Returns computed using this data are available only for the period February 1981 through the present. The Morgan Stanley Capital International indices are available for a longer period of time. However, the capital change component of the latter indices are computed on the basis of Laspeyres's index formula and do not necessarily reflect increment of value, while the income yield component is computed as one twelfth of the previous year's dividends expressed as a fraction of last month's index level. It is thus not entirely clear that the sum of the two yields are the appropriate measure of total return for this application. Other authors, notably Ferson and Harvey (1992) prefer the use of the MSCI indices for the reason that this index is available as early as 1970. The additional data is important for the GMM applications they consider.

15. The work by Chen, Roll, and Ross (1986) indicates that a small number of factors represent priced sources of risk in the United States. Hamao (1988) finds some evidence that the factors identified for the United States have some validity in Japan. Work by Brown and Otsuki (1990) shows that a slightly different set of factors represents priced sources of risk in Japan.

16. The objective of this analysis was to define a parsimonious model that explained a significant fraction of equity returns across different markets and was consistent across subperiods of the data. The criterion used was the Schwarz Criterion, that can be shown to be equivalent to the choice among models using a posterior odds ratio criterion with priors that are diffuse over the space of parameters that define the models [Klein and Brown (1984)]. Summary statistics, including both the Schwarz Criterion and alternative Akaike Information Criterion, for four contending models are available from the authors.

17. This procedure provides tail equivalent maximum likelihood estimates. It is fully described in McElroy and Burmeister (1988).

18. The system of equations was estimated with the Nonlinear Seemingly Unrelated (NLSUR) and Nonlinear Ordinary Least Squares (NLOLS). Imposing the restrictions implied by equation (5.7) on the time varying components of the risk premium yielded a likelihood ratio test statistic of 11.8, asymptotically distributed as Chi-square with 32 degrees of freedom, not significant at standard levels of significance. However, constraining the time varying components to equal zero yielded a highly significant Chi-square of 149.4, which with 20 degrees of freedom is significant at the one percent level.

REFERENCES

Brown, S. (1989). "The number of factors in security returns." *Journal of Finance.* 44, pp. 1247–62.

Brown, S., and T. Otsuki. (1990). "Macroeconomic factors and the Japanese equity markets: The CAPMD project." *Japanese Capital Markets.* E. Elton and M. Gruber, eds. New York: Harper and Row.

Brown, S., and M. Weinstein. (1983). "A new approach to testing asset pricing models: The bilinear paradigm." *Journal of Finance.* 38, pp. 711–43.

Campbell, J., and Y. Hamao. (1991). "Predictable stock returns in the United States and Japan: A study of long-term capital market integration." *Journal of Finance* (forthcoming).

Chan, K., G. Karolyi, and R. Stulz. (1991). *Global financial markets and the risk premium on U.S. equity.* Ohio State University working paper.

Chen, N-F., R. Roll, and S. Ross. (1986). "Economic forces and the stock market." *Journal of Business.* 59, pp. 383–404.

Connor, G., and R. Uhlaner. (1989). "A synthesis of two approaches to factor estimation." University of California, Berkeley working paper.

Dumas, B., and B. Solnik. (1991). "The world price of exchange rate risk." Wharton School working paper.

Fama, E., and J. MacBeth. (1973). "Risk, return and equilibrium: Empirical Tests." *Journal of Political Economy.* 81, pp. 607–36.

Ferson, W. (1990). "Are the latent variables in time-varying expected returns compensation for consumption risk?" *Journal of Finance.* 45, pp. 397–430.

Ferson, W., and C. Harvey. (1992). "The risk and predictability of international equity returns." University of Chicago working paper.

Ferson, W., and C. Harvey. (1992). "The risk and predictability of international equity returns." University of Chicago manuscript.

Gultekin, M., B. Gultekin, and A. Penati. (1989). "Capital controls and international capital market segmentation: The evidence from the Japanese and American stock markets." *Journal of Finance.* 44, pp. 849–69.

Hamao, Y. (1988). "An empirical examination of arbitrage pricing theory: Using Japanese data." *Japan and the World Economy.* 1, pp. 45–61.

Hansen, L., and K. Singleton. (1982). "Generalized instrumental variables estimation of nonlinear rational expectations models." *Econometrica.* 50, pp. 1269–86.

Hietala, P. (1989). "Asset pricing in partially segmented markets: Evidence from the Finnish market." *Journal of Finance.* 44, pp. 697–718.

Hodrick, R. (1987). *The Empirical Evidence on the Efficiency of Forward and Futures Foreign Exchange Markets.* Switzerland: Harwood Academic Publishers.

Klein, R., and S. Brown. (1984). "Model selection when there is "minimal" prior information." *Econometrica.* 52, pp. 1291–1312.

Korajczyk, R., and C. Viallet. (1989). "An empirical investigation of international asset pricing." *The Review of Financial Studies.* 2, pp. 553–85.

Litzenberger, R., and K. Ramaswamy. (1979). "The effect of personal taxes and dividends on capital asset prices: Theory and empirical evidence." *Journal of Financial Economics.* 7, pp. 163–96.

McCurdy, T., and I. Morgan. (1992). "Evidence of risk premiums in foreign currency futures markets." *The Review of Financial Studies.* 5, pp. 65–83.

McElroy, M., and E. Burmeister. (1988). "Arbitrage pricing theory as a restricted nonlinear regression model." *Journal of Business and Economic Statistics.* 6, pp. 29–42.

Shanken, J. (1987). "Multivariate proxies and asset pricing relations: Living with the Roll critique." *Journal of Financial Economics.* 18, pp. 91–110.

Wheatley, S. (1988). "Some tests of international equity integration." *Journal of Financial Economics.* 21, pp. 77–122.

CHAPTER 6

CURRENCIES AND LONG-TERM INTEREST RATES

Philippe Jorion

INTRODUCTION

Comparisons of capital costs across countries have increasingly attracted the attention of policy makers as part of the U.S. competitiveness debate. From the viewpoint of multinationals, sustained differences in capital costs have serious implications. Even within a single company, such differences will affect cross-border capital budgeting decisions, and thus plant location decisions. In turn, this will affect the balance of payments and political relations between trading partners. In this context, it is commonly asserted that U.S. firms cannot compete with Japanese firms because they are hobbled with a cost of capital that is higher than their Japanese counterparts. These arguments, eloquently summarized in a review article by Hatsopoulos, Krugman, and Summers (1988), are usually based on comparisons of the weighted cost of capital (WACC).

The WACC combines after-tax long-term debt costs with equity costs, and is measured in real terms, after accounting for the effect of inflation. Comparisons of the WACC therefore subsume international comparisons of real interest rates. Mishkin (1984) and Mark (1985) have provided tests of equality of short-term interest rates, using three-month Eurocurrency data. Such comparisons are useful for a number of reasons. First, focusing on real interest rates allows us to address a number of comparative macroeconomic issues, such as differences in the rate of investment across countries, or the efficacy of the conduct of activist monetary policies. Second, comparisons of real rates are useful to assess the appropriateness of theoretical models of open economies. Early monetary models, such as Frenkel (1976), assume that real rates are equalized across countries. Later models, such as Dornbusch (1976), Frenkel (1976) and Mussa (1982), assume sticky good prices which imply divergences in short-term real interest rates, but rely on flexible prices in the long run, as in monetary models, which imply long-run equal real interest rates. Finally, tests of the equality of real interest rates shed direct light on the question of international mobility of capital. Feldstein and Horioka (1980) started a long-lasting debate by observing that, with integrated capital markets, changes in national savings should be entirely offset by changes in foreign borrowing or lending, at an unchanged rate of return. As Frankel (1991a) argued, however, the question of international capital mobility can be more directly addressed by measuring rates of return across national markets.

Furthermore, international comparisons of the cost of capital are misleading if based solely on real costs. Multinational companies, offered with the choice of borrowing in several currencies, do not compare interest rates in different countries relative to the inflation rates of those different countries. In fact, debt costs are evaluated in terms of the same inflation rate, which drops out of any comparison, and in the same currency. What matters are *nominal costs,* translated into the same currency at prevailing exchange rates. Comparing rates in nominal terms can only be collapsed to comparing real rates if exchange rates move as predicted by Purchasing Power Parity.

In addition, previous studies of real interest rates, such as Mishkin (1984) and Mark (1985), only address short-term debt costs, which are not directly relevant if corporations finance long-term assets by long-term debt. Comparisons of long-term interest rates, in addition, are more interesting because it is commonly believed that central banks have a limited ability to affect long-term yields. which are more influenced by inflationary expectations. Therefore, differences in short-term real interest rates may not necessarily appear in long-term interest rates. Finally, short-term rates, especially in domestic credit markets, may not reflect market-clearing prices if governments impose capital controls, which are usually most effective for short-term assets.

In summary, this study presents evidence on debt costs measured over longer horizons than previously analyzed, and specifically adjusts for the impact of exchange rates.

THE COST OF CAPITAL AND REAL INTEREST RATES

Most of the early work on capital costs has been based on the Weighted Average Cost of Capital (WACC). The traditional measure of the corporate cost of capital is a weighted average of the cost of equity and of the cost of debt

$$k = k_e \; \frac{E}{V} + k_d \, (1 - t) \; \frac{D}{V} , \qquad (6.1)$$

where
    k_e = cost of equity.
    E/V = proportion of equity in project.
    k_d = cost of debt.
    τ = corporate income tax rate.
    D/V = proportion of debt in project..

The cost of capital is therefore determined by the required after-tax payments to a firm's debt and equity holders. This basic methodology, however, has serious limitations that make the results difficult to interpret.

A detailed analysis of the cost of capital across countries is provided in McCauley and Zimmer (1989). Measuring the cost of debt involves carefully documenting the share of capital raised as bank debt and bond issues, as well as the tax shield provided by interest payments. The cost of bonds is usually measured by the yield on high-grade corporate medium-term bonds, and the cost of bank debt is inferred from loan rates, after adjusting for the need to hold compensating balances.

Measurement problems with the cost of debt, however, pale in comparison with measuring the cost of equity. Averages of ex post returns could be used as estimates of expected equity returns, but unfortunately, the level of precision implied by ex post data is unacceptable given the volatility of stock returns. Typically, with an annual volatility of 15 percent, it would require 225 years of data to obtain an estimate of expected returns with a standard error of 1 percent, which is economically significant.

These statistical problems undermine the literature focusing on the pricing of risk in international stock markets. In an early paper on capital market segmentations, Stehle (1977) analyzes the pricing of risk for U.S. stocks using a CAPM framework, and cannot prove that U.S. stocks are priced relative to a domestic beta or to a world beta. Errunza and Losq (1985), on the other hand, explicitly model asymmetric investment restrictions, and provide some evidence of mild segmentation for less developed countries. Jorion and Schwartz (1986) apply domestic and international versions of the CAPM to Canadian stocks, and find the segmentation model to provide a better fit to the data. The more general Arbitrage Pricing Framework has been used by Cho, Eun, and Senbet (1986), and Korajczyk and Viallet (1989), who generally find evidence of segmentations, noting the models behave differently in later years, which suggests structural changes due to deregulations. Using a multifactor asset model, Gultekin, Gultekin, and Penati (1989) compare U.S. and Japanese stocks, and find that risk premia appear to be closer across the two markets after the relaxation of Japanese capital controls in 1980. Although the evidence generally seems to indicate structural differences in the pricing of risk across stock markets, the problem with all of these studies is that expected returns on common stocks are very imprecisely measured because of the volatility in stock returns. As a result, ex post estimates of the average equity cost of capital are of little use for measuring expected equity costs.

Instead of using market data, the cost of equity is usually inferred from price-earnings data. Unfortunately, comparing accounting earnings across countries has little meaning unless adjusted for different depreciation methods, different uses of reserve accounts, and cross-shareholding patterns, to name but a few problems. Fully accounting for these differences would require going back to detailed income data for all markets under consideration, and reconstructing earnings using the same method. Assuming comparable earnings measures, debt and equity costs must then be combined with market values for the outstanding amounts, debt, and equity in each country in order to arrive at an overall after-tax real cost of funds. This, however, results in estimates of the cost of capital that are based on average rather than marginal costs. Finally, these comparisons are only appropriate if U.S. and Japanese aggregates represent the same risk class.

An alternative approach to measuring the cost of capital is to decompose this cost into a real riskless rate plus a risk premium, in the spirit of Myer's (1974) adjusted present value approach. Assuming a similar risk premium across markets, it is then possible to focus directly on real interest rates, which can be measured much more precisely and are subject to much more powerful tests than previous estimates of the cost of capital. Admittedly, this decomposition ignores differences in the tax shield due to interest payments. Bernheim and Shoven (1987), however, have found that variations in real interest rates tend to swamp variations in corporate tax laws in the determination of the cost of capital. Therefore, focusing directly on real riskless interest rates avoids the problems associated with measurement errors of the weighted average cost of capital.

The real cost of debt, measured after the effect of expected inflation, is

$$k_d = E[\overset{\smile}{r}{}_t^m] = i_t^m - E[\overset{\smile}{\pi}{}_t^m], \tag{6.2}$$

where the m-year spot rate i_t^m, observed at time t, can be decomposed into an "ex post" m-year inflation component π_t^m, plus an "ex post" m-year real interest rate component r_t^m, both observed at time $t + m$. In what follows, returns are always measured in continuously compounded terms. The rate of inflation is usually taken from the increase in the Consumer Price Index. Assuming rational expectations, the expected inflation can be replaced with the actual realized inflation, subject to a confidence interval that reflects a small measurement error. This approach is vastly superior to other methods that use lagged inflation rates as measures of expected inflation, because it properly measures future inflation over an horizon that exactly corresponds to the investment horizon. Its drawback, however, is that the last few observations are used only to measure inflation, disregarding nominal rates; for instance, with 1973 to 1991 data, five-year real rates can be computed only up to 1986.

In previous studies, the long-term nominal cost of debt was usually taken from "A"-rated corporate bond yield, averaged over time. This approach, unfortunately, has severe shortcomings, because it ignores the term structure of interest rates. Because bond maturities are not explicitly controlled for, apparent differences in interest rates can arise because corporations across countries raise funds at different maturities. As U.S. corporations tend to issue longer-term debt than German or Japanese firms, this will induce a bias toward higher capital costs in the United States. if positively-sloped yield curves have been more prevalent during the sample period. Also, using a yield-to-maturity assumes that all intermediate cash flows will be funded at the same yield, which is inaccurate if the term structure of interest rates is not flat. More importantly, comparing bond yields implicitly assumes that the credit risk of foreign borrowers is similar to that of U.S. borrowers; this is difficult to control for, since foreign corporate bond markets are relatively small. Japanese bond yields, for instance, are usually taken from utilities, such as NTT, which really was a government agency, and cannot be directly compared to U.S. industrial corporations. Finally, bond yields may be distorted if bonds include options, such as the ability of the firm to call back the issue if interest rates drop. Since the holder of the bond requires a higher yield to compensate for being short this option, this again artificially inflates U.S. capital costs if such options are not present in foreign debt issues.

A simple solution to these problems is to use a sample of default-free, noncallable bonds issued by governments, from which a zero-coupon term structure can be recovered. Using zero-coupon yields, or spot rates, properly addresses the issue of maturity and reinvestment risk. Also, credit risk and call options are explicitly controlled for.

The raw data used in this paper consist of prices on government bonds issued in the U.S., Japan, and Germany over the flexible exchange rate period August 1973–December 1991. Because the Japanese bond market was illiquid in the 1970s and rates were controlled by the government, Japanese data only start in 1981. The methodology used to derive zero-coupon rates is described in Jorion and Mishkin (1991). This involves fitting a discount function by cubic splines, and solving for the parameters so as to minimize the deviations between market prices of all bonds and theoretical prices derived from the knowledge of the future cash flows, as well as of the discount function. In each market, one-year to five-year rates were recovered.

Figures 6–1 and 6–2 present one-year and five-year real riskless interest rates for the U.S. and Germany. Several interesting patterns emerge. During the 1970s, rates were higher in Germany, especially at longer maturities. This effect, however, was reversed in the early 1980s, when real rates were markedly higher in the U.S. More recently, differences have become smaller. Figures 6–3 and 6–4 present information for Japanese real interest rates. As in the case of Germany, Japanese rates during the early 1980s were lower than U.S. rates, especially so at long horizons, but differences seem to disappear over recent years. Note that these patterns are somewhat different from those described in Frankel (1991b), who reports that U.S. long-term real rates were systematically higher than in Japan over the latest twenty years. The difference is in part attributable to estimates of expected inflation, which in Frankel's case are based on past inflation rates; in situations of accelerating inflation, as was the case in the United States in the 1970s, using past rates of inflation seriously understates expected inflation, and overstates *ex ante* real interest rates.

Table 6–1 reports average one-year to five-year real rates over the 1973–1991 and 1981–1991 periods. These numbers confirm that rates were

FIGURE 6–1
One-Year Real Interest Rates: United States and Germany

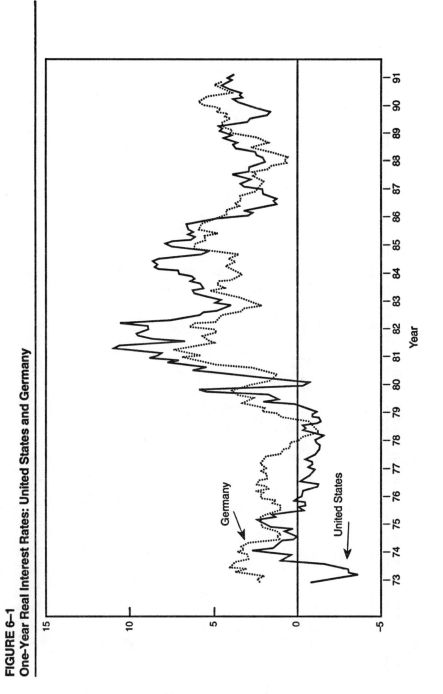

FIGURE 6–2
Five–Year Real Interest Rates: United States and Germany

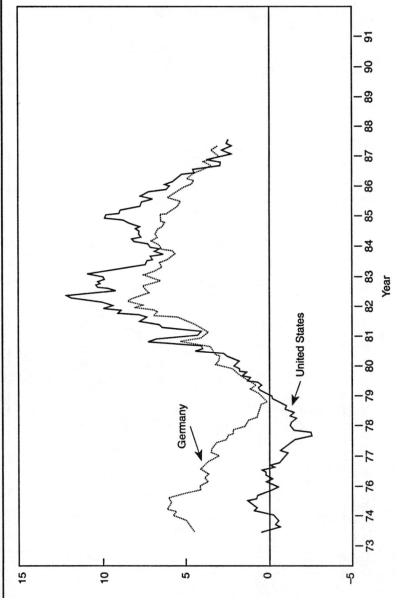

TABLE 6–1
Average Real Interest Rates Across Maturities (based on CPI data)

	1973–1991				
	1 Year	*2 Year*	*3 Year*	*4 Year*	*5 Year*
United States	3.0	3.3	3.5	3.7	3.8
Germany	3.2	3.6	3.9	4.2	4.5
	1981–1991				
	1 Year	*2 Year*	*3 Year*	*4 Year*	*5 Year*
United States	5.1	5.8	6.3	6.8	7.5
Germany	4.1	4.5	4.9	5.4	6.0
Japan	4.3	4.2	4.5	4.9	5.5

similar over the floating exchange rate period across countries, and higher in the United States in the last decade. These results are in line with those of Kester and Luehrman (1989), who show that, although real interest rates are not equal across the United States and Japan, the difference has favored the United States as often as Japan.

These results broadly correspond to different monetary regimes in the United States: first, lax monetary policy in the 1970s, followed by a period of more restrictive policy, initiated with monetary targeting from October 1979 to October 1982, and aimed at rooting out high levels of U.S. inflation. This was followed by a period of prolonged U.S. fiscal expansion, counterpoised to fiscal contraction in Japan and in some European countries. Given the prevalent view that central banks have more control over short-term rates, and that long-term rates primarily reflect future inflation, Figures 6–1 to 6–4 are somewhat astonishing, because they suggest that differences in real interest rates persist over five-year horizons, and that, overall, they are not that different from patterns observed from short-term real interest rates.

REAL INTEREST RATES AND EXCHANGE RATES

Comparing real interest rates across countries sheds light on specific macroeconomic issues, such as comparing the rate of investment across countries. However, real interest rates do not permit direct comparison of the cost of capital across countries because real rates do not account for exchange rate movements.

FIGURE 6–3
One-Year Real Interest Rates: United States and Japan

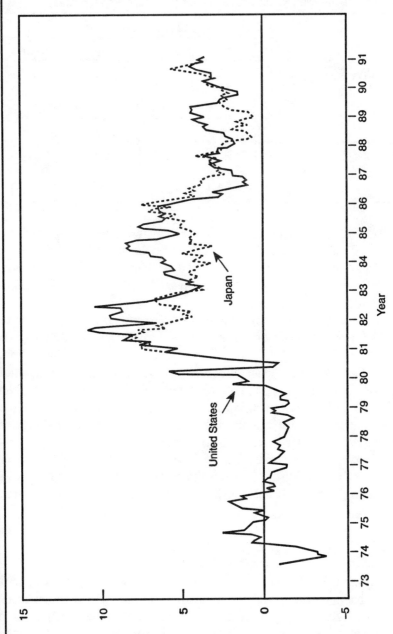

FIGURE 6–4
Five-Year Real Interest Rates: United States and Japan

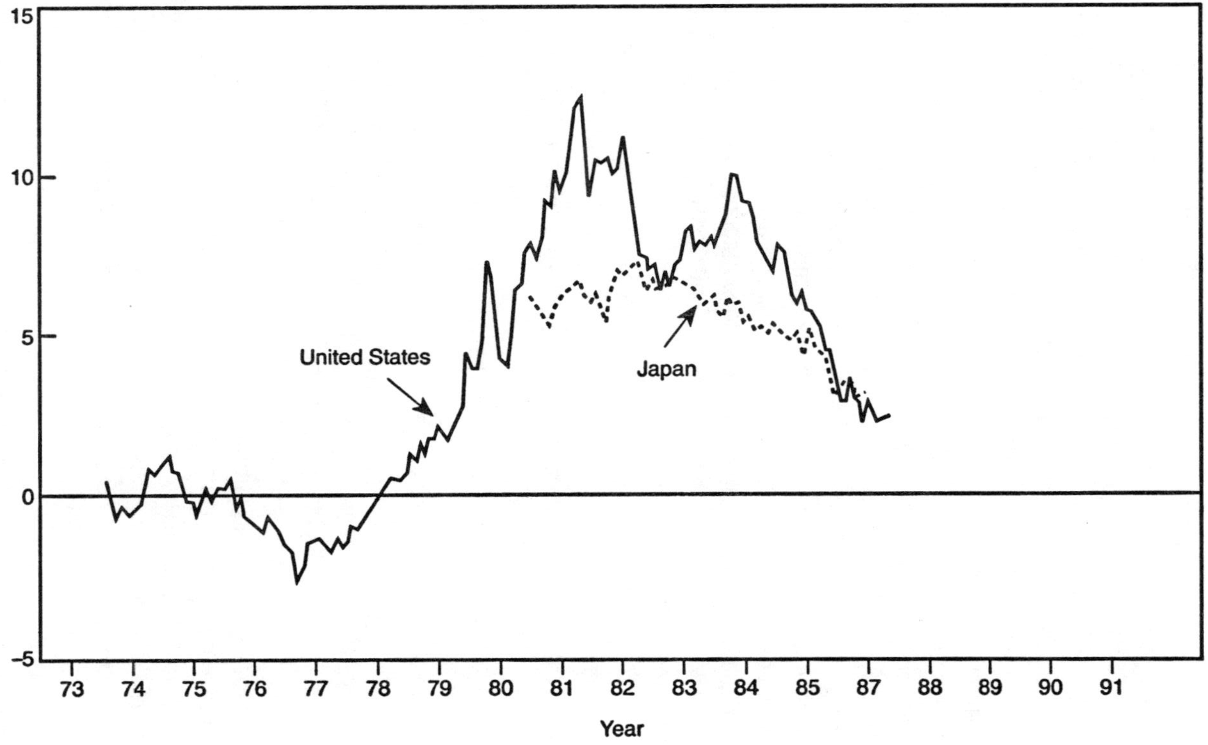

One of the central themes of the literature on international comparisons of capital costs is that Japanese real interest rates have been markedly lower than U.S. rates, which has created a cost of capital handicap for U.S. firms. This argument is fallacious for a number of reasons. First, if it was the case, U.S. firms could simply borrow in the yen Eurobond market, or alternatively, U.S. subsidiaries of Japanese firms would decide not to borrow in U.S. dollars. Given the ability of multinationals to raise funds in various currencies, it is hard to imagine how corporations could ignore a major difference in the cost of capital across currencies, if it existed. Another explanation is that low Japanese real rates may simply have offset the fact that the yen was expected to appreciate in real terms against the dollar. Therefore, what matters are capital costs measured in the same base currency. After all, foreign real interest rates are completely irrelevant for U.S. companies when measured in a foreign currency. Because the question of comparing the cost of capital across countries involves competition between multinationals selling in a common goods market, where prices are translated at prevailing exchange rates, real interest rates must be adjusted for exchange rate movements.

To further understand this point, decompose the difference in expected real rates, $E[\hat{r}] - E[\hat{r}*]$, into nominal rates and expected inflation components, and then introduce the expected currency appreciation $E[\Delta \hat{s}]$:

$$E[\hat{r}] - E[\hat{r}*] = (i - i* - E[\Delta \hat{s}]) - (E[\hat{\pi}] - E[\hat{\pi}*] - E[\Delta \hat{s}]), \quad (6.3)$$

where $\Delta \hat{s}$ measures the change in the logarithm of the spot rate S, defined in U.S. dollars per unit of the foreign currency, and where the asterisk arbitrarily refers to foreign currency units. The left-hand side in this equation might be called the deviation from real interest parity (RIP). The first term in the right-hand side of the equation measures the difference in the nominal cost of capital across currencies, and is sometimes called the deviation from uncovered interest parity (UIP). The second term represents the deviation from *ex ante* purchasing power parity (PPP). Therefore, even if capital costs were the same when translated into the same currency, deviations from real interest parity could occur if a currency was expected to appreciate in real terms against the reference currency.

A long-term real appreciation of a currency seems at odds with the strong belief most economists have in PPP, which is viewed as a fundamental tenet of international monetary economics. But in fact, PPP should be viewed as a first-order approximation that holds best when disturbances to the economy are primarily monetary in nature. This is the case in situations of high inflation or, in general, over the long-run. Abuaf and Jorion (1990), among others, have shown that real exchange rates tend to be mean-reverting over time, but only very slowly. Over the flexible exchange rate period, they find that a 50 percent over-appreciation of a currency with respect to PPP takes between three and five years to be cut in half. Similarly, analyzing annual data over the period 1900–1972 reveals that a period of three years is needed for such a reversal.

Even in the long term, PPP may be inaccurate when relative prices change over time. Such an explanation has been advanced by Belassa (1964), who shows that a rapidly growing country tends to experience higher productivity in the traded goods sector than for nontraded goods. As a result, the price of nontraded goods, P_N, tends to appreciate faster than the price of traded goods P_T, which leads to a real appreciation of the currency. In general, a country's overall price index contains traded and nontraded goods, and can be represented as in a geometric average of P_N and P_T: $P = P_N^{\alpha} P_T^{(1-\alpha)} = P_T (P_N/P_T)^{\alpha}$, and similarly for the foreign country. Assuming the law of one price holds for traded goods, $S = P_T / P_T^*$. Substituting for P_T, we have

$$S = (P/P^*) (P_N / P_T)^{-\alpha} (P_N^* / P_T^*)^{\alpha^*}. \tag{6.4}$$

The real exchange rate can be written as

$$SP^* / P = (P_N / P_T)^{-\alpha} (P_N^* / P_T^*)^{\alpha^*}. \tag{6.5}$$

As (P_N^* / P_T^*) increases in Japan because of productivity growth, the yen should appreciate in real terms. Therefore, PPP should be viewed as a useful first approximation of the relationship between exchange rates and prices, but will be inaccurate in situations where long-term changes in relative prices occur.

This analysis, in addition, highlights another problem with traditional comparisons of the cost of capital: the choice of the relevant price index. Presumably, these comparisons aim at comparing the cost of capital of competing firms located in different countries that produce tradable goods, such as automobiles. For policy reasons, comparisons of the cost of capital are applied to multinationals, rather than to purely domestic firms such as those providing domestic services with no foreign competition. For these multinationals, however, the relevant price deflator may be actually closer to an index of traded goods than to an overall consumer price index. For Japanese automobile manufacturers, for example, a substantial proportion of total costs include raw materials, energy, and parts, which are themselves traded goods. If labor costs also increase mostly in line with output prices, then the relevant "cost" index should be heavily biased towards traded goods. In this situation, an index more heavily weighted toward traded goods, such as the Wholesale Price Index, may be more appropriate. Differences in real interest rates could be much less apparent using the WPI index, rather than the usual CPI index, providing a better comparison of capital costs in the traded goods sector.

Table 6–2 reports estimates of the average real interest rate based on WPI index rather than the CPI index. The table shows slight differences from using the CPI measure. During the overall period, there is a 1.3 percent gap between U.S. and German five-year rates, using the CPI. This gap drops to −0.1 percent when using the WPI numbers. Over 1981 to 1991, U.S. real rates were up to 2 percent higher than in Japan, using the CPI inflation. This difference, however, drops to 0.5 percent using the WPI inflation. It appears, therefore, that some care should be used in the choice of the inflation rate. Using the WPI index rather than the CPI index decreases differences in the cost of capital across countries. In addition, there may be statistical or data consideration reasons to prefer the WPI index: the CPI index is subject to seasonal movements that do not appear in the WPI index and probably has more measurement errors due, for instance, to infrequent and less accurate sampling of housing costs that are, in addition, sometimes measured inconsistently across countries.

Returning to the effect of exchange rates, Figures 6–5 and 6–6 present total costs, measured in dollars, from U.S. and German riskless investments. Compared to the previous real rate graphs, dollars costs now appear to be much more volatile. Over one-year periods, there were wide swings in the dollar-measured cost of German debt, ranging from −25 percent to 45 percent and appearing to be equally often positive and negative. Five-year costs are somewhat less volatile, but also present periods of much higher and lower foreign costs. Although nominal capital costs are more appropriate for intercountry comparisons, estimates of capital costs are unfortunately very imprecisely measured, because they involve exchange rates which display substantial volatility. This translates into instability of estimates over subperiods.

Table 6–3 breaks down differences in average nominal capital costs across deviations from RIP and from PPP. From 1973 to 1991, deviations from UIP range from 0.2 percent at the one-year maturity to 0.5 percent at the five-year maturity for the DM/$ rate. These differences in nominal costs

TABLE 6–2
Average Real Interest Rates Across Maturities (based on WPI data)

	1973–1991				
	1 Year	*2 Year*	*3 Year*	*4 Year*	*5 Year*
United States	3.8	4.3	4.5	4.7	4.9
Germany	3.4	3.9	4.2	4.5	4.8
	1981–1991				
	1 Year	*2 Year*	*3 Year*	*4 Year*	*5 Year*
United States	7.5	8.0	8.4	9.0	9.7
Germany	4.8	5.3	5.7	6.3	6.9
Japan	7.3	7.4	7.7	8.3	9.2

TABLE 6–3
Decomposition of Dollar Cost of Debt Across Maturities (based on CPI data)

Germany/U.S.	*1973–1991*				
	1 Year	*2 Year*	*3 Year*	*4 Year*	*5 Year*
UIP	0.2	0.3	0.4	0.5	0.5
RIP	0.2	0.3	0.4	0.5	0.7
PPP	0.0	0.0	0.0	0.0	–0.2
Germany/U.S.	*1981–1991*				
	1 Year	*2 Year*	*3 Year*	*4 Year*	*5 Year*
UIP	0.3	0.8	1.0	2.0	3.1
RIP	–1.0	–1.3	–1.4	–1.4	–1.5
PPP	1.3	2.1	2.4	3.4	4.6
Japan/U.S.	*1981–1991*				
	1 Year	*2 Year*	*3 Year*	*4 Year*	*5 Year*
UIP	3.3	2.5	2.1	1.9	1.8
RIP	–0.8	–1.5	–1.8	–1.9	–2.0
PPP	4.1	4.0	3.9	3.8	3.8

are modest for the United States and Germany over the floating exchange rate period. These numbers are consistent with the real rate comparisons because, over this period, long-term movements in the DM/$ rate were quite in line with inflation rates differentials. Figure 6–7 describes the path of the nominal and PPP exchange rate between the DM and the dollar, and shows

FIGURE 6–5
One-Year Dollar Nominal Costs: United States and Germany

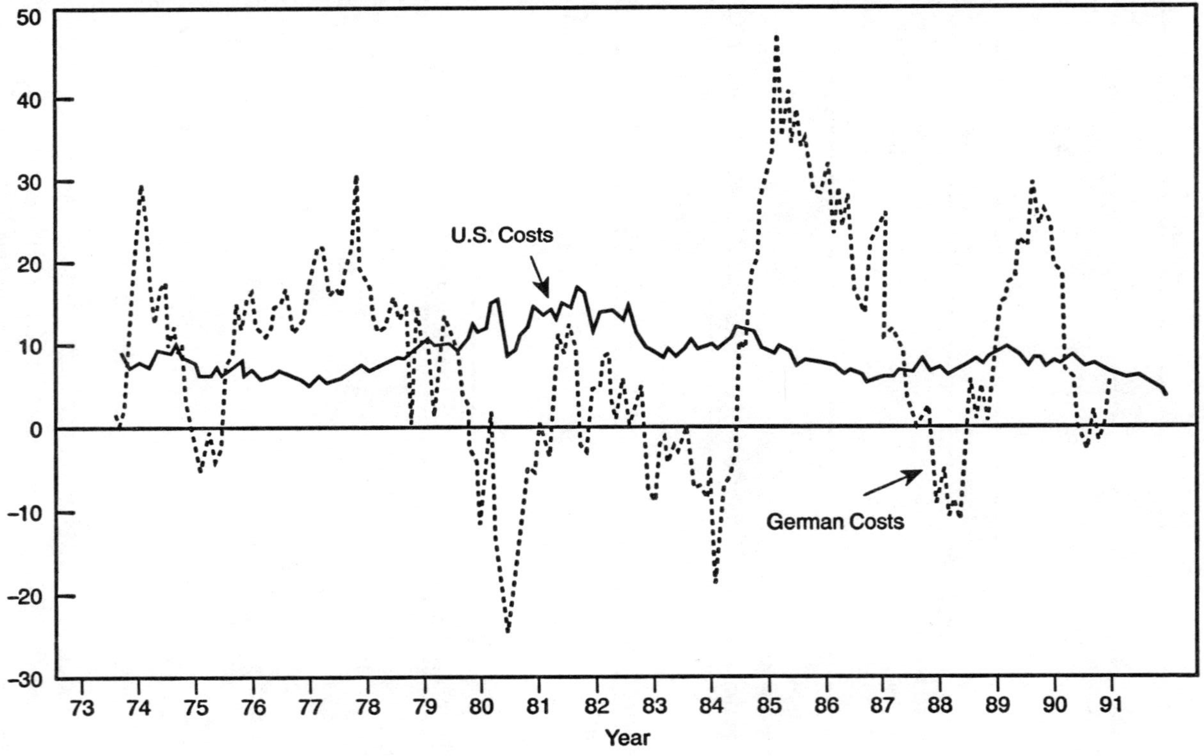

FIGURE 6—6
Five-Year Dollar Nominal Costs: United States and Germany

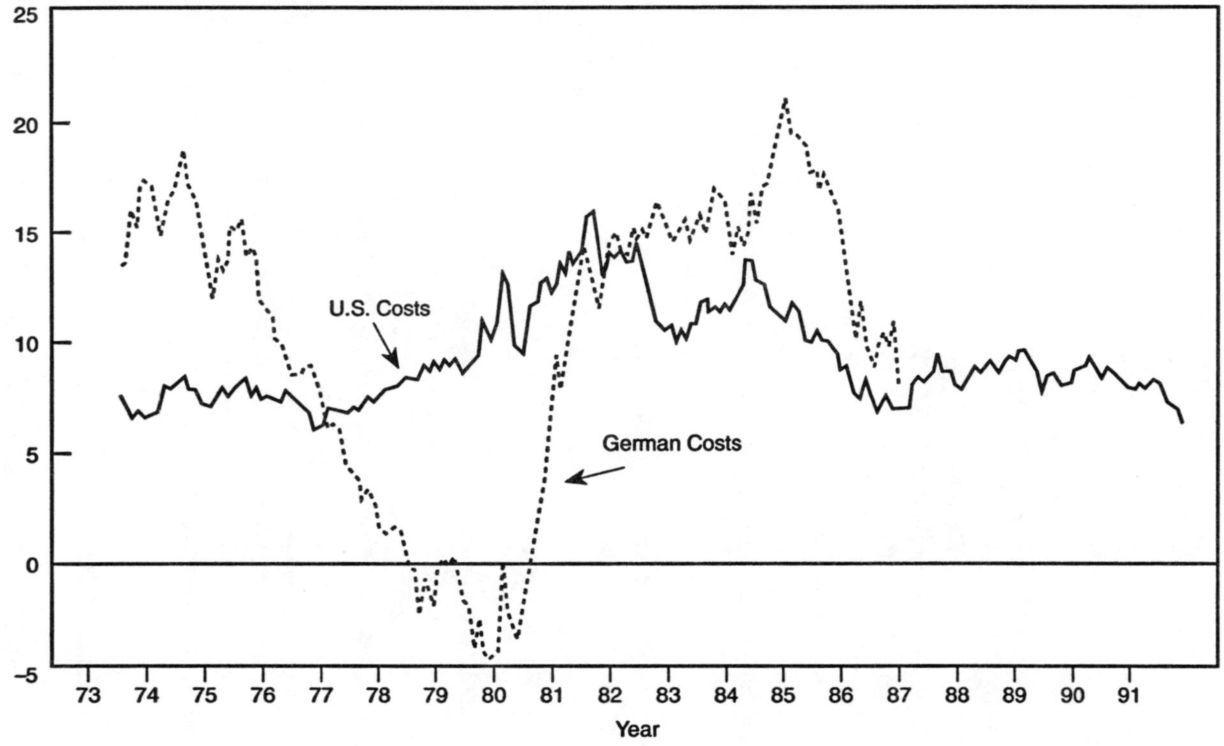

113

that the nominal price of the dollar depreciated by an amount quite close to the movement implied by PPP. Over this period, the deviation from one-year to four-year PPP was close to zero, and only −0.2 percent for the five-year horizon. For Germany, therefore, differences in nominal capital costs were close to differences in real capital costs, because purchasing power parity was essentially satisfied over the sample period.

Over the last decade, however, focusing on real rates would have mis-leadingly led to the conclusion that it was cheaper to borrow in Germany, by 1 percent to 1.5 percent per annum. But in fact, this difference was more than offset by an appreciation of the DM which ranged from 1.3 percent to 4.6 percent over different horizons, yielding nominal costs actually higher in Germany than in the United States. Across maturities, differences in capital costs were only 30 basis points higher at five-year horizons than at one-year horizons, which is a modest difference. This is consistent with the evidence in Jorion (1992), where expected term premiums across maturities, assumed constant, were found to be similar across the Eurodollar and Euromark markets.

The last part of the table decomposes the cost of capital for Japan over 1981–1991. Focusing solely on real costs would lead to the conclusion that real interest rates have been substantially lower in Japan, by as much as 2 percent at five-year horizons. This gap, however, is more than fully offset by a yen appreciation of about 4 percent; Marston (1987) shows that this appre-ciation is consistent with shifts in relative prices due to increased productiv-ity in Japan. Figure 6–8 shows that, over the period of floating exchange rates, the yen appreciated substantially more than was what implied by differences in inflation rates. The nominal rate went up by 58 percent, while PPP would have explained only an appreciation of 19 percent. Overall, the nominal cost of capital would have been systematically higher in Japan than in the United States. Since the opposite conclusion can be reached depend-ing on whether the focus is on real costs or on nominal costs, properly accounting for exchange rates appears to be essential in international com-parisons of the cost of capital.

CONCLUSIONS

Even though there are substantial variations over time in real and nominal interest rates, there is little evidence of systematically different capital costs between the United States, Germany, and Japan when averaged over long

FIGURE 6–7
DM/$ Exchange Rate and Purchasing Power Parity

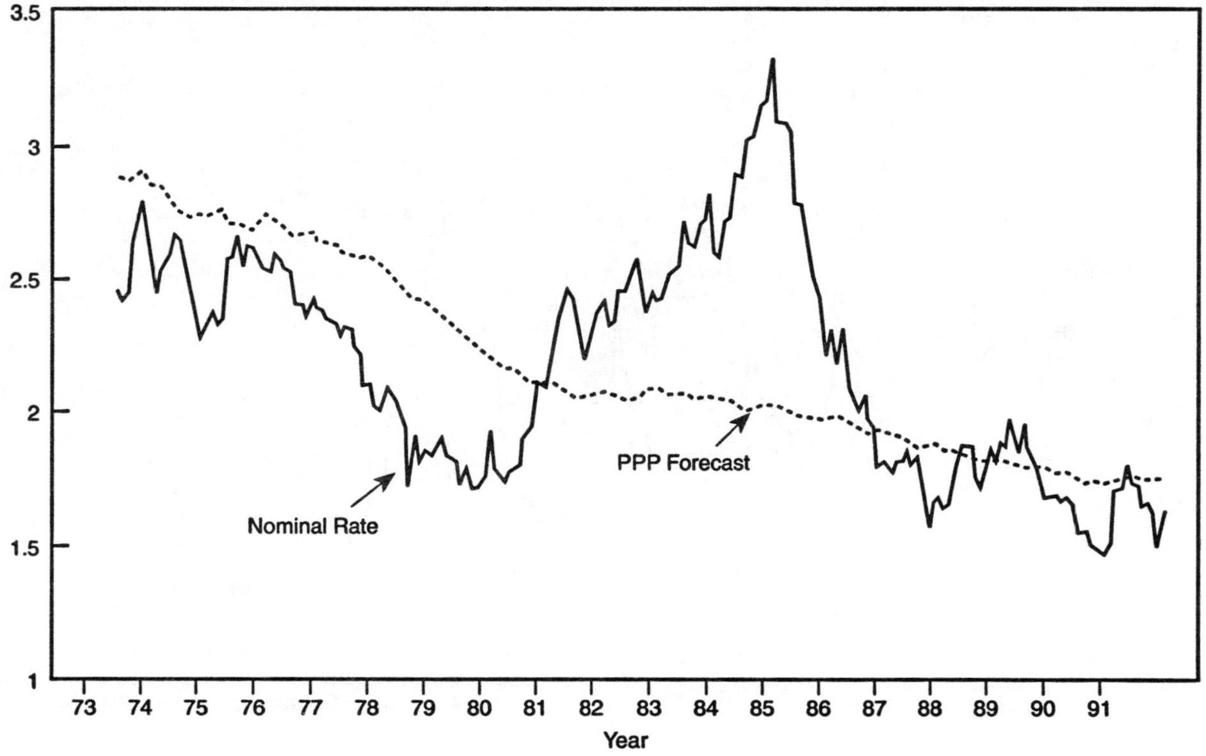

FIGURE 6–8
¥/$ Exchange Rate and Purchasing Power Parity

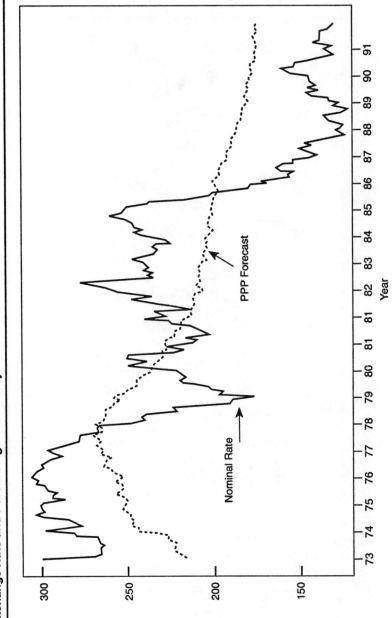

periods. Differences in interest rates have favored the United States as often as Japan or Germany. Further, it appears that differences in long-term real rates are no greater than differences in short-term real rates, especially when using the WPI to measure inflation.

Finally, this study has emphasized the importance of measuring debt costs in the same currency, rather than deflating nominal rates in each country by their respective inflation rates. Since multinationals have the ability to raise funds in different markets and currencies, capital costs should be translated into the same numeraire currency for comparison purposes. Differences in exchange-adjusted nominal costs are then related to differences in real costs through movements in the real exchange rate. Even though CPI-based Japanese real rates have been lower than U.S. real rates over the last decade, this difference has been more than offset by an appreciation of the yen in real terms. Therefore, there is little substance to the contention that U.S. companies have suffered a cost of capital handicap relative to foreign competition.

REFERENCES

Abuaf, N., and P. Jorion. (1990). "Purchasing Power Parity in the Long Run." *Journal of Finance*. March, pp. 157–74.

Belassa, B. (1964). "The Purchasing Power Parity Doctrine: A Reappraisal." *Journal of Political Economy*. 72, pp. 584–96.

Bernheim, D., and J. Shoven. (1987). "Taxation and the Cost of Capital: An International Comparison." *The Consumption Tax: A Better Alternative?* E. Walker and M. Bloomfield, eds. Cambridge, MA: Ballinger, pp. 61–85.

Cho, C., C. Eun, and L. Senbet. (1986). "International Arbitrage Pricing Theory: An Empirical Investigation." *Journal of Finance*. 41, pp. 313–29.

Dornbusch, R. (1976). "Expectations and Exchange Rate Dynamics." *Journal of Political Economy*. 84, pp. 1161–76.

Errunza, V., and E. Losq. (1985). "International Asset Pricing Under Mild Segmentation: Theory and Test." *Journal of Finance*. 40, pp. 105–24.

Feldstein, M., and C. Horioka. (1980). "Domestic Saving and International Capital Flows." *Economic Journal*. 90, pp. 314–29.

Frankel, J. (1979). "On the Mark: A Theory of Floating Exchange Rates Based on Real Rate Differentials." *American Economic Review*. 69, pp. 610–22.

Frankel, J. (1991a). "Quantifying International Capital Mobility in the 1980s." *National Saving and Economic Performance*. D. Bernheim and J. Shoven, eds. Chicago: University of Chicago Press. pp. 61–85.

Frankel, J. (1991b). "The Japanese Cost of Finance: A Survey." *Financial Manage-*

ment. 20, Spring, pp. 95–127.

Frenkel, J. (1976). "A Monetary Approach to the Exchange Rate: Doctrinal Aspects and Empirical Evidence." *Scandinavian Journal of Economics.* 78, pp. 200–24.

Gultekin, M., B. Gultekin, and A. Penati. (1989). "Capital Controls and International Capital Market Segmentation: The Evidence from the Japanese and American Stock Markets." *Journal of Finance.* 44, pp. 849–69.

Hatsopoulos, G., P. Krugman, and L. Summers. (1988). "U.S. Competitiveness: Beyond the Trade Deficit." *Science.* pp. 299–307.

Jorion, P. (1992). "Term Premiums and the Integration of the Eurocurrency Markets." *Journal of International Money and Finance.* 11, pp. 17–39.

Jorion, P., and E. Schwartz. (1986). "Integration vs. Segmentation in the Canadian Stock Market." *Journal of Finance.* 41, pp. 603–14.

Jorion, P., and F. Mishkin. (1991). "A Multi-Country Comparison of Term Structure Forecasts at Long Horizons." *Journal of Financial Economics.* 29, pp. 59–80.

Kester, C., and T. Luehrman. (1989). "Real Interest Rates and the Cost of Capital: A Comparison of the United States and Japan." *Japan and the World Economy.* 1, pp. 279–301.

Korajczyk, R., and C. Viallet. (1989). "An Empirical Investigation of International Asset Pricing." *Review of Financial Studies.* 2, pp. 553–85.

McCauley, R., and S. Zimmer. (1989). "Explaining International Differences in the Cost of Capital." *Federal Reserve Bank of New York Review.* Summer, pp. 7–28.

Mark, N. (1985). "Some Evidence on the International Inequality of Real Interest Rates." *Journal of International Money and Finance.* pp.189–208.

Marston, R. (1987). "Real Exchange Rates and Productivity Growth in the United States and Japan." *Real Financial Linkages in Open Economies.* S. Arndt, ed. Cambridge, MA: MIT Press. pp. 71–96.

Mishkin, F. (1984). "Are Real Interest Rates Equal Across Countries? An Empirical Investigation of International Parity Conditions." *Journal of Finance.* 39, December, pp. 1345–57.

Mussa, M. (1982). "A Model of Exchange Rate Dynamics." *Journal of Political Economy.* 90, pp. 74–104.

Myers, S. (1974). "Interactions of Corporate Financing and Investment Decisions." *Journal of Finance.* pp. 1–25.

Stehle, R. (1977). "An Empirical Test of the Alternative Hypotheses of National and International Pricing of Risky Assets." *Journal of Finance.* 32, May, pp. 493–502.

CHAPTER 7

EXCHANGE RATES AND INTERNATIONAL DIFFERENCES IN THE COST OF CAPITAL

Robert N. McCauley
Steven A. Zimmer

INTRODUCTION

Several years ago it became a commonplace to say that U.S. firms labored under the burden of heavier capital costs while competing in international markets. Now, with the Nikkei average having retraced its vertiginous steps to levels last seen five or six years ago, and with U.S. interest rates having fallen below half the level of those in Europe, the opposite view has acquired both currency and plausibility.

At the same time, much recent work comparing the cost of capital across countries has left many observers unsatisfied. The work seemed to take as its unstated premise that firms compete in international markets on the basis of their home capital costs. The capacity of large firms to borrow on very similar terms in the Eurobond and foreign bond markets seemed to be ignored. Perhaps worse, competition by multinational firms in the same market seemed entirely neglected.

Finally, comparisons of the cost of capital seemed to have nothing to

Robert N. McCauley is Assistant Vice President at the Federal Reserve Bank of New York. Steven A. Zimmer is Vice President of J.P. Morgan Asset Management. The views expressed are those of the authors and do not necessarily reflect those of the Federal Reserve Bank of New York or the Federal Reserve System.

say about exchange rates and exchange rate risks. This omission is odd in light of the fact that exchange-rate risk is a prime candidate among the forces that serve to distinguish national capital markets.

This chapter seeks to address all three concerns. First, we update our 1989 work comparing the cost of capital for industrial and commercial firms in order to answer the question of whether the new decade ushered in a new ranking of national capital costs. Second, we argue the primacy of the cost of equity in determining the capital advantage of multinationals from a variety of countries operating in the same economy. Third, we make some suggestions for the treatment of real exchange rate risk by the treasurer of a firm considering multinational expansion or acquisition.

CONCEPTUAL FOUNDATIONS

Several very useful and quite recent reviews of the literature relieve us of any such job here.[1] One point bears discussion, however.

We take the cost of equity to be a required profit rate. To measure this rate, we calculate an earnings-to-price ratio for broad, national stock market indexes, after adjusting reported earnings to render them comparable across countries. Recently, the substantial agreement of studies employing this method has been dismissed as reflecting no more than their common method.[2] While the finding that U.S. corporations face higher hurdle rates in evaluating investments remains controversial, it is worth noting that Malkiel (1992) adopted a distinct, and to many eyes, more acceptable approach and arrived at very similar results. Using the dividend discount model and analysts' medium-term earnings forecasts, he measured the cost of equity as highest for the United States, lower for Germany, and lowest for Japan, with rates that strikingly resembled ours over the 1980–88 period (Table 7–1).

TABLE 7–1
Estimates of the Cost of Equity Capital (United States vs. Japan and Germany, in percentage)

Average 1980–88	U.S.	Japan	Germany
Malkiel estimate	11.7	7.1	7.7
McCauley–Zimmer estimate	10.6	6.0	8.3

Source: Burton G. Malkiel, "The Influence of Conditions in Financial Markets on the Time Horizons of Business Managers: An International Comparison," *Federal Reserve Bank of New York*, p. 17.

NEW RESULTS SHOW CONSIDERABLE CONVERGENCE

Review of Our Approach: Cost of Capital, Cost of Funds, Cost of Debt.[3]

The cost of capital is the minimum before-tax real rate of return that an investment project must generate in order to pay its financing costs after tax liabilities. The cost of capital will be determined by the required payments to a firm's debt and equity holders (cost of funds), as well as by the economic depreciation of the investment, the tax treatment of that depreciation, the taxation of corporate earnings, and any fiscal incentives for investment.

Investment can be financed by two basic kinds of claims on the stream of returns from the investment project: debt or equity. The cost of funds is defined as a weighted average of a firm's debt and equity costs. We measure first the cost of debt, then the cost of equity, and then combine the two according to the shares of debt and equity in the capital structure of the representative firm. Our measurements aim to capture the cost to the aggregate of nonfinancial firms in the four economies.

The cost of debt is defined as the real, after-tax rate of interest faced by nonfinancial corporate borrowers. Estimating this cost begins with the nominal rate of interest paid by firms in the United States, Germany, Japan, and the United Kingdom on their mix of debt. Estimates of low or zero-yield compensating balances with banks are used to boost the cost of bank debt. Inflation, measured by the GNP deflator, is subtracted from the nominal interest rate to give a more comparable measure of real rates of interest. Finally, the allowable deductions from corporate income taxes for nominal interest payments in all four countries are netted to put these real rates on an after-tax basis.

Review of Our Approach: Cost of Equity

The cost of equity is much more difficult to measure and generates much more controversy. Our approach is to determine true, economic earnings by stripping off distortions of one kind or another and to compare those internationally comparable earnings to the respective market capitalizations. Our adjustments are four:[4]

Depreciation Earnings must be adjusted downward to reflect inflation's erosion of the historical values used for depreciation and upward to reflect acceleration of tax depreciation schedules. Economic earnings are overstated in an inflationary environment, because historical costs used in tax and accounting allowances fall short of replacement values for plant and equipment. Partly in response to this distortion, tax laws at times speed up permitted depreciation rates beyond economic rates. Earnings for all countries must be adjusted, although our procedures vary across the four countries.

Inventory profits   This adjustment reduces earnings to remove purely inflationary gains on goods in inventory. If a corporation uses first-in, first-out (FIFO) accounting, the real cost of goods sold will be understated by the extent of inflation over the inventory holding period. If the corporation uses last-in, first-out (LIFO) accounting, the real cost of goods sold will be understated when the firm reduces its inventory, with the size of the understatement dependent on the extent of the inventory rundown and on the age of the inventory.

Inflation's effect on nominal interest payments   The overstatement of borrowing costs in an inflationary environment finds a counterpart in the understatement of earnings. With no inflation, only real interest payments are subtracted from cash flow to arrive at earnings; with inflation, nominal interest costs represent not only the real interest rate but also a payment that compensates for inflation. In effect, this extra payment is a capital loss on a liability, not a current cost, and should not be accounted as a reduction in the firm's earnings.

Crossholding   Most telling for the U.S.–Japan comparison is the adjustment for extensive crossholding of shares in Japan. The need for this adjustment arises because a Japanese firm that holds less than a 20 percent share of a second corporation does not include the retained earnings of the latter corporation in its own reported earnings. At the same time, the crossheld shares are not excluded from the value of the outstanding shares of the second company. As a consequence, the outstanding value of shares overcounts the net value held outside the corporate sector when compared to reported earnings. Since listed firms own a large and rising portion of all shares, crossholding results in a serious understatement of profits in Japan.[5]

Results Through 1988

Increased international capital flows in the 1980s did not eliminate differences in real corporate borrowing costs (Chart 7–1). While the distortions of inflation are evident at the beginning of the decade, in 1983–88 real, after-

CHART 7–1
Effective Real After-Tax Cost of Debt

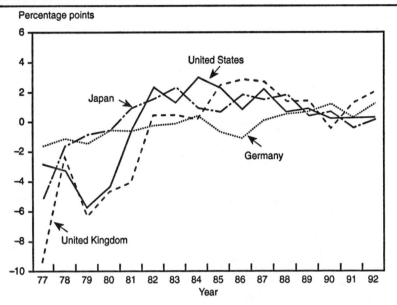

tax debt costs are similar for U.S., Japanese, and British firms at about 1.8 percent. German firms, however, enjoyed after-tax debt costs near zero.

This finding depends on the borrowing habits of corporations. Outside the United States, heavy reliance on bank debt renders short-term rates more important than long-term rates. Indeed, the German firms' advantage in the 1980s in the real, after-tax cost of debt compared to U.S. firms reflects more the mix of debt than any difference in either the cost of short-term debt or the cost of long-term debt.

Taking all our earnings adjustments into account, we obtain measures of the cost of equity in the four countries (Chart 7–2). Japanese corporations have generally enjoyed lower equity costs than the other three countries, and U.S. firms have generally faced the steepest equity costs. The effect of bull stock markets in the 1980s is evident in the generally declining trend of equity costs.

A comparison of debt and equity costs shows that debt is generally cheaper than equity. Only for Japan in the late 1980s are the two costs close, that is, within 1 percent.

Debt and equity costs are combined in proportions suggested by the debt-to-market equity ratios (Chart 7–3). By this measure, exchange-traded

CHART 7–2
Cost of Equity

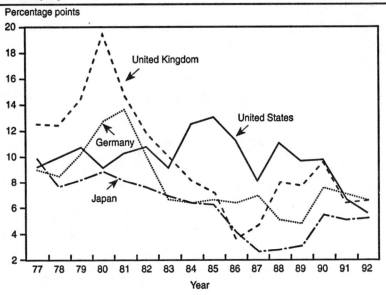

Japanese firms deleveraged very considerably in the 1980s.

German and Japanese firms' capital cost advantage is evident from the real after-tax cost of funds (Chart 7–4). Note, however, that the German firms' edge derived mostly from cheap, short-term debt in a capital structure rather lean on equity, while Japanese firms enjoyed cheap equity as well as higher leverage.

The international differences in the cost of funds generally carried over into the cost of capital (Table 7–2). The effect of tax policy is evident. Tax credits for research and development cheapened the costs for Japanese and U.S. firms in relation to those of German and British firms, respectively. Also, consider the U.S. cost of equipment before and after the Tax Act of 1986, which removed the investment tax credit: the cost of capital went up even though the cost of funds was falling.

Equity Costs Have Converged Substantially in the 1990s

In particular, Japanese and German firms' cost of equity have risen quite a bit since 1988. It may seem strange that the Japanese cost of equity has not risen by more, given the halving of equity prices since 1989, but it must be

CHART 7–3
Debt-to-Market Equity Ratios

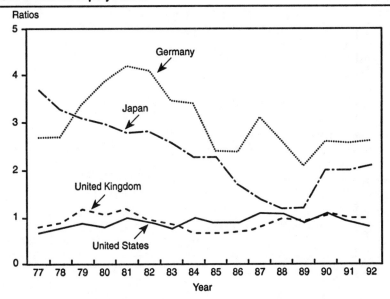

CHART 7–4
Real After-Tax Cost of Funds

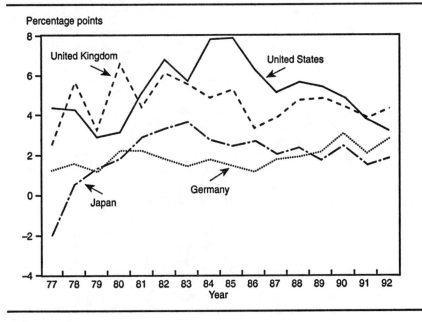

TABLE 7-2
Cost of Capital for Various Projects

	1977	1978	1979	1980	1981	1982	1983	1984	1985	1986	1987	1988	1989	1990	1991
Equipment and Machinery with Physical Life of 20 Years															
United States	11.2	11.7	11.2	11.5	11.5	11.5	10.6	11.3	11.1	9.1	10.2	11.2	10.3	9.7	8.5
Japan	5.9	6.9	7.6	8.8	8.8	8.5	11.3	8.4	8.3	7.8	7.0	7.3	7.4	8.2	7.1
Germany	7.7	7.3	7.5	8.6	8.8	7.8	7.0	7.2	7.1	6.9	7.0	7.0	7.3	8.5	6.5
United Kingdom	8.8	10.8	9.8	12.7	10.3	10.7	10.8	9.3	9.4	7.8	8.2	9.1	9.2	9.1	8.3
Factory with Physical Life of 40 Years															
United States	10.0	10.4	8.9	9.3	11.3	12.4	10.8	12.8	12.6	9.3	9.0	10.2	9.8	9.0	7.3
Japan	2.8	4.2	5.1	6.2	6.8	6.6	7.0	6.3	6.1	5.8	4.8	5.5	5.6	6.5	5.2
Germany	5.5	5.5	5.6	7.0	7.4	6.3	5.4	5.7	5.5	5.2	5.4	5.4	5.2	6.6	4.6
United Kingdom	6.7	9.9	7.8	12.2	7.7	8.7	8.8	7.6	8.3	6.1	6.6	7.9	8.0	7.7	6.8
Research and Development Project with 10-Year Payoff Lag															
United States	12.5	12.9	11.9	12.4	14.9	18.4	15.2	20.3	20.2	16.8	18.2	20.3	20.4	18.6	15.5
Japan	3.9	5.7	6.5	7.3	8.0	8.3	8.7	7.7	9.2	8.0	6.8	6.2	6.3	7.4	6.7
Germany	13.4	13.8	13.3	15.6	15.7	14.7	13.9	14.6	13.9	13.2	14.4	14.8	15.4	17.7	15.5
United Kingdom	18.2	28.4	21.1	33.4	24.2	29.5	29.2	24.4	25.4	18.9	20.6	23.7	23.8	22.6	20.5
Expensed Item with Physical Life of 3 Years															
United States	39.5	40.6	42.4	43.3	41.2	40.5	39.3	39.6	39.1	36.7	39.4	40.4	41.6	41.1	40.2
Japan	35.0	35.1	35.4	36.4	36.1	36.0	35.6	35.7	35.6	35.3	34.8	34.9	34.6	35.1	34.5
Germany	34.7	34.7	34.7	35.4	35.6	35.1	34.7	34.8	34.8	34.6	34.7	34.8	34.9	35.5	35.0
United Kingdom	39.4	40.6	41.4	42.5	40.5	40.0	39.6	38.4	37.7	36.1	37.0	37.4	37.4	37.2	36.8

borne in mind that Japanese corporate earnings have weakened as well. Meanwhile U.S. and British firms' equity costs have fallen.

Convergence is overstated by our measures because of the desynchronization of business cycles in 1989–91. The Anglo-Saxon economies entered recessions in 1990 while Japan and Germany boomed into 1991. As a result, U.S. and British firms' earnings fell short of permanent earnings. Moreover, U.S. and British investors appear to have priced their respective shares in anticipation of a recovery of profits.

The impact of the change in Japan's cost of equity on capital spending in Japan may well be magnified by the lack of sophistication in Japanese managers' views on cost of funds. They tended to ignore the equity options imbedded in convertible bonds and with warrant issues. As a result they tended to take the interest cost of such debt and equity packages, which might be near zero after a currency swap into yen, to be their cost of funds. Comparing the near zero cost of such instruments with, for instance, the current long-term prime rate, Japanese managers tend to conclude that their cost of funds has risen very substantially. Yet there is an argument that the real cost of long-term prime rate funding is at present lower than the cost of the hybrid instruments (Appendix to Chapter 7).[6]

The Costs of Funds Across Markets Have Converged, but to a Lesser Extent

The new decade of the 1990s was ushered in with striking timing by the breaching of the Berlin Wall and the fall of the Tokyo stock market. These events made their marks on the cost of funds. As the policy mix in Germany shifted to an expansive budget and tight money, German real interest rates at all points of the yield curve have risen to levels above those prevailing in the United States and Japan. And, as noted above, Japan appears to have little left to its cost of equity advantage, although ongoing differences in relative cyclic positions, not to say the volatility of the Tokyo Stock Exchange, make even a tentative conclusion hazardous. Taking all things together, a gap of two or more percentage points between the German and Japanese cost of funds, on the one hand, and that of the United States, on the other, may not characterize the 1990s the way such a gap characterized the 1980s.

British firms have not enjoyed a cheapening in the cost of funds in parallel with their transatlantic counterparts. In particular, as inflation has declined over the last year more than interest rates, the cost of sterling debt has risen.

The considerable convergence of equity costs means that the higher leverage of Japanese and especially German firms is a key force driving a wedge between the cost of funds of U.S. firms as compared with Japanese and German firms. For German firms, higher leverage represents more than all of any remaining cost of funds advantage in relation to U.S. firms. Moreover, since our measure of leverage is the ratio of debt-to-market equity, the decline in Japanese equity values is to some extent offset by the leaner mixture of relatively expensive equity in the capital structure of corporate Japan. The implication of the importance of leverage is that some large, low leverage German and Japanese firms must enjoy little or no advantage over their U.S. counterparts.[7]

COSTS OF EQUITY DIFFER IN A WORLD OF MOBILE CAPITAL?

The most direct answer is that the preference for home-market equities remains very strong. In fact, this preference is so strong that quite substantial portfolio reallocations away from the low cost of equity market to the high cost of equity market do not suffice to keep the valuation gap from widening. Thus, the modest foreign asset positions of major institutional investors provide a narrow basis for even fundamentally driven capital flows to reduce disparities in valuations.

Foreign Asset Shares of Institutional Investors Are Low

An idea of how xenophobic major, deep-pocketed institutional investors are can be gathered from Davis (1991). Life insurers in major countries show single-digit foreign asset shares with the brief exception of U.K. insurers and the more consistent exception of Japanese insurers[8] (Table 7–3). Looking down the years, the elimination of exchange controls in Britain at the beginning of the Thatcher years, and the liberalization of foreign asset constraints in Japan in the mid-1980s, emerge as the most noteworthy developments. Looking across the countries and down the years, a trend toward diversification may hardly be said to pervade the data.

The question immediately arises of whether insurers are constrained by law or regulation. Certainly, U.S. insurers are constrained by state regulation, although the constraint looks to be more like 10 percent of assets than 4 percent, and Canadian securities are often treated like U.S. securities.[9] The

TABLE 7–3
Foreign Assets in Life Insurance

Panel A: Percentage of Foreign Assets in Life Insurance Companies' Total Assets

	U.K.	U.S.	Germany	Japan	Canada	France
1980	4.3	4.0	0.6	2.7	3.3	–
1985	12.5	3.5	0.7	9.3	2.1	–
1986	11.9	3.2	0.7	11.7	2.7	–
1987	9.1	3.4	0.6	13.7	2.1	2.3
1988	9.5	3.5	0.6	14.2	2.2	2.0

Panel B: Foreign Assets of Life Insurance Companies End–1988

	Foreign Assets ($bn)	Percent of Total Assets	Foreign Bonds as Percent of Foreign Assets	Foreign Equities as Percent of Foreign Assets
United Kingdom	34.2	9.5%	18%	82%
United States	40.3	0.5%	(90%)[a]	(10%)[a]
Germany	1.2	0.6%	83%	17%
Japan	104.0	14.2%	79%	21%
Canada	1.9	2.2%	18%	82%
France	1.9	2.0%	(50%)[b]	(50%)[b]

[a] Division based on market estimates (equities are not separately identified in the data).
[b] Estimated.

Source: E. Philip Davis, "International Diversification of Institutional Investors," Bank of England *Discussion Papers,* Technical Series No. 44 (September 1991), p. 17.

Japanese authorities raised the permitted share of life insurers' foreign assets in 1986, but Japanese life insurers show a foreign asset share of only half of the 30 percent limit.[10] Legal and regulatory constraints are far from obviously binding.

Pension funds with long-duration liabilities might seem the natural bearers of foreign exchange risk and thus the natural holders of foreign assets. But again the data suggest a narrow base of foreign asset holding (Table 7–4). Apart from the bounce in foreign assets on the books of the British and Japanese pension funds in the early 1980s, a general trend toward more diversified portfolios is not in evidence.

Perhaps even less than the life insurers do pension funds appear to be straining against legal or regulatory constraints. While some U.S. state and local pension managers are doubtless constrained by law, regulation, or

TABLE 7-4
Foreign Assets in Pension Funds

Panel A: Percentage of Foreign Assets in Pension Funds' Total Assets

	U.K.	U.S.	Germany	Japan	Canada	France[a]
1980	8.2	0.7	0.4	0.5	4.1	5.0
1985	14.7	2.2	0.8	5.4	5.2	5.3
1986	16.8	3.2	0.7	0.5	0.3	5.8
1987	13.3	0.4	0.7	0.9	5.2	4.2
1988	13.9	3.8	0.4	7.0	5.3	4.0

Panel B: Foreign Assets of Pension Funds End-1988

	Foreign Assets ($bn)	Percent of Total Assets	Foreign Bonds as Percent of Foreign Assets	Foreign Equities as Percent of Foreign Assets
United Kingdom	53.8	13.9%	6%	94%
United States	62.8	4.0%	14%	86%
Germany	0.2	0.4%	93%	7%
Japan	65.2	7.1%	(50%)[b]	(50%)[b]
Canada	6.9	5.3%	7%	93%
France	1.2	4.0%	15%	85%

[a] Percent of securities holdings only
[b] Estimated

Source: E. Philip Davis, "International Diversification of Institutional Investors," Bank of England *Discussion Papers,* Technical Series No. 44 (September 1991), p. 23.

politics, U.S. corporate pension bulk far larger and are governed by the law's "prudent man" rule that is construed by some managers to permit foreign asset shares over a third. For their part, Japanese pension funds remain well below the same 30 percent limit that applies to life insurers.[11]

The proposition that these shares are all too low is given some support by their relation to the import shares of the respective economies. Import shares no more than proxy the larger traded goods sector, with its exposure to foreign price trends. Yet with the single exception of the Japanese life insurers, all the foreign asset shares fall short of the respective national import shares (Table 7-5). It is often remarked that "daily global movements of capital are huge compared with daily movements of goods" (Kester and Luehrman, 1992, p. 131). But underneath all the

TABLE 7–5
International Investment and Import Penetration (In percentage)

| | International Asset Share of Institutional Portfolios | | 1988 Imports as a Share of Gross Domestic Product | 1988 Imports as a Share of Total Final Expenditure |
	Life Insurance	Pension Funds		
United States	3.5	3.8	13	11
United Kingdom	9.5	13.9	27	21
Germany	0.6	0.4	27	21
Japan	14.2	7.0	10	9
Canada	2.2	5.3	26	20
France	2.0	4.0	21	18

Source: E. Philip Davis, "International Diversification of Institutional Investors," Bank of England *Discussion Papers,* Technical Series No. 44 (September 1991), p. 16.

churning it remains true nevertheless that the market for goods is more integrated internationally than the market for capital.

Even Portfolio Reallocations Driven by Fundamentals Could Not Close Valuation Gaps

This claim is well supported by equity flows in and out of Japan. International flows of funds in the late 1980s were consistent with investors' recognizing that the Tokyo market was out of line with the rest of the world's stock markets. Although Japan's largest foreign asset holders, the life insurers, are generally thought of as foreign bond buyers, they raised their portfolio weight on foreign equities from something below 1 percent to about 3 percent (Table 7–3). Koo (1992, p. 18) shows that they had accumulated foreign equities at the end of 1991 representing half the value of their foreign bond holdings (5.7 trillion yen *vs.* 11.5 trillion yen, but much of the foreign equity holding is, in fact, nontraded equity in foreign affiliates that hold portfolios of foreign bonds).

At the same time, foreigners underweighted Japanese shares very markedly. Foreigners as a group sliced their holdings of Japanese shares from 7 percent by value in 1986 to 4.3 percent in 1989.[12] Altogether data collected by the U.S. Treasury show that Japanese purchases of U.S. equity and U.S. sales of Japanese equities amounted to $28 billion in the period 1985-89.

Corporate Arbitrage of the Valuation Gap Bulked Larger than Portfolio Investors' Arbitrage

Japanese firms were net buyers of U.S. corporate assets in the late 1980s. In particular, the U.S. Commerce Department puts the net direct foreign investment flow from Japan to the United States at $50 billion in 1985–89.[13] The Japanese Ministry of Finance data show a 10 percent larger net inflow into the United States.[14]

Michael Adler has asked us how a major valuation gap could survive in a world of investment bankers actively seeking profits. An interesting, if relatively small-scale, form of arbitrage demonstrates that the investment bankers were not out to lunch. Investment bankers persuaded U.S. firms to cash in on the Tokyo market by carving out their Japanese affiliates. As shown by Fikre (1991), U.S. and British firms that floated shares in their Japanese subsidiaries or joint ventures on the Tokyo market commanded price-earnings ratios characteristic of the local market, rather than their home market (Chart 7–5).[15] By contrast, U.S. firms that merely listed their regular shares in Tokyo found their price-earnings ratios unaffected. Thus it seemed that Japanese investors were willing to put a high value on earnings of Japanese firms (apparently without respect to whether they were earned at home or abroad) *or on the earnings of firms in Japan.*

Stepping back, one can observe how the flow of equity from Tokyo to New York in both portfolio and direct form was very much of a piece with the broadest developments in corporate finance in the two countries. Thus while Japanese nonfinancial firms raised a net 11 trillion yen (about $90 billion) in equity in 1985-89, U.S. firms retired a net $500 billion in equity in the same years.[16] In other words, Japanese firms recognized a good thing, issued shares in volume (directly or round-about packaged with bonds and issued in London, Zurich and Frankfurt), used some of the proceeds to buy U.S. firms or U.S. corporate assets, and thereby contributed to the massive net retirement of equity in New York.

Segmented Equity Markets Permit National Factors to Affect Equity Costs

Given substantial but insufficient buy-side and sell-side flows, national economic differences can find expression in costs of equity. We have pointed to a number of factors. Japanese and German households save more of their income. Japanese and U.S. fiscal policy headed in opposite directions in the

CHART 7-5
Price-Earnings Multiples of Equity Carve-Outs Relative to U.S. and Japanese Markets[a]

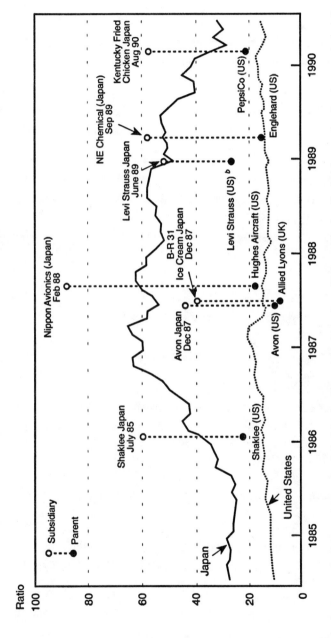

[a] Price-earnings ratios for Japan and the United States are taken from Morgan Stanley Capital International; price-earnings ratios for the subsidiaries, based on initial public offering prices, are computed using one-year lagged earnings.
[b] The parent company price-earnings ratio used for Levi Strauss is from September 1985, when management bought out the public shareholders.

133

1980s. Japanese economic growth was smoother than that of other countries in the 1980s.

If one understands the Japanese equity market as a bubble, one can argue that it was a national bubble in the sense that foreigners behaved as if they were not caught up in the mania. But note that if it was a bubble, it was a bubble from which the Japanese corporate sector extracted much equity.

Ignorance of how to analyze equity prices across countries may also play a role. For instance the professional literature on the crossholding adjustment is of recent vintage,[17] although some market participants long understood the basic point.[18]

In addition to the factors that can account for different equity valuations, one can ask why the mix of equity and debt varies across countries. We point to industrial organization differences—close relations between banks and corporations—to explain how Japanese and German firms can carry relatively high debt and interest burdens without incurring the dead-weight losses from distress that Anglo-Saxon firms show at such leverage.

DOES IT MATTER THAT PURELY DOMESTIC FIRMS CAN BORROW IN FOREIGN CURRENCY?

The question arises of how cost of funds can be sensibly defined on a national basis when firms can borrow in any number of currencies. In some ways this question misses the point of our findings for the 1980s. Differences in the cost of debt looked minor across the United States, Japan and Britain, and in the case of Germany the composition of the debt—largely short-term—provided the advantage in relation to the United States. And greater reliance on debt made a difference for Japan and Germany.[19]

Moreover, access to foreign currency debt finance does not in practice offer much of an alternative for most domestic producers. Even if foreign currency debt carrying a low real interest rate is identified, issuing liabilities in such a currency would expose the capital structure and income statement to the risk that foreign currency appreciation will more than wipe out the interest savings.[20] Firms that produce domestically but sell abroad or in competition with imports (like California wine producers) might well contract foreign currency (franc) debt to hedge their economic risks, but one has the impression that such behavior is sufficiently rare as not to render the costs of funds as calculated above uninteresting.

COST OF CAPITAL AND THE MULTINATIONAL FIRM

Multinational firms typically borrow locally when they are operating outside of their home country. It follows that the cost of funds as calculated above do not capture the constraints on, for instance, U.S. and Japanese firms operating in Britain.

As freely as multinationals can range across the world's debt (and derivatives) markets, in one respect they remain tethered to developments in their home capital markets. The cost of equity from its home-country stock market constrains the multinational firm in its consideration of acquisitions, establishments, expansions, divestments, or contraction of operations in foreign countries.

The Cost of Equity Theory of the Multinational

Aliber (1970) explained the preponderance of U.S. firms in the flow of direct foreign investment in the 1950s and 1960s by pointing to the New York Stock Exchange. If it capitalized a given stream of earnings at a higher multiple than the London, Frankfurt, Paris, or Tokyo stock exchanges, then U.S. multinationals could outbid British, German, French, or Japanese companies for corporate assets abroad.

This view did not convince everyone. It did not provide an account of the two-way flow characteristic of foreign direct investment; Hymer (1976) and Kindleberger (1969) offered an oligopoly perspective that better accounts for multinational oil companies buying gas stations in each other's back yard. In 1970 portfolio flows were relatively small, so that a theory that claimed that corporations were doing some of the unfinished work of institutional portfolio managers had some plausibility. But as portfolio flows increased against a backdrop of liberalized markets and portfolio regulation, many observers took a theory that depended on substantial and persistent differences in equity market valuations to be economically incorrect.[21]

As an account of the shifting balance of flows of direct foreign investment, the cost of equity hypothesis has aged well.

Foreign acquisitions in the United States rose sharply in the late 1970s when, as a result of the confounding effects of inflation, U.S. firms' cost of equity moved irregularly above that of major foreign competitors (Chart 7–2). The United States became the world's leading recipient of foreign direct investment after the New York Stock Exchange started to offer foreign firms easy pickings.

The timing and composition of the surge in direct investment into the United States in the late 1980s are mostly consistent with the cost of equity account. From the mid-1980s, foreign acquirers brought a significant cost-of-equity advantage to the bidding contests for U.S. corporate assets. And, by the end of the decade, foreign firms accounted for as much as a third of mergers and acquisitions by value. The country composition of the foreign acquisitions shifted toward Japan, which made sense in light of the low cost of equity there (Chart 7–6). The flux and reflux of Japanese net direct foreign investment in the United States followed Japanese firms' waxing and waning cost of equity advantage closely.

That British firms managed to increase their wonted share of acquisitions in the United States in the late 1980s was a little puzzling, and a deal-by-deal comparison of the price-earnings ratios of U.K. acquirer and U.S. acquisition does not suggest that the British firms were creating equity value by relocating earnings from New York to London; indeed, in 1988 and 1989 the target's exit multiple was generally higher than the acquirer's price-earning's multiple.[22] Overall, both the timing of the United States' receipt of a disproportionate share of the world's direct investment and the sources by country accord with Aliber's cost of capital hypothesis.

Banking Offers a Special Case[23]

It might seem that competition among banks, as highly leveraged firms, would be least affected by the cost of equity. But as a first approximation, internationally active banks issue deposits and debt instruments at similar rates and have similar leverage at the margin. So notwithstanding the very high leverage of banks, cost of equity differences (and international tax interactions), as expressed in different required spreads between marginal deposit and lending rates, are key to cost of capital differences in multinational banking.

In the 1980s the cost of equity offered a parsimonious account of developments in the U.S. commercial banking market. U.S. banks labored under a cost of equity disadvantage in relation to their foreign competitors and experienced a decline in their market share from about five-sixths to just over one-half.[24] Moreover, the nationality of the foreign banks that gained market share—Japanese and continental—accorded with measured cost of equity differences.

Multinational banking illustrates very nicely how uninformative affili-

CHART 7-6
Cost of Equity and Direct Foreign Investment Flows—United States and Japan

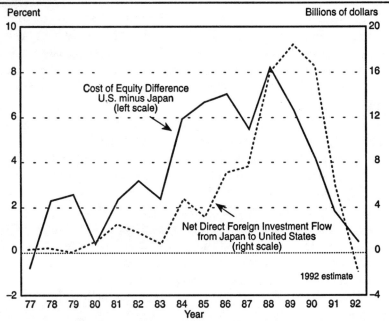

Sources: Department of Commerce and authors' estimates.

ate leverage can be. At the limit, a bank neither capitalizes nor lends anything to its foreign branch: it funds all of its assets with deposits. Yet depositors look to the parent for their funds ultimately. The equity ratio for the branch is thus better approximated by the equity ratio of the consolidated bank than by some ratio derived from the branch's balance sheet.[25]

Multinational banking also illustrates very nicely the insight that even direct investment motivated by cost of equity differences need not have much to do with international capital movements. Consider a foreign branch with a minimal obligation on its books to its overseas affiliates. On the basis of its parent's low cost of equity, the branch may book loans at spreads that leave local bankers scratching their heads. Does this not correspond to Kindleberger's (1969, p. 94) "general theory that direct investment is not so much a capital movement as an effort to take advantage of particular opportunities, open to the investing firm but not local business"?[26]

The Multinationals' Cost of Funds and Affiliate Leverage

The cost of funds for a multinational often compounds home-country debt and host-country debt. Certainly, multinationals can and do search for, and sometimes find, deviations from Fisher Open so that host-country debt costs are not relevant. Host-country debt provides a natural exchange-rate hedge and so empirically, host-country debt probably represents the modal choice.

The implications for competitive advantage in the cost of funds for multinationals operating in a single country are straightforward. Two multinationals headquartered in two different countries will differ in their cost of funds if their equity cost differs or if their leverage differs.

Conceptually, some reasons for international variation of leverage depend on the character of the host economy and others depend on the character of the home economy. If the Japanese economy grows more smoothly by virtue of the success of stabilization policy or by virtue of industrial organization, or the Japanese legal system imposes less catastrophic legal risk on firms operating there, then U.S. firms' Tokyo affiliates can leverage beyond home standards. In this case, however, Japanese firms would not get away with customary leverage in their foreign affiliates.

Home economy characteristics are probably more telling. If the German or Japanese economy is characterized by strong relations between banks and industry, firms from either country may carry higher leverage capacity to acquisitions and start-ups abroad. Foreign firms operating in Germany or Japan probably cannot partake of bank support, except perhaps through joint ventures. It is an open question whether the transplant of close bank-industry ties into the United States will be rejected by a hostile legal environment, particularly rules governing corporate distress.[27]

As a practical matter, varying leverage is not easily interpreted. Even excluding intercompany debt, observed leverage may amount to little more than tax avoidance and accounting convenience. Observed leverage can be more or less than true leverage. True leverage of an affiliate is the change in consolidated parent-firm debt and equity associated with an acquisition or an establishment—itself a concept hard to render operational.

Foreign firms operating in the United States do not obviously derive much advantage from leverage. Their debt-to-assets ratios have shown convergence with those of U.S. firms (Chart 7–7). These data, it might be noted, treat intercompany debt as equity, because taxes and accounting reasons are taken to determine the split between equity per se and intercompany debt.[28] Moreover, intercompany debt may be converted to equity or forgiven if the affiliate encounters difficulty.

CHART 7-7 Debt-to-Asset Ratios for American Corporations and Affiliates of Foreign Firms

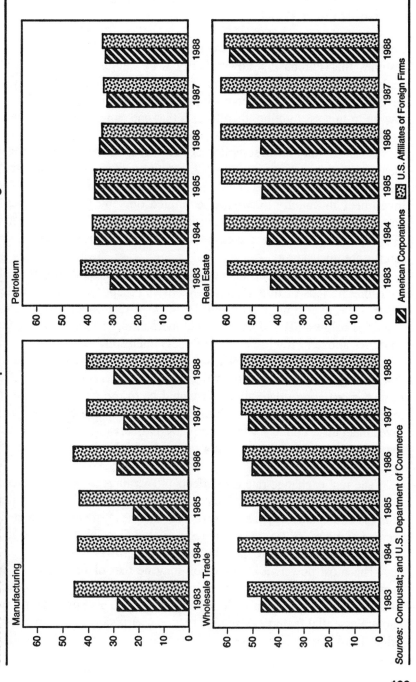

Sources: Compustat; and U.S. Department of Commerce

Cost of Capital and Exchange-Rate Risk: Relaxing Purchasing Power Parity

Cost of capital analysis in the case of multinational investment generally assumes that Purchasing Power Parity (PPP) holds. Lessard's (1985) analysis, for example, assumes no systematic exchange rate movements beyond those needed to account for differing inflation rates.[29] The follow-up to this assumption, therefore, is that one can discount real, leveraged foreign flows at the real cost of equity in the home country.

Consider what the assumption of PPP means for cross-border investment. If required returns in country A are higher than those in country B, then firms from country B should be more inclined to invest in A. Their investment in country A would be limited only by the difficulties of doing business in a foreign country. If one relaxes the assumption of PPP, however, it may be the case that measured differences in required returns are misleading.

It is an empirical fact that currencies deviate substantially from PPP over long periods of time (Chart 7–8). If we accept that currencies tend toward PPP over time, then it will be the case that direct investment in countries below PPP will be relatively more attractive and investment in countries above PPP will be relatively less interesting.

Given that significant PPP discrepancies exist, it may be incorrect to discount foreign, leveraged cash flows by the home country cost of equity. A more appropriate approach would be to use a discount rate that reflects some gradual trend back to PPP. For example, a firm making an investment in a country whose currency is overvalued on a PPP basis may want to use an equity discount rate that is higher than its own cost of equity.

The real exchange rate also affects the earnings to be discounted by a firm considering an international acquisition or establishment. If a currency is undervalued by the lights of PPP and the currency is expected to recover some of its real value, quite profitable firms in the traded goods sector may be expected to have weak earnings growth.[30]

The most powerful combination may be that of firms from a low cost of equity home country investing in the nontraded goods industries of a host country with an undervalued currency. This combination may capture essential features of the international diffusion of high real estate prices from Tokyo in the late 1980s.

CHART 7–8
Deviation from $–DM PPP (Current Real Exchange Rate vs. 10-Year Average)

CONCLUSIONS

The gap of two or more percentage points between the Japanese and German costs of funds on the one hand, and that of the United States, on the other, may not characterize the 1990s the way such a gap characterized the 1980s. Although cyclic differences render comparisons hazardous, Japanese equity costs and German debt costs appear to have risen while U.S. equity costs have fallen. Higher debt costs distinguish British firms from their U.S. counterparts in mid-1992.

Cost of equity differences are key to competition among multinational corporations, whether financial or nonfinancial firms. The timing and national composition of the surge in direct investment into the United States in the 1980s reflect U.S. firms' cost of equity disadvantage.

Deviations from purchasing power parity should be taken into account by firms acquiring or establishing foreign operations. In particular, a firm purchasing leveraged assets in a country with an undervalued exchange rate might lower its cost of equity hurdle; a firm purchasing leveraged assets in a country with an overvalued exchange rate might raise its cost of equity hurdle.

NOTES

1. Poterba (1991, pp. 20–32), Mattione (1992b) and Frankel (1991).
2. Kester and Luerman (1992, p. 134).
3. Those who are familiar with McCauley and Zimmer (1989, pp. 7–28), may skip to "Equity costs have converged substantially in the 1990s," below.
4. McCauley and Zimmer (1989, pp. 7–28).
5. French and Poterba (1991).
6. McCauley and Zimmer (1992, pp. 12–28).
7. Hodder (1991, p. 588) notes that the largest firms in Japan, as in many other countries, tend to have lower leverage than industry as a whole.
8. Historical accounting of domestic equities may have seriously overstated the foreign asset share of Japanese insurers in the 1980s.
9. McCown and Martinie (1988).
10. Koo (1992, pp. 17–18).
11. Koo (1992, pp. 22–23).
12. Tokyo Stock Exchange (1991, p. 60). Note that the floatation of NTT shares, which were until recently not open to foreign ownership, might have tended to reduce the foreign share.
13. The disparity between the portfolio flows and direct investment flows is understated if some of the Japanese direct foreign investment into the United States was highly leveraged with U.S. borrowing, as with real estate.
14. U.S. accountants Kenneth Leventhal & Company (1992), however, put Japanese investment in U.S. real estate alone at $50 billion in the same years, an amount that is hard to reconcile with the gross flow reported by either the Commerce Department or the Ministry of Finance.
15. Note that if the funds raised in these floatations were repatriated to the United States, they would have contributed to the net flow of direct foreign investment from Japan to the United States.
16. It appears that the Bank of Japan's flow of funds data understate the net equity issuance by the corporate sector because they count only shares actually issued and neglect the value of options imbedded in convertible bonds or bonds with equity warrants.
17. French and Poterba (1991) and McDonald (1989).
18. Aron (1981–87).
19. Some have argued, however, a more subtle point. It is sometimes said that access to international debt markets by successful firms from bank-dominated financial systems can weaken the nexus of understandings and support between firms and banks that supports higher leverage without attendant distress costs. This force for weaken-

ing bank-industry links is easy to overstate: Japanese banks often guaranteed the Eurobonds of Japanese industrial borrowers and bought ex warrant bonds. But this argument is really about the tension between relationship banking and securities issuance, rather than about foreign currency borrowing per se.

20. Nissan could presumably handle the losses it incurred when it financed its plant in Tennessee by borrowing one billion yen in the early 1980s when the yen was 250 to the dollar as compared to 125 now. See Misawa (1985, pp. 5–12).

21. Concludes Gray (1982, p. 191): "Aliber's theory adds little to the state of the art unless the argument is restricted to FDI between the bloc of rich nations, in which sophisticated capital markets exist, and poor nations. As an explanation of FDI among developed nations Aliber's theory is weakened by the growing integration of capital markets." Concedes McClain (1983, p. 299): "However, the timing of 'waves' of foreign direct investment by multinationals from developed countries, and the predominance of certain small hard-currency countries (e.g., the Netherlands, Switzerland) as source countries, have a less straightforward explanation; here Aliber's theory, even resting as it does on other capital-market imperfections, has some appeal."

22. McCauley and Eldridge (1990, pp. 319–52).

23. Zimmer and McCauley (1991, pp. 33–59).

24. McCauley and Seth, 1992.

25. By contrast, a subsidiary is separately capitalized. But no one is surprised when NatWest recapitalized Nat West USA after an accumulation of troubled real estate loans in New Jersey.

26. The Basle Accord on minimum capital assets ratios for internationally active banks has created pressure for capital flows in association with foreign-currency assets and liabilities. Matching foreign currency assets and liabilities is taken to be the norm, with "open" foreign exchange positions monitored closely. But since the international agreement on bank capital standards, an argument has been joined over whether a structural long position in foreign currency might not be justified (and not be treated as a bet attracting so-called position risk capital) in order to hedge the capital asset ratio against fluctuations in foreign exchange rates. See Fukao (1991, pp. 33–59). For example, a Japanese bank with a large U.S. dollar book might take a structural long position in the U.S. dollar. If the dollar appreciates against the yen, the gains on the open position might offset the rise in the yen value of the dollar assets. But note that the open dollar position would only increase the economic exposure inherent in the presumably positive net interest margin in dollars.

27. Note legal hazards to import of close bank-industry ties in the United States: equitable subordination risk of "busy" banks and lender's control. See McCauley (1990, pp. 232–35).

28. Caves (1982, pp. 160–94).

29. Lessard (1985, pp. 570–84).

30. By contrast, Aliber in the "Multinational Paradigm" emphasizes the role of an undervalued exchange rate in spurring capital expenditure on the assumption of more static expectations regarding the real exchange rates.

APPENDIX TO CHAPTER 7

COST OF CAPITAL AND EQUITY-LINKED BONDS

Equity issues by Japanese firms in the late 1980s were often embodied in convertible bonds and bonds with warrants. This combining of debt and equity in a single instrument gave rise to a great deal of confusion. In particular, a low coupon dollar five-year bond with a detachable five-year warrant attached could be swapped back into yen at an annual interest rate of 1, zero, or even minus 1 percent. It seemed like free money.

It was not: cash-flow does not accurately measure cost. Consider how the huge issue of $1.5 billion in five-year Eurodollar bond with warrants by Mitsubishi Corporation traded at its launch in London in late April 1989. The 4.4 percent coupon bond sold ex warrants at $81 per $100 par bond while the naked warrants sold at $22.* (The underwriters had only paid Mitsubishi $98 for the package, so they appear to have done well.)

Any notion of the cost of the warrant bond must not neglect the equity embodied in the warrant. At the very least, $22 of equity was raised. If Mitsubishi's share price were to rise by 1994, the firm would issue $100 dollars in equity; if the price were to fall, the firm would issue no shares but would keep the $22 premium for the warrant. Calculation of the precise share of equity and debt in the warrant bond is beyond the scope of this review. It is surely closer to the truth to take the warrant bond as half debt and half equity than as pure debt, however.†

The true cost of the $81 of debt is the interest plus the amortized cost of the $19 discount from par. This works out to be the then-prevailing cost of a five-year corporate note in dollars. Swapped into yen, the cost was something around or above the yield on a new five-year NTT bond.

The cost of the equity embodied in the warrant may be taken at the cost of equity as we have measured it. This may seem wrong: after all, new shares might not be issued. But the $22 that Mitsubishi Corporation would keep if the warrant expires unexercised in the event of poor share performance just compensated the firm for the possibility that shares might be

---

* "Celebratory Feast," *International Financing Review*, 773 (April 29, 1989), p. 38.
† One measure of the equity content is the hedge ratio for the warrant, the exercise price of which is set at 2.5 percent premium over the share price at issue. In the particular case of the Mitsubishi Corporation warrant, the hedge ratio would be unusually high: the exercise price on the warrant was to be reset on January 31, 1992, at the lower of a 2.5 percent premium over the average price of the last six trading in January 1992, or 75 percent of the original exercise price. Note that with cost of equity and cost of debt quite close, the cost of the warrant bond is not very sensitive to the choice of weights.

issued at a discount from market price in the event of good performance.

Taking the after-tax cost of debt as above to be 1.8 percent and taking the cost of equity to be, say, 3 percent in the late 1980s, the cost of the warrant bond may be taken as:

$$.5 \ (1.8 \ \text{percent}) + .5 \ (3 \ \text{percent}) = 2.4 \ \text{percent}.$$

Note that this cost of funds of the with warrant issue is little different from our computed cost of funds for Japanese industry. The cost of the bond with warrant was cheap by international standards because of the low cost of its equity component, not because of the low cost of the debt component.

Now it is often lamented that warrants are expiring unexercised and that the low cost warrant bonds will have to be refinanced with high cost debt.[*] Neither of these claims can be taken at face value.

If Japanese managers had known ahead of time that warrants would expire unexercised, they should have sold more, not less. As for the refinancing cost, it is true that reported profits will fall—7 percent for a sample of 240 firms.[†] This income drop, however, reflects bad accounting rather than any fundamental deterioration in corporate performance. In effect, the proceeds of (stochastic) equity issues were being added to net income. In other words, the net income of Japanese firms that sold warrant bonds and convertible bonds has been overstated, because interest expenses had been held down by virtue of the packaging of debt with equity. The adverse fundamental development for Japanese firms is the rise in the cost of equity owing to the stock market plunge in 1990, which currently discourages further issues of equity-linked debt.

In fact, despite the step-up in cash payments there is no extra economic cost of replacing the warrant bonds with new debt. If a firm borrows at long term prime rate, 6.2 percent, the after-tax real cost of the funding is:

$$6.2 \ (1 - t) - \text{GNP deflator} = 6.2 \ (.44) - 1.8 = 0.9,$$

which is, if anything, less than the cost of the warrant bond. If the firm did not lose the proceeds of the equity-linked bond in *zaitech*, its capital structure should be able to bear the debt.

---

[*] Mattione (1992b, p. 5).
[†] Mattione (1992b, p. 24).

REFERENCES

Adler, M. (1974). "The Cost of Capital and Valuation of Two-Country Firm." *Journal of Finance.* 29, no. 1, March, pp. 119–32.

Adler, M., and B. Dumas. (1975). "Optimal International Acquisitions." *Journal of Finance.* 30, no. 1, March, pp. 1–19.

Aliber, R. (1970). "A Theory of Direct Foreign Investment." *The International Corporation: A Symposium.* C. Kindleberger, ed. Cambridge: Massachusetts Institute of Technology Press.

Aliber, R. (1992). "The Theory of Foreign Direct Investment and the Multinational Paradigm." *The Multinational Paradigm.* Chapter 5.

Aron, P. (1987). "Japanese Price Earnings Multiples," Daiwa Securities America, 1981-87 reports.

Caves, R. (1982). *Multinational Enterprises and Economic Analysis.* Cambridge: Cambridge University Press.

"Celebratory Feast." *International Financing Review.* 773, April 29, 1989, p. 38.

Davis, E. (1991). "International Diversification of Institutional Investors." Bank of England *Discussion Papers,* no. 44. September, pp. 1–53.

Fikre, T. (1991). "Equity Carve-outs in Tokyo." Federal Reserve Bank of New York *Quarterly Review.* 15, Winter, pp. 60–64.

Frankel, J. (1991). "The Japanese Cost of Capital: A Survey." *Financial Management.* 20, no. 1, Spring, pp. 95–127.

French, K., and J. Poterba. (1991). "Were Japanese Stock Prices Too High?" *Journal of Financial Economics.* 29, pp. 337–63.

Fukao, M. (1991). "Exchange Rate Movements and Capital-Asset Ratio of Banks: On the Concept of Structural Positions." Bank of Japan *Monetary and Economic Studies.* 9, September, pp. 91–103.

Gray, H. (1982). "Macroeconomic Theories of Foreign Direct Investment: An Assessment." *New Theories of the Multinational Enterprise.* A. Rugman, ed. New York: St. Martin's Press.

Hodder, J. (1991). "The Cost of Capital for Industrial Firms in the U.S. and Japan." *Japanese Financial Market Research.* W. Ziemba, W. Bailey and Y. Hamao, eds. Amsterdam: North-Holland.

Hymer, S. (1976).*The International Operations of National Firms: A Study of Direct Foreign Investment.* Cambridge: Massachusetts Institute of Technology Press.

Kester, C., and T. Luehrman. (1992). "The Myth of Japan's Low-Cost Capital." *Harvard Business Review.* May-June, pp. 130–38.

Kindleberger, C. (1969). *American Business Abroad: Six Essays on Direct Investment.* New Haven, CT: Yale University Press.

Koo, R. (1992). "Japan and International Capital Flows," Nomura Research Institute, processed (April).

Lessard, D. (1985). "Evaluating International Projects: An Adjusted Present Value Approach." *International Financial Management*. D. Lessard, ed., 2nd ed. New York: John Wiley & Sons, 570–84.

Leventhal, K., & Co. (1992). *1991 Japanese Investment in United States Real Estate*.

Malkiel, B. (1992). "The Influence of Conditions in Financial Markets on the Time Horizons of Business Managers: An International Comparison," processed (January).

Mattione, R. (1992a). "A Capital Cost Disadvantage for Japan?" *Journal of the International Securities Markets*. 6, Summer, pp. 173–98.

Mattione, R. (1992b). "A Dangerous Dependence?: Equity Linked Bond Issues, Corporate Profitability and Economic Activity in Japan." Morgan Guaranty (Tokyo branch), prepared for 67th Annual WEA International Conference, San Francisco, California (July).

McCauley, R. (1990). "Policies Toward Corporate Leverage." *Studies on Corporate Leveraging*. E. Frydl, ed. New York: Federal Reserve Bank of New York, pp. 176–240.

McCauley, R., and D. Eldridge. (1990). "The British Invasion: Explaining the Strength of U.K. Acquisitions of U.S. Firms in the Late 1980s." *International Capital Flows, Exchange Rate Determination and Persistent Current-Account Imbalances*. Basle: Bank for International Settlements, pp. 319–52.

McCauley, R., and R. Seth. (1992). "Foreign Bank Credit to U.S. Corporations: The Implications of Offshore Loans." Federal Reserve Bank of New York *Quarterly Review*. 17, Spring, pp. 52–65

McCauley, R., and S. Zimmer. (1989). "Explaining International Differences in the Cost of Capital." Federal Reserve Bank of New York *Quarterly Review*. 14, Summer, pp. 7–28.

McCauley, R., and S. Zimmer. (1992). "International Comparisons of the Cost of Capital" [in Japanese]. *Security Analysts Journal*. 30, no. 3, March, pp. 12–28.

McClain, D. (1983). "Foreign Direct Investment in the United States: Old Currents, 'New Waves,' and the Theory of Direct Investment." *The Multinational in the 1980s*. C. Kindleberger and D. Audretsch, eds. Cambridge, MA: MIT Press, pp. 278–333.

McCown, W., and S. Matinie. (1988). "State Regulation of Life Insurance Companies." *Association of Life Insurance Counsel Proceedings*. p. 27.

McDonald, J. (1989). "The *Mochiai* Effect: Japanese Cross-Holdings." *Journal of Portfolio Management*. Fall, pp. 90–94.

Misawa, M. (1985). "Financing Japanese Investments in the United States: Case Studies of a Large and a Medium-Sized Firm." *Financial Management*. Winter, pp. 5–12.

Poterba, J. (1991). "Comparing the Cost of Capital in the United States and Japan: A Survey of Methods." Federal Reserve Bank of New York *Quarterly Review*.

15, Winter, pp. 20–32.

Shapiro, A. (1989). "The Cost of Capital for Foreign Investments." *Multinational Financial Management.* 3rd ed. Boston: Allyn and Bacon, pp. 602–24.

Stanley, M. (1990). "Cost of Capital in Capital Budgeting for Foreign Direct Investment." *Managerial Finance.* 16, pp. 13–16.

Tokyo Stock Exchange. (1991). *Fact Book, 1990.*

Zimmer, S. (1992). "Cost of Capital and Technology: Where Do We Stand?" statement before Subcommittee on Technology and Competitiveness, House Committee on Science, Space and Technology, *Investment Incentives and Capital Cost: Hearing.* 102nd Congress, 2nd session, March 3, 1992, pp. 69–81.

Zimmer, S., and R. McCauley. (1991). "Cost of Capital for Banks in International Competition." Federal Reserve Bank of New York *Quarterly Review.* 15, Winter, pp. 33–59.

COMMENT

EXCHANGE RATE VOLATILITY AND EQUITY RETURNS

James N. Bodurtha, Jr.

Brown and Otsuki are concerned with the equity component of international capital costs. They show, convincingly, two major results. First, common sources of global financial risk are related to observed differences in equity returns across countries. Second, the risks associated with U.S. yield spreads, Japanese yield spreads, U.S. inflation, and U.S. dividend account for significant differences in estimated equity capital costs.

The following diagram summarizes the components of the cost of capital estimates:

PANEL 1: Explanatory Factors

Expected Return	YSUS	YSJAP	IUS	DIV	SML	TUK	XJAP
SML	↓	↑		↑			
TUK						↑	↑
XJAP			↑		↑		

PANEL 2: Risk Premia

Cost of Capital	Constant	YSUS	YSJAP	IUS	DIV
SML	↓			↓	↑
TUK		↑	↓		↓
XJAP	↓		↓	↑	
MKT	↑			↑	

In the first panel, sources of expected return changes are depicted. Among the global and country portfolios, U.S. small firm (SML) , U.K. money market (TUK), and yen (XJAP) related results are summarized. Findings of significant predictability in these returns are indicated by appropriately pointed arrows.

For example, U.S. small returns are significantly related to the beginning of return-period spread levels (YSUS, negatively), Japanese yield spreads (USJAP, positively), and U.S. dividend yield (DIV, positively). Short-term U.K. money market returns are positively related to their own initial returns (TUK, positively), and to the previous-period yen value changes (XJAP, positively). Yen value changes are related to previous-period U.S. inflation rates (IUS, positively), and U.S. small firm portfolio returns (SML, positively). These results are indicative of the general predictability of the full or cross-section of returns examined.

A finding of predictive power for a particular factor is not, however, sufficient to conclude that this factor affects the cross-section equity returns and associated costs of capital. The sufficient condition is that the factor must significantly increase or decrease a relatively broad group of returns. Otherwise, the factor is idiosyncratically related to only a few returns. In this case, portfolio-based investors will be able to diversify sufficiently to make these idiosyncratic factors insignificant in the equity pricing-capital cost context.

In the second panel of the table, a summary of the evidence on significant "risk premium" estimates is presented. The positive estimates indicate factors which add to both the perceived and priced riskiness of particular return series.

The U.S. inflation factor (IUS) has the most significant return and capital cost impact. Higher U.S. inflation is associated with lower U.S.

small-firm (SML) equity cost, high broad U.S. market (MKT) equity cost, and higher yen (XJAP) expected returns. This finding points to U.S. small firms being a relatively good hedge against U.S. inflation, and especially so relative to the broader market. Based on this factor alone, the inflation-associated costs of small-firm equity capital are lower than those estimated for the broad market. Analogously, the yen does not provide an inflation hedge.

Higher expected dividend yield (DIV) adds to the estimated cost of small-firm equity capital, while lowering the cost of U.K. short-term paper. As dividend yields rise in two ways (dividends up, prices down), the economic interpretation of this factor is not particularly clear. Nevertheless, the positive predictive relationship between dividend yields and small-firm returns (shown in the first table panel) suggests that this factor is a measure of market sensitivity. To the extent that it is, the positive risk premium indicates an incremental risk in small stock returns and relativley less risk in short-term U.K. paper.

A steeper U.S. yield curve (YSUS) is significantly associated with higher expected short-term U.K. investment returns, while a flatter Japanese yield curve is associated with increases in these expected returns. All else equal, increasing yen forward premia are associated with higher costs of issuing U.K. short-term paper.

Given that the other risk factors are at their expected levels, the "constant" equity return-cost estimates indicate average risk premiums. For U.S. small-firms and the yen, the estimates are negative. For the broader U.S. market, the estimate is positive. Contrary to most previous studies of international returns, these estimates are not some unexplained cost. Instead, the appropriate combination of time-series sensitivity, b's, and cross-sectional contribution to prices of risks, a's, identifies this additional cost of capital component.

Generally, Brown and Otsuki's approach yields significant new insights into international costs of equity capital. Particularly, the joint modeling of time-series and cross-section aspects of the returns process is appealing. As noted in Professor Brown's remarks, and as highlighted in *The Economist* review of this work, some puzzles are cast in a completely new light in their context. For example, their estimates of the required Japanese cost of equity capital is actually higher than average Japanese equity returns over their sample period. Their work must certainly be added to the set of potential explanations for this cost-of-capital conundrum.

In the context of other symposium papers, the Brown–Otsuki approach and results provide a sharp and specific perspective on the equity segment of the firm's international macroeconomic environment and associated costs of capital. These other works help to place the Brown–Otsuki paper in context, and also suggest some further extensions.

At a broad level, the Levi, Adler–Prasad, and Knetter works all address the form of the returns relations treated. Relative to the linear structure of returns presented by Brown-Otsuki, the other works' firm level focus points to more complicated relationships between returns and the factors that generate significant risks. These works, like the work of Dornbusch and Amihud also indicate potential concern with additional risk factors, which are omitted in the Brown-Osuki study. In the context of corporate exchange rate risk, changes in real currency values, or deviations from purchasing power parity, and changes in capital market restrictions are likely to be important.

Past and ongoing research addresses the set of factors that differentiate the cross-section of international equity returns. This work has focused on exchange-rate risk and implications of various forms of capital market segmentation.

Though some works, such as Jorion (1991), do not find evidence of a significant exchange-rate risk component in equity returns, other work, such as Bekaert and Hodrick (1991), Bodurtha (1990), Korajczyk, and Viallet (1991) do identify significant exchange rate-related factors. Like the Brown–Otsuki analysis, all of these works are based on linear relationships between return and risk. The particular specification of this risk and its relation to other potential money market factors should be evaluated further. (See Ferson and Harvey (1992) for such factors.)

Recent work examines both general (Bansal, Hsieh, and Viswanathan [1992]), and specific (Mark [1988], Giovannini [1989], and Jorion [1991] and Chan, Karolyi, and Stulz [1991]) nonlinear return relations. Under appropriate specifications, the general approach holds out the possibility of fitting the relationships akin to those hypothesized by Levi, Adler–Prasad, and Knetter. The nonlinear pricing approach also suggests further directions for specification testing.

The question of capital market segmentation has also received direct attention. There have been two types of tests; those based on the factor pricing models (analogous to, though less dynamic than, the Brown–Otsuki one) and those based on direct calculation of price or rate differences. Evidence for the CAPM tests generally points to a degree of equity market segmentation, for example, Bodurtha, Cho, and Senbet (1989), Cho, Eun, and Senbet (1986), Errunza and Losq (1985), Heston, Rouwenhorst, and Wessels (1992), Jorion and Schwartz (1986), Stehle (1977), and Wheatley (1988). A possible extension of the Brown–Otsuki approach would be to test the robustness of their cost of equity estimates to potential regional differences. Roll's (1992) concern with international industrial linkages is also relevant.

Direct tests of cost of capital differences, of which the MacDonald (1989), Eun and Jannakiramanan (1991), and Stulz and Wasserfallen (1991) are examples, also point to significant differences historically. In this body of work, the Jorion and McCauley–Zimmer symposium works each add a significant point.

First, Jorion shows clearly that Japanese and German costs of debt have been far higher than U.S. debt costs. Simply put, had the Japanese and Germans funded their investment in dollar bonds (albeit gross speculation) their resultant home currency costs of debt would have been marketedly lower (due to dollar depreciation). For some reason, this fundamental observation has not, till now, been considered in the international cost of capital debate.

Second, McCauley and Zimmer conduct their cost of capital analysis over the 1977–1991 period. Their results point to narrowing cost of capital differences during the final ten years of the 1977–1991 observed period. Alternative dynamic structures have been posted and documented by Gultekin, Gultekin and Penati (1989) and Bonser–Neal, Brauer, Neal and Wheatley (1990). These results, taken together, point to a narrowing of international equity capital cost differences over time.

REFERENCES

Bansal, R., D. Hsieh, and S. Viswanathan. (1992). "A New Approach to International Arbitrage Pricing." working paper.

Bekaert, G., and R. Hodrick. (1991). "Characterizing Predictable Components in Excess Returns on Equity and Foreign Exchange Markets." Kellogg Graduate School of Management Department of Finance working paper no. 99.

Bodurtha, Jr., J. (1990), "International Factors and U.S. Equity Excess Returns," University of Michigan working paper.

Bodurtha, Jr., J., D. Cho and L. Senbet. (1989), "Economic Forces and the Stock Market: An International Perspective." *The Global Finance Journal.* 1, pp. 21–46.

Bonser-Neal, C., G. Brauer, R. Neal, S. Wheatley. (1990). "International Investment Restrictions and Closed-end Country Fund Prices." *Journal of Finance*. 45, pp. 523–47.

Chan, K., A. Karolyi, and R. Stulz. (1991). "Global Financial Markets and the Risk Premium on U.S. Equity." working paper.

Cho, D., C. Eun, and L. Senbet. (1986). "International Arbitrage Pricing Theory." *Journal of Finance*. 41, pp. 313–29.

Eun, C., and S. Jannakiramanan. (1991). "International Ownership Structure and Firm Value." working paper.

Errunza, V., and E. Losq. (1985). "International Asset Pricing under Mild Segmentation: Theory and Test." *Journal of Finance*. 40, pp. 1173–88.

Ferson, W., and C. Harvey. (1992). "The Risk and Predictability of International Equity Returns." working paper.

Giovannini, A. (1989). "Time Variation of Risk and Return in the Foreign Exchange and Stock Markets." *Journal of Finance*. 44, pp. 307–25.

Gultekin, B., M. Gultekin, and A. Penati. (1989). "Capital Controls and International Capital Market Segmentation: Evidence from the Japanese and American Stock Markets." *Journal of Finance*. 44, pp. 849–69.

Heston, S., K. Rouwenhorst, and R. Wessels. (1992). "The Structure of International Stock Returns." working paper.

Jorion, P. (1991). "The Pricing of Exchange Risk in the Stock Market." *Journal of Financial and Quantitative Analysis*. 26, pp. 363–76.

Jorion, P., and E. Schwartz. (1986). "Integration vs. Segmentation in the Canadian Stock Market." *Journal of Finance*. 41, pp. 603–13.

Korajczyk, R., and C. Viallet. "Equity Risk Premia and the Pricing of Foreign Exchange Risk." *Journal of International Economics*, forthcoming.

MacDonald, J. (1989). "The Mochiai Effect: Japanese Corporate Cross Holdings." *Journal of Portfolio Management*. Fall, pp. 90–94.

Mark, N. (1988). "Time-Varying Betas and Risk Premia in the Pricing of Forward Foreign Exchange Contracts." *Journal of Financial Economics*. 22, pp. 335–54.

Roll, R. (1992). "Industrial Structure and the Comparative Behavior of International Stock Market Indices." *Journal of Finance*. 47, pp. 3–42.

Solnik, B. (1983). "The Relation between Stock Prices and Inflationary Expectations: The International Evidence." *Journal of Finance*. 38, pp. 35–48.

Stehle, R. (1977). "An Empirical Test of the Alternative Hypothese of National and International Pricing of Risky Assets." *Journal of Finance*. 32, pp. 493–502.

Wheatley, S. (1988). "Some Tests of International Equity Market Integration." *Journal of Financial Economics*. 21, pp. 177–212.

COMMENT

EXCHANGE RATE VOLATILITY, HEDGING, AND THE COST OF CAPITAL

Ian H. Giddy

INTRODUCTION

This comment argues that exchange risk management as currently practiced does little to reduce a firm's cost of capital; on the contrary, more volatility may increase shareholders' required rate of return for firms that hedge selectively relative to those that do not. Instead, it may benefit the firm by reducing expected taxes and the deadweight costs of financial distress. If this is so, when and how should a firm hedge? Finally, when should a firm use foreign exchange options rather than symmetrical hedges such as futures and forward contracts?

Textbooks such as those by Shapiro (1989) and Eiteman, Stonehill and Moffett (1992) offer a lot of detail but very little convincing justification for hedging exchange risk in multinational firms. Such a rationale has been sought by Froot, Scharfstein and Stein (1992), Lessard (1990), Smith, Smithson, and Wilford (1990), Smith and Stulz (1985), and Stulz (1984). Drawing on these papers, we will show that if there is a rationale for hedging, it depends on the nature of taxes and of possible costs of bankruptcy faced by creditors and shareholders, rather than on direct risk-reduction desired by shareholders. Moreover, the kind of hedging that is justified may be quite different from that which is done by many firms. It may also be that out-of-the-money options may have a far more important place in corporate exchange risk management than is commonly accorded it by corporate treasurers.

DOES HEDGING REDUCE THE REQUIRED RETURN ON EQUITY?

There is reason to believe that under many conditions hedging may not reduce the cost of equity capital for a firm.

The foundation of this argument relies on the classic "Modigliani–Miller" framework: the value of a firm is determined by its assets, and no amount of reshuffling of liabilities or superimposition of derivative contracts will alter this value. If investment decisions are fixed, and there are no taxes or transaction costs (including bankruptcy costs), investors can replicate any foreign exchange hedging that the corporation can do. They do not need the company to perform risk management on their behalf. Even if one introduces transaction costs to hedging activities, institutional investors can plausibly reduce costs through diversification and by using forward contracts and the like to hedge only the residual exchange risk in a portfolio.

In short, the market does not reward the corporation (in the form of a lower required return on equity) for devoting resources to the elimination of diversifiable or hedgable risk.

Indeed, the corporate treasurer may actually damage the interests of the shareholder if he undertakes unwanted hedging. Although dividends are paid in a particular currency, shareholders do not necessarily want the firm's management to hedge with respect to that currency. Equity, after all, does not bear a currency sign. Its value reflects the complex mix of economic and firm variables, many of which the investor is deliberately seeking when he invests in the company's stock. If I buy shares in Ciba-Geigy, the Swiss chemicals firm, it is not because I want a Swiss franc-denominated security. Whether or not I am a Swiss investor, I am seeking the mix of business and currency cash flows that Ciba represents, and very little of this is of Swiss franc origin. So it would be wrong for Ciba to hedge all its dollar and yen exposure into Swiss francs, even if it could identify what the true exposure was. The investor would just have to unhedge what the corporate treasurer has misguidedly hedged.

A related reason to beware of hedging nominal cash flows is that different investors may want a different currency mix in their portfolios, perhaps because their consumption baskets are denominated in different currencies or capital market barriers constrain their portfolio choices in different ways. The results reported by McCauley and Zimmer in this volume offer support for this notion: there appear to be systematic differences in the cost of equity between countries, differences that may in part be explained by real exchange risk. If the corporate treasurer cannot guess what the investor's "base currency" is, he cannot know which cash flows to hedge and which to leave alone.

Finally, investors may penalize firms that hedge if the hedging is discretionary rather than consistent. Anecdotal evidence supports the view that the more sophisticated the financial management of a company, the greater is the role played by their own views on direction and volatility in selecting the kind and timing of exchange risk management. Whether or not this adds volatility to the firm's reported earnings, it creates an uncertainty for investors who may be perfectly capable of doing their own, consistent, hedging.

Now consider the effect of exchange rate volatility in the light of the last three comments. Greater volatility suggests more active hedging and more uncertainty about selective hedging, both of which we have argued, may be detrimental to investors' interests. *Hence the penalty imposed by investors on firms that engage in undesired selective hedging will tend to be greater, the more volatile are nominal exchange rates.*

DOES HEDGING REDUCE THE REQUIRED RETURN ON DEBT?

Despite the arguments offered above, there is ample evidence that the majority of large, international firms do hedge exchange risk, and that they do so selectively rather than fully. The results reported by Brown and Otsuki, for example, are consistent with the hypothesis that investors expect a higher return in exchange for taking currency risk.

An answer may be found by relaxing the MM assumptions of no transactions costs or taxes. Consider first the effect of costs of financial distress on the return required by the firm's creditors.

Exchange rate volatility may make earnings volatile and thus increase the probability of financial distress. If hedging reduces the nominal volatility of the firm's earnings, it will in turn reduce the expected value of the costs of financial distress (including bankruptcy), as is shown in Figure 1. Some

FIGURE 1

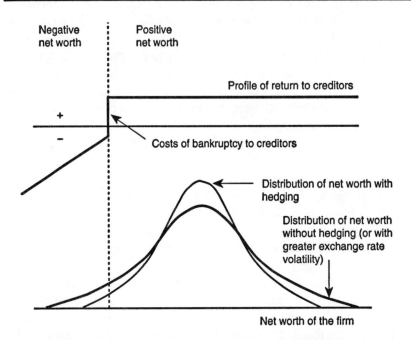

Negative net worth | Positive net worth

Profile of return to creditors

+

−

Costs of bankruptcy to creditors

Distribution of net worth with hedging

Distribution of net worth without hedging (or with greater exchange rate volatility)

Net worth of the firm

Note: Creditors incur bankruptcy costs if exchange rate variations drive the firm's net worth below zero, so they will charge a lower risk premium if hedging reduces the probability of this happening.

of these costs are borne by creditors ("Costs of bankruptcy to creditors" in Figure 1), in which case a reduction in expected distress costs will reduce lenders' required rate of return. In addition, for a given level of debt, lower earnings volatility will entail a lower probability of a negative net worth.

In Figure 1, the probability distribution of the value of the firm is mapped against the return to creditors. In this context, creditors are regarded as writers of a put option on the value of the firm, an option that is in the money for negative values of the firm's net worth (to the left of the dotted line). At this point creditors face a one-shot bankruptcy cost, reducing their returns. As the firm's net worth turns out to be even more negative, creditors' losses increase. Lower inherent volatility of exchange rates or effective hedging lowers the probability of bankruptcy and so a lower option premium (margin for risk) could be charged.

DOES HEDGING INCREASE AFTER-TAX EARNINGS?

Exchange rate volatility may matter because of the tax shield benefit of leverage in double-taxation countries. Consider the following simple framework:

Value of Firm to Shareholders
= Value of Assets – Value of Debt
+ Present Value of Tax Shield
– Present Value of Expected Costs of Financial Distress.

The last two are a function of leverage, among other things. The double taxation of corporate income and the worldwide practice of tax deductibility of interest payments provide an incentive for debt finance. This incentive, however, is weakened by the direct and indirect costs of financial distress and bankruptcy, which are greater the greater the volatility of earnings. More leverage means more volatile earnings, so the tax-shield gains from leverage are, at some point, offset by the deadweight costs of financial distress.

The greater the probability of distress, the lower the leverage level that is optimal for the firm and the lower the tax shield. *Since currency risk hedging reduces the probability of financial distress, it allows the firm to have greater leverage and therefore a greater tax shield.* Thus the greater the degree of bankruptcy-cost-reducing hedging, the greater the value of the firm and the lower the cost of capital.

A RATIONALE FOR HEDGING WITH OPTIONS

The argument so far has been that shareholders do not necessarily value hedging for its value in reducing risk for its own sake, but only insofar as it can (a) reduce the risk premium charged by lenders, or (b) reduce the expected value of distress costs, or (c) reduce taxes by allowing greater tax-shielding leverage. One way to achieve these is to shrink the distribution, as shown in Figure 1. A better way may be to truncate the distribution by purchasing out-of-the-money options, as shown in Figure 2.

Assume for simplicity's sake that the only source of variability of a firm's net worth is the variability of the nominal exchange rate. Then we can map the distribution of the exchange rate onto the distribution of the firms's

FIGURE 2

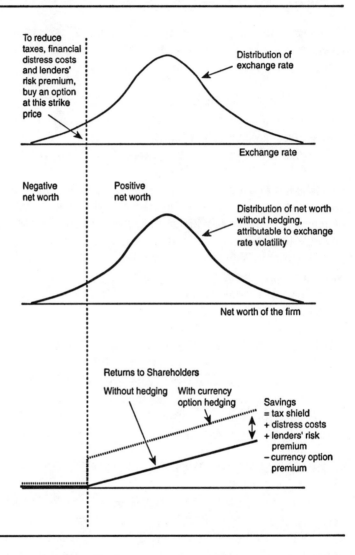

net worth. At some (presumably extreme) value of the exchange rate the firm is bankrupt, and incurs financial distress costs of C_{FD}. In addition, the possibility of bankruptcy raises creditors' charges by P_{FD} and taxes by T_{FD}. If the firm can buy a risk-free, out-of-the-money option for a fair price less than $C_{FD}+P_{FD}+T_{FD}$, then the value of the firm to shareholders should increase, as shown in the bottom third of Figure 2.

CONCLUSIONS

This comment suggests that companies that hedge exchange rates selectively may be doing their shareholders a disservice. Such hedging may at best substitute for what the shareholders can do as well themselves, and at worst create duplicate costs and uncertainties for which shareholders and lenders alike would penalize the firm in the form of a higher cost of capital.

Yet hedging can under some circumstances reduce the cost of debt; that is, if it reduces the expected costs of bankruptcy to creditors or of financial distress to shareholders, or if it allows greater leverage and hence increases the tax shield afforded by debt finance. It can be shown that where fluctuations in the firm's value can be directly attributed to exchange rate fluctuations, the firm may be best off buying out-of-the-money currency options—that is, buying insurance only against the extreme exchange rate that would put the firm into bankruptcy.

One implication of these arguments is that companies who do not hedge exchange risk should not necessarily have a higher before-tax cost of equity capital. Another is that the degree of hedging should be greater, the greater the value of the tax shield to the company. Conversely, companies should not hedge if they cannot use the tax shelter because they have enough or are not profitable: for example, General Motors (no profits), General Electric Capital (plenty of shelters), or the tax rate is low, or if the expected deadweight losses from bankruptcy are low.

REFERENCES

Eiteman, D., A. Stonehill, and M. Moffett. (1992). *Multinational Business Finance.* 6th ed. New York: Addison-Wesley.

Froot, K., D. Scharfstein, and J. Stein. (1992). "Risk Management: Coordinating Corporate Investment and Financing Policies." NBER Working Paper no. 4084.

Lessard, D. (1990). "Global Competition and Corporate Finance in the 1990s." *Continental Bank Journal of Applied Corporate Finance.* pp. 19–28.

Shapiro, A. (1989). *Multinational Financial Management.* 3rd ed. New York: Allyn and Bacon.

Smith, C., C. Smithson, and D. Wilford. (1990). "Five Reasons why Companies Should Manage Risk." *The Handbook of Currency and Interest Rate Risk Management.* R. Schwartz and C. Smith, eds. New York Institute of Finance. pp. 19.3–19.14.

Smith, C., and R. Stulz. (1985). "The determinants of Firms' Hedging Policies." *Journal of Financial and Quantitative Analysis.* 20, December, pp. 391–405.

Stulz, R. (1984). "Optimal Hedging Policies." *Journal of Financial and Quantitative Analysis.* 19, June, pp. 127–40.

PART THREE

EXCHANGE RATES AND CORPORATE STRATEGIC MANAGEMENT

CHAPTER 8

EXCHANGE RATE PLANNING FOR THE INTERNATIONAL TRADING FIRM

Michael Adler

INTRODUCTION AND OUTLINE

This chapter deals with interactions between the strategic and the exchange rate hedging decisions of an international trading firm. We count as strategic the firm's pricing policies or, obversely, its output decisions. The choice among production locations is also strategic but is not considered here. Strategic decisions generally depend on the level of the exchange rate. When wages and prices in different countries are sticky, movements in the *level* of the exchange rate can affect competitiveness and hence strategic decisions. Corporate hedging decisions, in contrast, are designed to reduce the variance of the firm's cash flows, *conditional on the level of* the exchange rate. The effectiveness of hedging for protecting the firm against shifts in the conditional *cash flow distribution itself* is limited. A firm must therefore take its possible future strategic decisions into account when designing its hedging policy.

Much of the earlier international trade and finance literature implies that firms which have access to the forward currency market can completely

The author thanks Bernard Dumas, Larry Glosten, and Bruce Greenwald for pertinent suggestions; and especially, Bhaskar Prasad for insightful assistance.

hedge the effects of currency variations: see Ethier (1973) and Baron (1976). The volume of international trade is then unaffected by exchange rate variability. This view is questionable in the face of recent contributions which show that exchange rate changes, serving as a metaphor for deviations from the law of one price of the marginal costs of imperfectly competitive firms, cause variations in firms' optimal sales decisions: for example, see Dornbusch (1987) and Froot and Klemperer (1989). When such firms do not hedge, exchange rate changes can, in principle, affect both the volume of trade and sales prices in various locations. The question then is whether hedging can completely insulate firms from these effects. Our answer is that, in general, it cannot.

The idea that strategic responses to exchange rate movements and hedging decisions can serve different purposes is beginning to take hold in the corporate finance literature. Mello, Parsons, and Triantis (1992) consider a perfectly competitive firm's option to shift production abroad. They argue that this option is valuable and has the effect of shifting the firm's production possibility frontier outwards. In contrast, financial hedging, at most, increases the firm's value along a production possibility frontier, by reducing expected bankruptcy costs. These considerations make it necessary to simulate the production-transfer and hedging decisions simultaneously. Brealey and Kaplanis (1991) and Dumas (1992) also allow for the exogenous possibility of moving production between locations and make the point that this prospectively causes firms' exposures to vary over time. Dumas further emphasizes that options and forward contracts are imperfect instruments for hedging cash flows that are correlated with levels, rather than with changes, of the exchange rate. An implication of these papers is that currency hedging does not remove or replace the need for strategic decisions that anticipate, or respond to, changes in the level of the exchange rate.

We explore these matters further in what follows. The objective is to obtain a clearer idea of precisely how the hedging decision should accommodate strategic adjustments to the firm's operating plans. The vehicle for the inquiry is a multi-period modification of the Cournot model of oligopolistic competition formulated in Dornbusch (1987). We introduce additional dates to allow for hedging in advance. Home and foreign firms compete in the foreign market over sales of a homogeneous product. Purchases, processing, and shipping take place at each of times 0 and 1. Sales revenues are realized with a one-period lag, at times 1 and 2. Hedging first occurs at time 0, at which point the quantities processed and exported at time 1, together with the time-1 and time-2 exchange rates, are all random. The initial hedge can be revised at time 1. We study the variance-minimizing hedges of the exposures at times 1 and 2.

The principal implications of this analysis are twofold. First, the home firm cannot achieve a perfect time-0 hedge of its foreign currency cash flows at either future date. This is because the quantity of the exposures, that is, the amounts of foreign currency on hand at each date, are random. This exposure uncertainty has two components. One arises from uncertainty as to the physical volume of future shipments and the other from uncertainty as to the foreign market price. Consequently, the exposures are nonlinear in the future spot rate. Perfect hedges are thus precluded, as forward hedges have linear payoffs. This is one sense in which perfect hedges are impossible when cash flows are functions not only of variations but also of levels of the exchange rate.

Second, foreign firms competing in the foreign market are exposed to the exchange rate even though all their transactions are conducted in local currency. This result provides substance to the observation of a Weyerhauser executive that he had found the firm's domestic U.S.$ cash flows to be exposed to the Swedish Krona, Weyerhauser's chief competitors' home currency. The reason in our model is that foreign firms also face exchange-rate related uncertainty because their U.S. competitors' uncertain future decisions affect sales prices and time-1 outputs. In principle, local firms too should hedge their domestic operations with foreign currency contracts. However, as with U.S.-based firms, their hedges also cannot be perfect.

These results are sufficient for a first cut at embedding a firm's strategic behavior into its hedging decision analysis in the third section. What is required is analogous to contingency planning. Imagine the exchange rate to be the only state variable and forecast its distribution. Analyze the industry equilibrium conditional on the level of the exchange rate in each state and derive the firm's cash flow in that state. Finally, regress the state-contingent cash-flow outcomes on the exchange rate across states to determine the minimum-variance hedge. Roughly speaking, strategic decisions in this perspective serve to change the size of the firm's financially hedgeable exposure. As strategic exposures can be expected to vary from period to period, currency hedges have to be revised over time.

While firms' hedging decisions depend on their strategic reactions, the reverse is not the case: to this point, firms' real decisions are independent of their financial hedging decisions. This does not arise from the simplicity of our model. Such is the case even in the more elegant formulations of Dixit and Stiglitz (1977) and Froot and Klemperer (1989). The reason is that the hedging decision variable disappears from the first order conditions, regardless of whether profits are maximized with respect to quantities or prices.

The competitive reaction model must therefore be modified if it is to address more complicated issues: whether firms can design currency hedges that affect their trading decisions and their market values. Dumas (1978) concludes that firms' real decisions can remain independent of exchange rate volatility even when costly bankruptcy is possible. An implication of Adler and Dumas (1983), Smith and Stulz (1985), and Froot, Scharfstein, and Stein (1992) is that they do not. We leave these issues to be dealt with elsewhere.

THE MODEL

We can display the dependence of exposure on strategic decisions most easily with a relatively standard multiperiod Cournot oligopoly model. There are n identical home (U.S.) firms and n^* foreign firms competing for sales of a homogeneous product in the foreign market, with sales per firm of q and q^* respectively. Both groups of firms are assumed to be alive at three dates: 0, 1, and 2. A firm in a given group decides its quantity using a constant marginal cost function, wq_t and $w^* q_t^*$, $t = 0$, 1, where w is paid in dollars and w^* in foreign currency. Each firm's marginal costs in its own currency are assumed to be sticky in the short run. Quantity decisions are derived from maximizing profits at each date, assuming that all the other firms are doing the same. The entire quantity is sold and shipped to customers immediately. Sales are made on credit: payment for time-0 sales is received at time 1 and for time-1 sales at time 2.

Aggregate sales at times 0 and 1 take place subject to a linear demand curve which remains constant over time:

$$nq_t + n^* q_t^* = a - bp_t^*, \quad t = 0, 1$$

so that the product's market price at each date is:

$$p_t^* = (a - nq_t - n^* q_t^*) / b \qquad (8.1)$$

No generality is to be obtained for our purpose by letting the foreign demand function either shift or be random. Note that if $p*$ is dimensioned in foreign currency, b has dimension (1/FC).

Both firms face exchange rate uncertainty at each production date. Interest rate parity, covered and uncovered, holds. The financial markets are assumed to price forward contracts, written at time t for maturity $t + k$, such that they are worth zero at time t. Letting F and S denote the forward and spot rates, $V_t\,({}_tF_{t+k}) = V_t\,(S_{t+k})$, where V_t is the market's valuation functional at time t. Consequently, each firm uses the current forward exchange rate, in US\$/FC, as the planning equivalent of the random future spot rate for making real decisions. Hedging is possible at each decision date. Forward contracts are available for all relevant maturities.

Since foreign firms all make decisions in their own currency, let us focus first on a representative U.S. firm. Its unhedged cash flows at each future date are:

time 2:
$$C_2 = p_1^* q_1 S_2$$

time 1:
$$C_1 = p_0^* q_0 S_1 - w q_1$$

Viewed from time 0, all of S_2, p_1^* and q_1 are random.

At each of times 0 and 1, all firms maximize "hedged" profits. This requires a little explanation. As there is no intertemporal link between q_1 and q_0, profit maximization at time 1 is independent of the optimal q established at time 0. Each firm therefore maximizes profits at time 0 using the initial, one-period forward rate, ${}_0F_1$, as its planning equivalent. Similarly, it maximizes profits at time 1 using ${}_1F_2$, independently of any time-0 hedge. At time 0 however, the firm can anticipate two cash flows. It immediately hedges both, with two contracts, in an amount ${}_0X_1$ for C_1 and ${}_0X_2$ for C_2. Subsequently at time 1, it can revise its hedge of C_2 by the amount ${}_1X_2$.

At time 0, the profit functions to be maximized by each firm are given by

$$\pi_0 = (p_0^* {}_0F_1 - w)q_0, \text{ and}$$

$$\pi_0^* = (p_0^* - w^*)q_0^*$$

Following Dornbusch (1987), these can be rewritten as

$$p_0 = (p_0^* \, _0F_1 - w)[a - bp_0^* - (n-1)q - n^*q^*]$$

$$p_0^* = (p_0^* - w^*) \, [a - bp_0^* - nq - (n^* + 1)q^*]$$

With $N = n + n^* + 1$, maximization produces reaction functions that, after some algebra, provide the solution:

$$q_0 = \frac{a}{N} + \frac{n^*(bw^*)}{N} - (\frac{n^* + 1}{N}) (\frac{bw}{_0F_1}) \tag{8.2a}$$

$$q_0 = \frac{a}{N} + \frac{n}{N} (\frac{bw}{_0F_1}) - (\frac{n+1}{N}) (bw^*) \tag{8.2b}$$

$$p_0^* = \frac{a}{bN} + \frac{n}{N} (\frac{w}{_0F_1}) - \frac{n^*}{N} w^* \tag{8.2c}$$

Equations (8.2a) through (8.2c) confirm the intuition that an FC appreciation tends to raise q, and reduce both q^* and p^*. Subsequent profit maximization at time 1 differs from the initial program only in that it takes $_1F_2$, the forward rate at time 1 with maturity at time 2, as the planning-equivalent exchange rate. It should therefore be apparent by inspection of (8.2a) through (8.2c), that q_1, q_1^*, p_1^* and $_1F_2$ are all random when viewed from time 0.

Let us now consider the hedging problem of each firm in turn, starting with a U.S. firm. From (8.1), the U.S. firm's time-1 hedged cash flow is given by:

$$C_1 = p_0^* \, q_0 S_1 - wq_1 + \, _0X_1 (\, _0F_1 - S_1) \tag{8.3}$$

Similarly, its time-2 hedged cash flow is:

$$C_2 = p_1^* \, q_1 S_2 + \, _0X_2(\, _0F_2 - S_2) + \, _1X_2(\, _1F_2 - S_2) \tag{8.4}$$

We are interested in the precision of the hedge at each point in time. After substituting into (8.3) the optimal time-1 solution for q_1, equation (8.3) can be decomposed into constant and random terms:

$$C_1 = [(\, _0X_1)(\, _0F_1) - (w/N)(a + n^*bw^*)] + (p_0^* \, q_0 - \, _0X_1)S_1 + (\frac{n^* + 1}{N}) [(bw^2)\frac{1}{_1F_2}]$$

The optimal time-0 hedge that minimizes the variance of C_1 is:

$$_0X_1 = p_0^* q_0 + (\frac{n^* + 1}{N})[\frac{\text{cov}_0(\frac{bw^2}{_1F_2}, S_1)}{\text{var}_0(S_1)}] \qquad (8.5)$$

where the time subscripts on the covariance and variance in (8.5) indicate that they are conditioned on time-0 information. Equation (8.5) tells us that at time 0 the firm can achieve a perfect hedge only of the part of the time-1 cash flow that is determined by time-0 decisions. The component of C_1 that depends on time-1 decisions cannot be hedged perfectly, but only up to the regression coefficient of $bw^2/_1F_2$ on S_1. Note that $bw^2/_1F_2$ is an uncertain amount of dollars: (1/FC) ($\$^2$) (FC/$\$$). The negative covariance in (8.5) can be rewritten as: $\text{cov}[b(w/_1F_2)^2 {}_1F_2, S_1] = \text{cov}[g(_1F_2) {}_1F_2, S_1]$ where g is a nonlinear foreign currency function. Even if $_1F_2$ were perfectly correlated with S_1, as would be the case with constant interest rates, a perfect forward hedge would require continuous revisions. In discrete time a perfect hedge with a linear instrument is impossible.

We now turn to designing $_0X_2$, the time-0 hedge of the time-2 cash flow. As dates after time 2 are ignored, the firm at time 1 can choose $_1X_2$ once it knows $p_1^* q_1$ so as to hedge C_2 perfectly. $_1X_2$ itself, however, is random when viewed from time 0. The resulting dynamic programming problem can be simplified in the following way to bring out the intuitions. First we rewrite $_1X_2$ as the revision in $_0X_2$ conditional on time-1 information:

$$_1X_2 = (p_1^* q_1 - {}_0X_2 \mid I_1)$$

This allows us to rewrite equation (8.4) as:

$$(C_2 \mid I_0) = (p_1^* q_1 S_1 \mid I_0) + [_0X_2(_0F_2 - S_2) \mid I_0] + [(p_1^* q_1 - {}_0X_2)(_1F_2 - S_2) \mid I_1 \mid I_0] \qquad (8.6)$$

The law of iterative expectations then permits us to simplify (8.6):

$$C_2 = (p_1^* q_1) {}_1F_2 + {}_0X_2(_0F_2 - {}_1F_2) \qquad (8.7)$$

where all terms are conditional on time-0 information. Minimizing the variance of C_2 w.r.t. $_0X_2$ and setting the derivative equal to zero then provides:

$$_0X_2 = \frac{\text{cov}_0\{[(\frac{n^*+1}{N})^2 + (\frac{n^*+1}{N})][b(\frac{w}{_1F_2})^2 \,_1F_2], \,_1F_2\}}{\text{var}_0(_1F_2)} \tag{8.8}$$

Two things about (8.8) are notable. Once again, the optimal hedge involves the covariance between a nonlinear function and the forward exchange rate so that a perfect hedge cannot be achieved from the start. Second, the time-0 hedge for time 2 is determined using only time-1 data. Time-2 data do not enter the estimate. In general when hedge revisions are taken into account, the terminal-date spot exchange rate is never needed, as one or more earlier forward rates always replace it. The number of forward rates that enter the picture depends on the specifics of the distributed lag structure of the particular firm's cash flows. In our model only one lag is present.

Let us now briefly consider the situation of a representative foreign firm. Even though it prices its output and pays its costs in its home (i.e., foreign) currency, it is nonetheless strategically exposed to the exchange rate used by its U.S. competitors to compute their decisions. In principle, therefore, it should hedge. The foreign firm's time-1 hedged cash flow is as follows:

$$C_1^* = p_0^* q_0^* - w^* q_1^* + _0X_1^* (S_1 - _0F_1)/_0F_1 S_1$$

where asterisks denote foreign currency quantities and the firm is hedging back into its own currency. The foreign firm uses $1/F$ as the planning equivalent of $1/S$ in the future. After substituting its optimal time-1 output quantity conditional on $1/_1F_2$ and minimizing the variance of C_1^* its optimal hedge is:

$$_0X_1^* = \frac{\text{cov}_0\{[(\frac{n}{N})(\frac{bww^*}{_1F_2})], \frac{1}{S_1}\}}{\text{var}_0(1/S_1)} \tag{8.10}$$

In contrast with (8.5), equation (8.10) contains no constant term. There is no need for the foreign firm to hedge $p_0^* q_0^*$, its time-1 home-currency revenues from its time-0 decisions. Notably, however, (8.10) brings out the foreign firm's exposure to the U.S. firm's marginal costs, $w/_1F_2$, measured in foreign currency. Further analysis reveals that, as in the previous case, the hedge in (8.10) is not perfect. Analyzing the time-2 cash flow adds no further insights.

In summary, the principal implication of this section is that all time-0 hedges are imperfect. Our U.S. firm has the opportunity for a perfect hedge only one period prior to the terminal date. In futures markets jargon, future costs and future decisions that lead to random revenues introduce quantity uncertainty that cannot be hedged away solely with forward currency contracts. Moral hazard issues preclude forward contracts written on individual firms' outputs. It is therefore safe to conjecture that the aforementioned quantity uncertainty cannot be hedged by financial means at all.

While the firm's real decisions depend on the future exchange rate level, the volatility of the exchange rate, as such, does not directly affect them. This is a consequence of the use of the contemporaneous forward rate as the planning-equivalent of the random spot rate. We have here an echo of proposition 2 in Baron (1976). Intuitively, the firm assigns its strategic decisions to exchange rate levels as embodied in the conditionally-known forward rate and manages volatility separately via currency hedging decisions. As strategic plans are independent of volatility in this model, the imperfectness of the hedges does not affect them.

Consequently, the currency hedging decision itself is not a component of a firm's competitive arsenal. We conjecture that this characterization is true for many if not most firms. There is however, the possibility that currency hedging policy may matter competitively in some situations. We do not investigate this issue here. Let us therefore turn to the practical matter of how firms can take strategic plans into account when designing their currency hedges.

HEDGING AROUND STRATEGIC DECISIONS

Integrating strategic decisions into the analysis of financial hedging is reasonably straightforward in the absence of feedback effects from financial hedging to real decisions. Chew (1988) reports the view of the treasurer of Jaguar that dollar hedging buys Jaguar the time to make adjustments to sales plans and production structures to preserve profitability. This report is rare, however. Informal surveys seem to suggest that most firms plan their real strategies independently of their treasurers' currency hedging activities. Whether or not they should is matter for future research. What they actually do is set their real strategies first and let their treasurers hedge around them. This behavior is consistent with the model of the last section.

We consider the practical implementation problem in what follows. We use the cash-flow structure of the trading firm in the second section to develop a binary probability/decision tree. The treasurer can use this to calculate the hedge, conditional on the strategy in each state of nature. This formulation corresponds closely to the approach underlying the numerical examples in Adler and Dumas (1980, 1982). We emphasize, however, that the outlined procedure is no more than a blueprint. The structure of the tree varies with the specifics of the particular firm.

Exhibit 8–1 is a schema of the trading firm's hedging problem. A state of nature is a pair of the levels (or ranges) of the future spot and coincident one-period forward exchange rates. The notation is straightforward. For example, Y_{ts} is the value of Y at time t in state s, while $_tZ_{sk}$ is the value of Z at time t in state s for maturity $t + k$. A strategic plan is a set of contingent output and hedging decisions or scenarios, each of which is conditional on a state of nature. The distribution of states at each point in time is known and is assumed to be binary for simplicity.

Each scenario is exploded into a forecast of (state-contingent) unhedged cash flows, projected in U.S. dollars. With these data in hand, the time-0 hedges can be calculated. Consider $_0X_1$ first: its foreign currency face

EXHIBIT 8–1
Binary Hedging Decision Tree for the U.S. Trading Firm

Time-0		Time-1	Time-2
Decisions	*States*	*Decisions/Outcomes*	*Outcomes*

$$_0X_1$$
$$_0X_2$$

$$\left\{ \begin{array}{l} S_{11} \\ _1F_{12} \end{array} \right\}$$

$$\left\{ \begin{array}{l} q_{11} \text{ given } _1F_{12} \\ _1X_{12} \text{ given } _1F_{12} \\ C_{11} = \$CF \text{ given } S_{11} \end{array} \right\}$$

$$P_{11}{}^*q_{11}S_{21} = C_{21}$$
$$P_{11}{}^*q_{11}S_{22} = C_{22}$$

$$\left\{ \begin{array}{l} S_{12} \\ _1F_{22} \end{array} \right\}$$

$$\left\{ \begin{array}{l} q_{12} \text{ given } _1F_{22} \\ _1X_{22} \text{ given } _1F_{22} \\ C_{12} = \$CF \text{ given } S_{12} \end{array} \right\}$$

$$P_{12}{}^*q_{12}S_{23} = C_{23}$$
$$P_{12}{}^*q_{12}S_{24} = C_{24}$$

value [cf. equation (8.5)] is simply:

$$_0X_1 = \frac{C_{11} - C_{12}}{S_{11} - S_{12}} \tag{8.11}$$

In the binary case, the form of the variance-minimizing regression hedge is identical to that of the delta hedge in the options literature.

Consider $_0X_2$ next. Exhibit 8–1 displays four possible cash-flow outcomes at time 2. One could conceivably estimate the hedge by regressing the four outcomes on the four associated levels of the time-2 spot rate. In the present case, the procedure can be simplified. The firm can anticipate revising its time-0 hedge at time 1 as in (8.8). Having arrived at time 1, only two planning equivalent time-2 cash flows are possible:

$$\hat{C}_{21} = (p_{11}^* q_{11}^*)\,_1F_{12}\,;\; \hat{C}_{22} = (p_{12}^* q_{12})_1 F_{22}$$

Consequently, with the possibility of revision taken into account, (8.8) in the binary case becomes:

$$_0X_2 = \frac{\hat{C}_{21} - \hat{C}_{22}}{_1F_{12} - _1F_{22}} \tag{8.12}$$

Exhibit 8–1, together with equations (8.11) and (8.12), suggests how currency hedges that take strategic decisions into account can be planned in practice. Careful contingency planning is the key to the procedure. The firm must determine in advance its responses in different scenarios. These given, the calculation of the initial variance-minimizing hedges, one for each future cash flow in the planning horizon, is fairly mechanical.

It is useful at this point to contrast the corporate hedging problem with that of hedging portfolios of foreign securities [see Dumas (1992)]. Exchange rate changes and securities' rates of return both take the form of vectors which are approximately identically and independently distributed and whose covariances can often be assumed to be reasonably stable. These covariances can therefore be evaluated with past data. Unconditional portfolio variance can be minimized by hedging the portfolio forward, one period at a time. Owing to the i.i.d. assumption, little is to be gained from taking out an n-period hedge with the prospect of interim revisions. Dumas conjectures that, if what is desired is a hedge at a future time T, there may be no point to hedging in advance of time $T-1$.

In the corporate setting, the prospect of future, state-contingent strategic decisions that change the probability distributions of cash flows, makes the i.i.d. assumption untenable. Time series estimates of optimal hedges based on past data are therefore not likely to be of much use. If firms want to be hedged they cannot wait to do so. They must start now and recalculate their entire portfolio of hedges as information and strategic decisions, evolve. This comes out clearly as an implication of our approach.

In one respect, to be sure, our trading firm model oversimplifies a more complex reality. The simplicity of the optimal hedge calculations in (8.10) and (8.11) is due in part to our assumption of only one lag, the one between invoicing and receipts. In practice, additional lags show up in the production-inventory-shipment-payment cycle. This creates a distributed lag relationship between cash flows and current and past exchange rates. A treasurer should ideally be completely familiar with the details of this sequence before putting together the structural plan for his hedge: it can be expected to be more complex than Exhibit 8–1.

Let us now consider what is needed to implement such an exposure measurement program. One proposition is clear at the outset. Designing currency hedges in our approach requires that management be willing to project cash budgets along at least two exchange rate paths. This requirement stopped one firm from even attempting exposure measurement along our lines. Its cash budgets took the form of point cash-flow projections for each future period and were treated as contracts or quotas. The firm was unwilling to let its cash budget vary with the exchange rate on the grounds that top executives were unwilling to give their subordinates uncertainty as an excuse for budget variances. When cash budgets can consist of only one set of numbers, our procedures cannot be carried out.

A second requirement implied by our approach is that managers abandon the transaction by transaction approach to hedging. The periodic cash flows targeted for hedging should include receipts and payments for goods to be sold or purchased, as well as cash flows linked to purchases and sales of capital equipment and the issuance or repurchase of securities. The planning horizon should be long enough for the effect of early decisions on later cash flows to enter the picture. The output of the exposure measurement system is a time-stream of future exposures, some positive and others negative. Each one represents the hedgeable foreign currency content of a given period's cash flow. Hedging policy at time 0 consists of taking out a portfolio of options or forward contracts with different maturities, one for every cash flow in the stream. In this setting, there is no call for targeting any single transaction separately. The technical problem of estimating streams of time-varying conditional exposures is certainly formidable. That it is difficult does not justify picking out one transaction in the stream, just because it is large or the only one that is already recorded.

Managing a portfolio of hedges through the revisions called for by our procedure can prove cumbersome. The question then is whether one can hedge the entire time-stream of exposures starting with a single contract (of whatever maturity), which is then rolled over. The answer is that in principle one can in either of the two equivalent ways. The size of the initial hedge, with maturity equal to the rollover date, is the FC exposure during the period plus the present value, as of the rollover date, of all the regression-coefficient FC exposures computed for each cash-flow posterior to the rollover date. Alternatively, the hedge can be estimated as the regression coefficient obtained by regressing the distribution of the present value of the subsequent cash-flow stream on the distribution of the exchange rate, as of the rollover date. These last are colloquially termed "value hedges." The value-hedging approach does not remove the need to revise the firm's estimates of its future strategy-conditional cash flows as time passes. And it runs up against the usual difficulties associated with valuing nontraded cash flows. From the perspective of implementability, it may not be easier than the alternative.

Designing currency hedges correctly is obviously hard work. A legitimate question is whether it is worth the effort. This can be answered by comparing the effectiveness of alternate hedging policies. Only Brealey and Kaplanis (1991) have studied this issue. They work out the unconditional variance associated with several possible policies for a particular i.i.d. process of incoming information regarding future cash flows. When strategic reactions are ruled out, they find that all alternatives are inferior to value hedging but say nothing about its implementability. Permitting strategic reactions breaks down the simplicity of their conclusion but seems to leave value hedging as the best choice. The question awaits further research.

CONCLUDING OBSERVATIONS

We conclude the chapter with some remarks regarding its testable implications. These primarily concern the effects of changing exchange rates on international trade.

The simple model of the second section above confirms that movements in the level of the exchange rate, anticipated by firms using the forward rate for planning outputs, affect the volume of trade. This prediction is substantially in conformity with the recent pass-through literature. It also predicts more refutably that the volumes of bilateral trade should not respond to changes in the volatilities of exchange rates between pairs of trading partners. This hypothesis is due to the model specific result that firms with access to forward markets ignore exchange rate volatility when making their real decisions regardless of whether or not they actually hedge.

If exchange rate volatility is found to be associated with trade volume, the reason is to be sought in models that link real decisions to hedging possibilities.

REFERENCES

Adler, M., and B. Dumas. (1980). "Foreign Exchange Risk Management." *Currency Risk and the Corporation*. B. Antl, ed. London: Euromoney Publications, Ltd., pp. 145–57.

Adler, M., and B. Dumas. (1982). "Accounting Standards and Exposure Management." *Management of Foreign Exchange Risk*. B. Antl and R. Ensor, eds. London: Euromoney Publications, Ltd., pp. 35–42.

Adler, M., and B. Dumas. (1983). "International Portfolio Choice and Corporation Finance: A Synthesis." *Journal of Finance*. 38, no. 3, June, pp. 925–84.

Baron, D. (1976). "Flexible Exchange Rates, Forward Markets, and the Level of Trade." *American Economic Review*. 66, no. 3, June, pp. 253–66.

Brealey, R., and E. Kaplanis. (1991). "Discrete Exchange Rate Hedging Strategies." London Business School working paper. December.

Chew, L. (1988). "Damage Control." *Risk*. 1, April, pp. 34–40.

Dixit, A., and J. Stiglitz. (1977). "Monopolistic Competition and Optimum Product Diversity." *American Economic Review*. 67, no. 3, June, pp. 297–308.

Dornbusch, R. (1987). "Exchange Rates and Prices." *American Economic Review*. 77, no. 1, March, pp. 93–106.

Dumas, B. (1978). "The Theory of the Trading Firm Revisited." *Journal of Finance*. 33, no. 3, June, pp. 1019–30.

Dumas, B. (1992). "Short and Long Term Hedging for the Corporation." The Wharton School working paper. March 30.

Ethier, W. (1973). "International Trade and the Forward Exchange Market." *American Economic Review*. 63, no. 3, June, pp. 494–503.

Froot, K., and P. Klemperer. (1989). "Exchange Rate Pass-through when Market Share Matters." *American Economic Review*. 79, no. 4, September, pp. 637–54.

Froot, K., D. Scharfstein, and J. Stein. (1992). "Risk Management: Coordinating Corporate Investment and Financing Policies." M.I.T. working paper.

Mello, A., J. Parsons, and A. Triantis. (1992). "An Integrated Model of Multinational Flexibility and Hedging Policies." University of Wisconsin working paper. March.

Smith, C., and R. Stulz. (1985). "The Determinants of Firms' Hedging Policies." *Journal of Financial and Quantitative Analysis.* 20, no. 4, December, pp. 391–405.

CHAPTER 9

EXCHANGE RATES AND CORPORATE PRICING STRATEGIES

Michael M. Knetter

Since the breakdown of the Bretton Woods system of fixed exchange rates, firms engaged in international trade of goods and services have been confronted with relative cost shocks of unprecedented magnitudes. The wide swings in the value of the U.S. dollar against the currencies of most major industrial countries during the 1980s illustrate the point. At the beginning of the 1980s, the dollar was worth roughly 1.7 German marks. By early 1985 it had risen above 3.3 marks, an increase of nearly 100 percent in its value relative to the mark, in spite of the fact that U.S. inflation exceeded German inflation during this period. It then fell dramatically to less than 1.6 marks by late 1987. The changes in the yen/dollar exchange rate were nearly as large over this same period. Research in international finance has shown that these movements in exchange rates are not easily explained by changes in observable fundamentals. Clearly, the fluctuations are too large to be consistent with the underlying differences in productivity growth across countries.[1] Consequently, these changes have induced huge shifts in the relative production costs of U.S.,

The author thanks James Dana and Joe Gagnon for helpful discussions, Kristine Knetter for research assistance, and Science Center Berlin for a pleasant research environment.

Japanese, and German firms across the entire spectrum of traded goods industries. These shifts in relative production costs across firms provide fertile ground for empirical research on pricing behavior.

The topic of this chapter is the impact that exchange rate changes have on the pricing decision of firms whose factor payments are denominated primarily in the home currency and who earn at least some share of their revenue in foreign markets. Two interesting analytical issues arise with regard to pricing in the context of these huge exchange rate swings. The first is whether firms' production costs in domestic currency are sensitive to exchange rate fluctuations. This can arise if either some inputs are priced in foreign currency units, or if cost varies with the quantity produced which in turn varies with exchange rates. For example, since Japan imports many raw materials that are priced in dollars and traded in relatively integrated world markets (e.g., oil), an appreciation of the yen reduces input costs measured in yen. Thus, we would expect yen prices of Japanese-produced autos to fall as the yen strengthens against the dollar. It is also likely that fluctuations in the value of the yen can result in a change in total production of autos in Japan if relative prices change in foreign markets. If auto production does not exhibit constant returns to scale, then the change in the quantity produced will affect marginal (and average) costs of the Japanese producers. This will be potentially more important for exchange rate changes vis-à-vis large export destinations. Note that the effects exchange rates have on costs should affect yen export prices to *all* markets. Although yen/dollar exchange rate changes may have the greatest effect on Japanese production costs relative to other currency movements, the resulting price changes via this channel are not destination-specific.

The second issue is how a change in the exchange rate affects the markup of price over cost. In order to maximize profit in either an integrated world market or segmented export markets, firms may adjust markups in response to exchange rate changes. In the segmented, imperfectly competitive markets case, which is probably applicable to most manufactured goods, destination-specific markup adjustment that is triggered by exchange rate changes is referred to as "pricing-to-market" (PTM).[2] This is a form of third-degree price discrimination in which buyers are separated by geographic, information, legal, or other barriers.[3] Since this chapter is about pricing policies, theory and evidence on PTM will be my main focus.[4]

The combined sensitivity of costs and markups to exchange rate changes ultimately determines the "pass-through" of exchange rate changes from the exporter to the importer. Pass-through is typically defined as the elasticity of the local currency price of a foreign-produced good with respect to a change in the exchange rate between the local currency and the currency of the exporter.[5] If local currency prices move in proportion to the exchange rate, then there is "full pass-through" of exchange rate changes to local currency prices. The low pass-through of exchange rate changes to dollar prices of foreign-produced goods in the United States in the 1980s stimulated new interest in goods prices and exchange rates. Since pass-through combines information about both cost and markup changes, it does not have a precise economic interpretation. Low pass-through in the 1980s could have been due to: (1) offsetting cost movements due to both the role of the dollar in world commodity trade and the fact that the United States is a large country or in (2) destination-specific markup adjustment in a world with segmented, imperfectly competitive markets. This may explain why PTM has become the focus of more research in recent years.

Measures of PTM can provide us with useful information on firm strategies. In particular, how do different firms/industries strike the balance between price and quantity adjustment? What industry characteristics are associated with different adjustment patterns? Are price and/or quantity adjustments consistent with the predictions of standard economic models? It also enables us to address whether behavior in a given industry is different across exporting countries. For example, is the response of markups to exchange rate changes different for U.S. and German chemical exporters? Evidence on this point might provide some information about the importance of differences in the labor market, financial market, and other economy-wide institutions in determining firm behavior.[6]

This chapter consists of two main sections. The first section summarizes theoretical issues with respect to exchange rate fluctuations and export pricing. I will also discuss some some critical assumptions of standard models of pricing that may complicate interpretation of the empirical evidence. The second section will summarize and extend recent empirical work on industry-level export price adjustment. In this section I will study markup adjustment on shipments to a cross-section of export markets for approximately 60 German and 20 U.S. 7-digit industries. The third section concludes.

EXCHANGE RATE FLUCTUATIONS AND EXPORT PRICES IN THEORY

This section of the chapter will show in detail the effects of exchange rate fluctuations on traded goods prices for simple noncompetitive market structures, and then discuss how the relationship is complicated by more sophisticated market structures and the role of dynamic factors. I will begin by analyzing exchange rate pass-through for a monopolist selling to a single foreign market, to show how pass-through depends on cost and demand functions in a precise way. Next, I analyze the pricing problem of a monopolist selling to multiple destinations. This shows how prices to multiple buyers can isolate demand characteristics in principle. Third, I discuss how more complex market structures would complicate the revenue function of the exporter and the optimal pricing policy. Fourth, I examine how dynamic factors can complicate pricing strategies. Finally, I review some important caveats that apply to almost all of the theoretical models of PTM that will be particularly important in interpreting the empirical results.

Exchange Rate Pass-Through Under Monopoly

This section derives the elasticity of import price with respect to the exchange rate for a monopolist. It can be viewed as an extension of Bulow and Pfleiderer's (1983) results on the effect of cost changes on price for a domestic monopolist and parallels Feenstra (1989). While the results are not new, they illustrate the identification and interpretation problems inherent in empirical research on goods prices and exchange rates. This analysis is partial equilibrium in nature in that the producer's actions are assumed to have no effect on the exchange rate, a standard assumption in other research on this topic. In addition, I abstract from transportation costs, trade barriers, adjustment costs, and uncertainty.

Let q denote the quantity produced for sale in the foreign market, $p*$ the price in foreign currency (referred to as the import price), and e the exchange rate (in units of foreign currency per unit of the exporter's currency). Without loss of generality, assume the monopolist employs a single factor of production at domestic currency price w. The inverse demand function which gives the import price as a function of the quantity sold will be denoted by $p^*(q)$. The domestic currency profits, Π, from sales in the foreign market are given by:

$$\Pi(q) = \frac{p^*(q)q}{e} - C(q, w) \tag{9.1}$$

where $C(q,w)$ is the firm's cost function. The optimal export quantity must satisfy the first-order condition:

$$\frac{d\Pi}{dq} + \frac{p^{*'}(q)\,q + p^*}{e} - C_q(q, w) = 0 \tag{9.2}$$

Assuming that the cost and demand functions are twice continuously differentiable, one can apply the implicit function theorem to the first-order condition to determine the response of import price with respect to a change in the exchange rate:

$$\frac{dp^*}{de} = \frac{dp^*}{dq}\frac{dq}{de} = -p^{*'}\frac{\Pi_{qe}}{\Pi_{qq}} \tag{9.3}$$

where Π_x denotes the derivative of the profit function with respect to x. Exchange rate pass-through is defined to be the elasticity representation of this derivative. Letting η $(1 < \eta < \infty)$ denote the absolute value of the elasticity of demand with respect to price and assuming for the moment that factor prices are independent of the exchange rate, the pass-through coefficient can be expressed as[7]:

$$\frac{d \ln p^*}{d \ln e} = \frac{-\eta + 1}{-\eta + 1 - \frac{d \ln \eta}{d \ln p^*} - \eta \frac{eC_{qq}}{p^{*'}}} \tag{9.4}$$

This expression reveals the channels affecting the pass-through relationship for a monopolist. Both the slope and the degree of convexity of the import demand schedule are important, indicated by the presence of both the elasticity of demand and the *elasticity of the elasticity* with respect to import price. In addition, the denominator is a function of the slope of marginal cost. If the domestic factor price faced by the monopolist were affected by the exchange rate (as in the case of an imported input), then the resulting shift in the cost function would further complicate the pass-through relationship. In reality, all of these effects are likely to be operative to some extent.

There are several points worth noting about the implications of equation (9.4) for exchange rate pass-through. First, with constant marginal cost and constant elasticity of demand, the monopolist will fully pass-through exchange rate changes to import prices. This can be seen by noting that the last two terms in the denominator are zero under the stated conditions. The result is independent of the particular value of elasticity and thus, of the markup of price over marginal cost. Consequently, even under these restrictive assumptions about functional form, the pass-through coefficient reveals nothing about the degree of market power for a monopolist.[8]

Second, with constant marginal cost, the convexity of the demand schedule dictates whether pass-through exceeds, equals, or is less than one.[9] The pass-through coefficient would exceed one for demand schedules more convex than a constant elasticity schedule with equivalent slope. Pass-through is less than one for demand schedules less convex than the constant elasticity schedule. This would include the linear case.

Third, if the slope of marginal cost is not known, knowledge of the pass-through coefficient alone is insufficient to determine even the convexity of the demand schedule.[10] Even when demand is less convex than a constant elasticity schedule, pass-through could exceed one if marginal costs were falling sufficiently in the neighborhood of the optimum. On the other hand, pass-through may be incomplete in spite of demand schedules having more convexity than a constant elasticity schedule, provided marginal costs were increasing sufficiently at the optimal output level. This suggests that pass-through could vary dramatically across industries and within a particular industry over time as capacity utilization changes.[11]

Multi-Market Monopoly and Pricing-to-Market[12]

Consider a firm that produces goods for sale in n separate destination markets, indexed by i. The profits of the firm are given by:

$$\Pi(p_1,\ldots,p_n) = \sum_{i=1}^{n} p_i q_i (e_i p_i) - C\left[\sum_{i=1}^{n} q_i (e_i p_i), w\right] \qquad (9.5)$$

where p is the export price (i.e., price in the exporter's currency), q is quantity demanded (a function of the price in the buyer's currency), and e, w and $C(q,w)$ are defined as in the previous section.[13] The first order conditions for profit maximization imply that the firm equates the marginal revenue from sales in each market to the common marginal cost. Alternatively, the export price to each destination is the product of the common marginal cost and a destination-specific markup:

$$P_i = C_q \left(\frac{-\eta_i}{-\eta_i + 1} \right) \forall_i \qquad (9.6)$$

where the arguments of C_q are suppressed and η is the absolute value of the elasticity of demand in the foreign market with respect to changes in price. A change in the exchange rate vis-à-vis the currency of country i can affect the price charged to market i in two ways: by affecting either marginal cost (through changes in quantity or input prices) or the elasticity of import demand. The former effect will spill over to the other destination markets as well, while the latter is destination-specific. Both effects determine pass-through, while PTM refers to the second effect only.

These two effects are revealed more clearly by taking the log of (9.6) and totally differentiating the resulting expression with respect to export prices, input prices, and exchange rates:

$$\frac{dp_i}{p_i} = \frac{C_{qq} [\Sigma q_j' (p_j de_j + e_j dp_j)] + C_{qw} dw}{C_q} + \frac{\eta_i' e_i p_i}{\eta_i (-\eta' + 1)} \left(\frac{dp_i}{p_i} + \frac{de_i}{e_i} \right) \forall_i$$

where the arguments of q' and η' are suppressed. Defining: $\qquad\qquad (9.7)$

$$\beta_i = \left| \frac{\dfrac{\partial \ln \eta_i}{\partial \ln p_i^*}}{(-\eta_i + 1) - \dfrac{\partial \ln \eta_i}{\partial \ln p_i^*}} \right|$$

where $p^* = ep$ is the price in the buyer's currency and letting (dC_q/C_q) equal the total differential of the log of marginal cost, equation (2.3) simplifies to:

$$\frac{dp_i}{p_i} = (1 + \beta_i) \frac{dC_q}{C_q} + \beta_i \frac{de_i}{e_i}, \forall_i \qquad (9.8)$$

Two important observations can be made about export price elasticities on the basis of (9.8). The first is stated in the following proposition.

Proposition. *The elasticity of export price with respect to the exchange rate, net of the effect of any associated changes in marginal cost, is less than (greater than) zero as demand is less (more) convex than the constant elasticity form.*

This follows by inspection of the simplification of the total differential in equation (9.7) and the relationship between convexity and the response of elasticities to changes in price. For demand schedules less convex than the constant elasticity class, elasticity of demand increases with price, causing the numerator to be positive and the denominator negative in the expression for β. The intuition is the same as in the problem of the first section.

The simplification given by (9.8) also reveals an implication for the relationship between the effect of marginal cost changes and exchange rate changes on the export prices. Changes in marginal cost and changes in exchange rates *net of their effect on marginal cost* have an identical effect on prices in the importer's currency. Equation (9.8) is in terms of the export price changes, so the coefficients on changes in exchange rates and marginal cost differ by one, since exchange rate movements automatically change import prices proportionately. This is intuitively appealing. Since it is the interplay with arguments of the cost function that in general causes exchange rates to have potentially different effects from pure input price shocks, it is reasonable that when they are accounted for separately, marginal cost changes and exchange rate changes have symmetric effects on import prices.

The sections above illustrate two things: (1) even with simple market structures, the relationship between exchange rates and goods prices is complicated and depends on the functional forms of cost and demand as well as the sensitivity of input prices to exchange rates, and (2) by introducing multiple markets and focusing on relative export prices, it may be possible to isolate the "demand-side" effects of exchange rates from those effects that work through the cost function. In other words, PTM may in principle provide more useful information than a simple pass-through coefficient.[14]

Alternative Market Structures

Moving from monopoly to other imperfectly competitive market structures further complicates the relationship between prices and exchange rates. In the multimarket framework, the same principles concerning the convexity of demand will apply to price adjustment, but the demand schedule must now be thought of as a residual demand which incorporates the response of competitors to changes in the exchange rate (or other factors that affect the export price). Unfortunately, obtaining closed form solutions for the pricing equation based on the properties of residual demand is typically not possible. Nonetheless, the link between market demand and residual demand will vary with the number of firms, where they are located, and the nature of strategic interaction. I will focus on how price adjustment varies with these factors for a given market demand schedule.

Dornbusch (1987) provides a clear analysis of the pass-through problem for a number of models of market structure. These models can easily be extended to multiple segmented markets to consider the implications for PTM. I will focus my discussion on the Cournot oligopoly model.

The Cournot model reinforces the points made in the foregoing sections and illustrates how the location and number of firms affects pass-through and PTM. Dornbusch's version of the model is geared toward studying pass-through to the "home" market. I will change the orientation of the model to study pass-through from home firms to a foreign market, in order to be consistent with notation from the previous sections and in the empirical work to follow. The foreign market is assumed to be perfectly sealed from other markets for the output of n identical home and n^* identical foreign firms. To keep things simple, Dornbusch initially assumes constant marginal cost (w for home firms and w^* for foreign firms in units of their local currencies) and linear market demand. Given these cost and demand conditions, we know from the first section above that if the foreign market were served by a home monopolist, then pass-through of exchange rate changes to goods prices in the foreign market would be incomplete. With linear demand, markups increase proportionately less than costs.

In the homogeneous products Cournot model with quantity as the strategic variable, Dornbusch shows that pass-through can be expressed as:

$$\frac{\partial \ln p^*}{\partial \ln e} = \varphi = \left(\frac{n}{N} \right)\left(\frac{ew}{p^*} \right)$$

where $N = n^* + n$ is the total number of firms serving the market. Both terms are fractions, so pass-through is less than one.

Since the equilibrium markup is a decreasing function of the total number of firms, one must be careful in interpreting how the pass-through expression is affected by changes in market structure. The effect of the location of firms is seen by holding N (and thus the markup) constant, but increasing the share of home firms. Pass-through increases since the first term gets larger while the second remains constant. Home firms have greater influence on foreign price as their share of the market increases. To see the role of the number of firms, we allow the total number of firms to increase (which will decrease the markup), while holding the market share of the home firms (n/N) constant. It is clear that this will increase pass-through. Prices become more sensitive to costs when markups are small.

The extension of this framework to the study of PTM is straightforward. Since the model assumes constant marginal costs and no imported inputs in production, the translation from pass-through to PTM only requires that we shift focus to how export prices measured in the home currency change with exchange rate changes. Clearly, full pass-through implies that export prices are unaffected by exchange rate changes, while low pass-through implies exchange rates have a relatively large effect on export prices. Consequently, low pass-through is synonymous with a high degree of PTM. Therefore we expect to observe a great deal of PTM when either: (1) the domestic firms have a small share of the foreign market(s) or (2) the market is not very competitive in the sense that markups are large.

In thinking about these two principles, note the ambiguity in the relationship between "market power" and PTM. PTM is greatest if the industry as a whole has a great deal of monopoly power (high markups over cost), but the home firms have a relatively small share of the foreign market and thus less influence over the equilibrium price. PTM is lowest when the industry as a whole is rather competitive (markups are small), but home firms tend to dominate the industry (they have relatively more market power), so that pass-through is nearly complete to all markets.[15]

Dynamic Models

Krugman (1987) rightly pointed out that most observers intuitively sense that both the actual and expected duration of an exchange rate change has an important effect on the degree of PTM. The models I outlined in the sections above do not have this property. In order for PTM to be duration-dependent, models must have intertemporal linkages in demand or supply—today's prices somehow affect tomorrow's demand or cost. I will briefly review two models to illustrate supply- and demand-side dynamics, respectively .

Baldwin and Foster (1986) and Krugman (1987) have emphasized the potential role of *market-specific* distribution costs in explaining PTM.

Baldwin and Foster refer to it as the "marketing bottlenecks" model. Suppose an exporter faces identical constant elastic demand in several foreign markets so that normally full pass-through (or no PTM) would be expected in the absence of capacity constraints. Further assume that distribution outlets, each having a fixed capacity, are required to sell output for the product. If the exporter's currency depreciates relative to one destination market, he would leave the export price unchanged and allow the destination market currency price to fall proportionately provided there was sufficient capacity. If capacity constraints are binding however, the exporter would only pass-through the exchange rate change to the point where demand equalled capacity. The export price would be increased temporarily to this destination until more capacity could be put in place. Thus, PTM might be observed vis-à-vis other export destinations until capacity expanded sufficiently to meet the demand that would result with full pass-through.

The example implicitly assumes that the exchange rate change is permanent, or at least perceived to be so by the exporter. If the exporter believes the exchange rate change to be temporary or that it will at least partly reverse itself, then additions to capacity may be smaller or nonexistent. We would then expect to observe PTM lasting until the exchange rate returned to a level at which sales in the foreign market did not exceed capacity at the original export price. It is not immediately obvious how the bottlenecks model generates PTM for permanent appreciations of the exporter's currency, since constraints on decreasing shipments are harder to justify.[16]

Froot and Klemperer (1989) present a model in which demand-side dynamics influence the pass-through relationship. One motivation is Klemperer's (1987) switching cost model which has the implication that current profits are a function of past sales (i.e., market share matters). This concern about market share affects the pricing strategy, since the optimal price today depends on all past prices. In an international context this model has an additional implication: because of the effect exchange rates have on the home-currency value of foreign-currency profits, firms' expectations about future exchange rates will affect the value of today's market share. Consequently, currency fluctuations that are expected to be reversed in the future will have a different impact on pricing behavior from those that are expected to be permanent. The degree of pass-through and thus PTM may be related to expectations about future exchange rates, as well as present.

Some Caveats

In this section I will briefly discuss a number of factors likely to affect pricing behavior which are typically not addressed in models of PTM or pass-through.

Invoicing Decisions

Models of pass-through or PTM typically ignore the choice of invoice currency. In practice, trade requires the parties involved to choose an invoice currency and specify the value and quantity of goods in advance of actual exchange. Baron (1976) has analyzed the problem of choosing the optimal invoice currency as a function of supply and demand uncertainty. If contracts specify the invoice currency and a price that is not contingent on the exchange rate, then the invoice currency obviously matters a great deal for the observed pass-through of exchange rate changes. If the exporter invoices in his own currency, then pass-through is complete. If the exporter invoices in the foreign currency, then there is no pass-through.

If contract prices can be adjusted frequently, then the choice of invoice currency is of little consequence for pass-through or PTM. No matter which currency is chosen, the appropriate adjustment of the contract price could yield identical outcomes. To the extent that desired pass-through dictated by market constraints is near one extreme or the other, the optimal invoice currency would seem to be the one that necessitated the least adjustment of the contract price. In other words, if full (no) pass-through is optimal, this can be achieved by invoicing in the exporter's (importer's) currency. If some intermediate level of pass-through is desired, this could in principle be achieved by invoicing in a combination of the two currencies. I am not aware of such contracts in practice, although Whitaker (this volume) notes that GE Medical Systems invoices in the ECU for some transactions. This has apparently become a more common practice in recent years.[17] Choice of invoice currency should depend on the same factors that determine pass-through. It should not have unintended effects on pass-through apart from the very short run.

Foreign Subsidiaries and Transfer Pricing

Another issue that is typically ignored in the literature on pass-through and PTM is the possibility that multinational firms sell output to a foreign subsidiary. In this case, the price may reflect the firm's preferences over where it realizes profits which will depend on tax laws in different countries. For example, a firm that wished to realize all profits in the market of final sale would charge a price equal to unit cost in the domestic currency and let the subsidiary adjust the markup over cost. In this case we would expect to see full pass-through (or no PTM) with respect to the transaction between the home firm and foreign subsidiary. If we measured prices at the consumer level, however, we may see that the subsidiary does adjust markups, so that pass-through is not full. In general, transfer pricing, where it exists, would probably bias measures of PTM downward, since some markup adjustment may occur between the subsidiary and the ultimate customer that is not captured in the international transaction.

Endogenous Market Structure and Hysteresis
In recent research, Baldwin (1988) and Dixit (1989) among others, have considered the possibility that market structure itself depends on realizations of exchange rates, since exchange rates will affect the entry and exit decisions of firms. More significantly, if there are sunk costs associated with these decisions, then temporary swings in exchange rates can have permanent effects on market structure and thus on the relationship between prices and exchange rates. Baldwin (1988) presented some empirical support for this idea in his work. The data were consistent with the hypothesis that U.S. product markets became somewhat more competitive as a result of the overvaluation of the dollar in the early to mid-1980s. Subsequent research by Hooper and Mann (1989), Ohno (1989), Knetter (1991b), and Parsley (1991) has shown less support for this proposition. For investigations with long-time series data sets, structural breaks may be an important issue, but it does not appear to be a significant factor for empirical work with post–Bretton Woods data.

Trade Policy
Another issue that may affect the data, but has received little attention empirically is the notion that there may be significant feedback between firms' pricing policies and governments' trade policies. Feenstra's (1988, 1989) work is one example where exchange rates and trade policy are both taken into account. He has documented the quality upgrading of Japanese auto exports in response to VERs (and its associated effect on unit values of exports to the United States) and the symmetric pass-through of tariff and exchange rate changes.

There are two levels at which trade policy will affect PTM. First, binding quantity restrictions would give rise to rigid prices in the buyer's currency and therefore a high degree of PTM. This is something that seems very evident in the data on Japanese auto exports to European and North

American markets, as shown in Gagnon and Knetter (1991). More subtle is the notion that the mere threat of trade restrictions may alter the pricing strategy of firms engaged in trade. Anti-dumping law in the United States, for example, may serve to constrain the extent to which foreign firms choose to pass-through depreciations of their currency against the dollar. In general, protectionist pressure seems to increase most in countries whose currency has appreciated against its trading partners. If true, there may be an asymmetry in pass-through: firms may be reluctant to pass-through devaluations for fear of provoking trade restrictions in the importing country, which may be hard to reverse.[18] Knetter (1991b) finds weak support for such asymmetries in the data.

Imperfectly Sealed Markets

Perhaps the most important qualification to bear in mind before moving to empirical work is that national markets are not perfectly sealed, as is typically assumed in theoretical models of pass-through and PTM . While it is possible to price discriminate between different markets of final sale in most manufactured goods industries, there may be bounds on how large price differentials can become before arbitrage becomes a profitable activity or new entry is encouraged in some markets. The characteristics that determine the ability of a firm to segment foreign markets are also important determinants of the competitiveness of the industry. Product differentiation and geographic and legal barriers to arbitrage tend to permit discrimination across markets and increase the market power of firms in the industry.

Empirically, we might expect to observe that price differentials across buyers in different markets are closely related to exchange rate changes as long as exchange rates stay within some band. Once exchange rates wander outside the band, the price differentials cannot increase further and the relationship with exchange rates thus breaks down in this region. The band width itself should depend on characteristics of the product. Automobiles should have a much wider band than Vitamin C, since the degree of product differentiation and barriers to arbitrage are much greater in the automobile industry.

Pricing Strategies and Observed Behavior

While economists are most interested in whether evidence on pricing to market can be used to support particular models of market organization, perhaps business people are more concerned with what the data say about strategies that firms use to cope with exchange rate fluctuations. In theory, once a model is fully articulated, choosing the optimal pricing policy is a matter of maximizing the present discounted value of the stream of profits the firm expects under alternative policies.

Although there may be a single optimal strategy in theory, we may expect to observe different behavior in practice. Does different behavior imply different strategies? Suppose we observe Toyota and BMW engaging in different pricing responses to exchange rate changes. One possibility is that the firms face objectively similar situations (e.g., number of competitors, market demand schedule, etc.) but choose different courses of action based on different subjective factors, such as beliefs about the responses of foreign government policy, consumers, or competitors, or discount rates. Another possibility is that the situations are not objectively similar (BMW may face less competition than Toyota in most markets), and that Toyota would choose the same strategy as BMW were it confronted with the same objective situation, and vice versa. In the former case, we might think of the different behavior as resulting from firms pursuing different strategies, whereas in the latter case the different behavior results from a different environment.

In reality, firms are probably very uncertain about the reaction of competitors, consumers, and government policies to price changes. Firms that give more weight to the potential impact of price changes on future demand and cost and/or those that have lower discount rates are more likely to choose pricing strategies that involve relatively more PTM and less pass-through, all else equal. But the "all else equal" qualification looms large, given the variety of "objective" factors that can influence optimal behavior. By careful organization of empirical evidence, it may be possible to determine whether firms facing basically similar market constraints are choosing different strategies. Different behavior across industries may be more likely to reflect different objective environments, whereas different behavior across countries within an industry may reveal differences in strategies.

EMPIRICAL EVIDENCE ON EXPORT PRICES AND EXCHANGE RATES

Empirical studies of how exchange rates affect prices have a much longer tradition than the theoretical work surveyed in the previous section. The period of volatile exchange rates in the early and mid-1980s and the coincident incorporation of imperfect competition into trade theory has led to a new burst of empirical research in this area. Progress in the more recent work shows up on three fronts: (1) measurement and interpretation have been sharpened by the shift from pass-through to PTM, (2) more sophisticated methods in time series econometrics have been brought to bear on the data, and (3) more detailed data, especially in terms of country and industry variation, has been examined.

While these advances have been important, it remains true that econometric research to date has not been successful in measuring the influence of all of the possible channels through which exchange rates might affect goods prices under imperfect competition. Disentangling the separate roles of market demand, strategic interaction, and intertemporal linkages (let alone the factors theory has largely neglected) in the price adjustment process will require industry studies at a level of detail not yet seen in the literature on pass-through or PTM. Nonetheless, the reduced-form equations that have been estimated do provide general information about the relationship between exchange rates and prices for specific industries and therefore shed some light on pricing strategies.

This section of the chapter is divided into four subsections. I first summarize recent evidence on exchange rates and prices at the industry level. Next, I discuss the empirical framework used in this paper to study export price adjustment to exchange rate changes. Third, the data are described. Fourth, I present the results of estimation and offer some interpretations of the main findings.

Recent Studies

At the macroeconomic level, empirical research on exchange rate pass-through flourished around the collapse of the Bretton Woods system, although evidence from aggregate data says little about pricing strategies. Dunn's (1970) paper on Canadian prices was one of the earliest studies at the industry level, and was followed by Isard (1977), Kravis and Lipsey (1977), and Richardson (1978). While much interesting work was done in the 1970s and early 1980s, I will concentrate on industry-level research that has been done since Goldstein and Kahn's article (1985), which reviews the earlier work in great detail. There have been many new studies since 1985, stimulated in part, no doubt, by the large swings in the value of the dollar and the puzzling behavior of the U.S. current account in this period.

Based on the movement in various four-digit industry U.S. import prices relative to a trade-weighted average of foreign production costs, Mann (1986) concluded that foreign profit margins are adjusted to mitigate the impact of exchange rate changes on dollar prices of U.S. imports. Somewhat surprisingly, a sample of U.S. exporters showed no tendency to adjust markups in response to exchange rate changes.[19]

Giovannini (1988) shows that large deviations from the law of one price are correlated with exchange rate changes for monthly export and domestic prices of narrowly defined Japanese manufactured goods—ball bearings, screws, and nuts and bolts. The deviations in some cases exceed 20 percent of the mean levels for the sample period, and persist for well over one year. Using monthly price indexes for Japanese export and domestic prices from 1980–87, Marston (1990) finds strong evidence of PTM in a sample of eight transport equipment and nine consumer goods industries at the four-digit level. The degree of PTM (the change in domestic/export price ratio in response to an exchange rate change) is over 50 percent for both sets of goods on average.

Knetter's (1989) study of export pricing in U.S. and German seven-digit industries documents evidence of PTM on German exports to a variety of destinations. As in the work of Mann, there is no evidence of PTM for U.S. exports. In a comparative analysis of PTM in autos, Gagnon and Knetter (1991) estimate Japanese auto exporters offset approximately 70 percent of the effect of exchange rate changes on buyer's prices through markup adjustment. The comparable number for German auto exports varies by engine size: for small autos, about 40 percent of the effect of exchange rate changes are offset by destination-specific markup changes, whereas for large autos adjustment is minimal. They find no evidence of PTM for U.S. auto exports.

Knetter (1992) addresses the issue of whether there are country-specific differences in the degree of PTM. In a sample of U.S., U.K., Japanese, and German industries, I find that within a particular industry, the hypothesis that behavior is the same across exporting countries cannot be rejected. While most U.S. industries in the sample again show little evidence of PTM, corresponding industries in the other countries behave similarly. There is little statistically significant evidence that PTM varies by destination, either. In particular, the United States does not appear to experience more PTM as a buyer than other destinations for Japanese and German exports.

Regarding the appropriate dynamic specification of prices and exchange rates, the evidence is much harder to read. There seem to be three separate issues. First, does the law of one price hold in the long run, so that

PTM is merely a short-run phenomenon? Second, are there important lags in the price adjustment process that must be recognized in estimation? Third, does the price response to exchange rate changes depend on whether the changes are perceived to be temporary or permanent? Under certain conditions, the dynamic models described in the first section above imply that this distinction matters a great deal. If those conditions hold and exchange rate changes differ greatly in terms of the permanence of an innovation, then it is important to account for this empirically.

While the first question may appear to be more basic, it is probably the one which we can say least about. Price discrimination based on age of consumer, time of day, and bundling of products is pervasive and persistent, but can geographic price discrimination persist over the long run? The existence of firms selling output at uniform delivered prices within domestic markets attests to the possibility, provided differentials do not exceed transport costs.[20] It is certainly easier for differentials to persist across countries than within them, since differences in customs, language, and regulations, as well as fluctuations in currency values, increase the cost of arbitrage. Fluctuations in currency values over the floating rate period are such that we cannot hope to get reliable sample information about whether PTM-induced price differentials across countries would vanish if exchange rates stopped changing. In a sense, volatile exchange rates have probably facilitated the segmentation of national markets while making it difficult for research to determine if that segmentation can persist.[21]

Regarding lags in price adjustment, the work of Giovannini (1988) and Marston (1990) provides the most thorough evidence. Giovannini explicitly allows for the possibility that prices may be set in advance of sales and that price discrimination may be observed simply due to exchange rate surprises. He finds that preset prices alone cannot account for the violations in the law of one price, although they appear to be part of the story. Marston also finds price presetting to characterize a number of the transport equipment categories, but that it is less important for consumer goods. The estimated share of exports with preset prices exceeds 50 percent in only three of the 17 industries in Marston's study. Given the monthly frequency, it is somewhat surprising a larger share of products do not exhibit preset prices.

Froot and Klemperer's (1989) empirical framework can address both the first and third issues raised above. They test for the presence of cost effects (the only channel by which exchange rates affect prices in static models) and "interest rate effects" in price adjustment. The latter arise from dynamic considerations alone and exist only in the event of temporary exchange rate changes. The interest rate and cost effects work in opposite directions, so the fall in the dollar price of imports after a temporary appreciation will be less than after a permanent appreciation. The parameter estimates imply that *purely* temporary exchange rate changes lead to perverse price adjustment: as the dollar appreciates temporarily, foreign firms increase profit margins enough to more than offset the effect of the depreciation, leading to an increase in dollar import prices in this case. The authors cannot reject the null hypothesis that permanent changes in exchange rates leave relative prices across export markets unaffected,that is, there is no PTM in the long run. It is fair to say that the evidence for both of these propositions is rather weak, given that very few specifications yield significant coefficients. The 1981–86 sample of annual observations may be too short to uncover true long run relationships, but provides the best chance for identifying the temporary/permanent distinction.

The Multimarket Framework

The empirical framework adopted here follows Knetter (1989). It is motivated by the first-order conditions of a monopolist selling to multiple export destinations. One can view the first-order conditions of the firm as a set of pricing equations, where price charged to each destination market is the product of marginal cost and a markup term. Marginal cost is common to all destinations, whereas the markup may be common or destination-specific. In imperfectly competitive markets, it is natural to think of markups as being destination-specific and therefore influenced by destination-specific variables, such as exchange rates, income, and other prices.

The general model of export price adjustment I estimate for a seven-digit industry in a given source country can be written as follows:

$$p_{it} = \theta_t + \lambda_i + \beta_i x_{it} + \gamma_i y_{it} + \varepsilon_{it} \tag{9.9}$$

where $i = 1,..., N$ and $t = 1,...,T$ index the destination market for exports and time, respectively, p is the log of destination-specific export price (measured in units of the exporter's currency at the port of export), x is the log of the destination-specific exchange rate (expressed as units of the buyer's currency per unit of the seller's divided by the destination market price level), y is the log of income in the destination market and θ_t, λ_i, γ_i and β_i are $(T + 3N - 1)$ parameters to be estimated.[22] The θ_t are coefficients corresponding to a set of time effects, and the λ_i are coefficients corresponding to a set of destination market effects.[23] The error term, ε_{it}, is assumed to be independent and identically distributed with mean zero and variance σ_ε^2.

The model given by (9.9) is an analysis of the covariance model in which the intercept term is allowed to vary due to unobservable factors that are constant across individuals but vary over time (captured by the θs) and unobservable factors that are constant over time but vary across individuals (captured by the λ's). The primary factor underlying the time effects is the marginal cost of the exporter. It is likely that some common movement in prices is due to changes in the markup over marginal cost that are common to all destination markets.[24] The primary factor underlying the destination effects will be geography, trade policy, and other institutional features of destinations that vary across countries but are constant over time. One can think of these factors as determining the "competitiveness" of the destination market and thus its average level of markup over cost. As written in equation (9.9), the model allows for the destination-specific response of prices to exchange rate and income changes to vary across destinations. Knetter (1992) shows that it is almost never possible to reject the hypothesis that the export price response to exchange rates is identical across destinations for a given industry. In accordance with that finding, equality constraints will be imposed on these coefficients in most of the estimation which follows.

The errors in equation (9.9) can arise for many reasons. Measurement error in the dependent variable is perhaps the primary source, since unit value data will be used to measure prices. Many of the theoretical models mentioned in the first section of the chapter imply either non-linearities in the relationship between exchange rates and prices, or that responses are conditional on the nature of exchange rate changes, so (9.9) may suffer from mis-specification as well. Nonetheless, the linear fixed effects model seems to be a sensible first pass at data from a wide range of industries. No single specification is likely to be best for all of them.

The statistical interpretation of the β's is straightforward. A value of zero implies that the markup to a particular destination is unresponsive to fluctuations in the value of the exporter's currency against the buyer's. Thus, changes in currency values are fully passed through to the buyer apart from any possible impact they may have on the common marginal cost. Negative values of β imply that markup adjustment is associated with stabilization of local currency prices. For example, a value of $-.5$ means that in response to a 10 percent appreciation (depreciation) of his currency, the exporter would reduce (increase) his markup by 5 percent.

Assuming constant costs, the price paid in units of the buyer's currency would rise (fall) by only 5 percent. Positive values of β correspond to the case in which destination-specific changes in markups amplify the effect of destination-specific exchange rate changes on the price in units of the buyer's currency. The estimated value of g would be interpreted similarly. It gives the destination-specific response of price to changes in destination market income. I will constrain the response of prices to real income changes to be identical across countries, in part to conserve on degrees of freedom.

The economic interpretation of the β's depends on what one assumes about market structure. Obviously, PTM cannot occur in a frictionless, competitive model of trade. Export market segmentation is a necessary condition for the existence of price discrimination in general, and PTM in particular. Some possible explanations for segmentation were discussed in the first section of this chapter. Estimates of β reveal whether exporters in a given industry are attempting to offset the effects of currency fluctuations on prices, but we cannot be certain of the underlying reason for the behavior. The explanation is likely to differ by industry.

Before presenting the data and estimation, some discussion of dynamic and time series issues is in order. Work by Giovannini (1988), Kasa (1990), and Marston (1990) has addressed the dynamics of price responses with monthly data. Since annual data will contribute little to that debate, I ignore price adjustment lags. The appropriate dynamic specification of the model depends on the true time series properties of the variables. With only 13 annual observations on price to each destination in each industry, it is impossible to uncover the true time series relationship between the variables. Here I will present the regressions in log levels. Two caveats should be kept in mind: (1) strictly speaking, these results should be interpreted as long-run relationships and (2) standard errors are suspect. The relationships are quite robust—similar estimates have been obtained using differenced data. Thus, we can be confident these are not spurious relationships, although we may not know the exact dynamic specification.[25]

Data

The data used in this study are based on the annual value and quantity of exports to selected destination countries for a number of seven-digit industries from two source countries: the United States and Germany. The sample period is 1973–1987 for U.S. exports and 1975–1987 for German exports.[26] The data are taken from customs declaration forms at the port of export. The values are in units of the exporter's currency net of transportation, insurance, and tariffs. That makes them ideal measures for price comparisons, provided the level of aggregation is fine enough. Data in the markets of final sale for the product may seem a better source of detailed price information, but price differentials on products in different locations do not provide good evidence on PTM, since trade barriers and transportation costs can inhibit arbitrage within a range of prices and retail competition may differ across countries.

For each source country-industry pair, data on exports to a number of relatively large (in terms of sales) export destinations are collected. Eligible destination markets are those that have currencies that fluctuate in value against the exporter's currency, to the extent possible.[27] The aim in choosing large export destinations is to improve the accuracy of the unit values (the value of exports divided by the quantity) as a measure of price, and to minimize the number of periods in which price is not observed because of a lack of shipments. These criteria for data collection imply that sampling over destinations is not random. As a result, caution should be taken in drawing inferences about other trading relationships.

The industries were selected with several factors in mind. One aim was to provide variation in terms of the types of products: durables, nondurables, intermediate goods, and so forth. Another was to try to choose some products that are important export industries in the source countries being studied. The data are available at higher frequencies in some cases. In the United States and Germany, they are available monthly. The choice of annual frequency reflects primarily the need to economize on data collection effort. Lower frequencies may actually be preferred in constructing unit values, since erratic variation in shipments at high frequencies could increase the amount of noise in the unit value series. This is particularly likely in cases where there is heterogeneity in the product category.

The exchange rate series used as an independent variable is expressed in units of the buyer's currency per unit of the exporter's and is based on the annual average nominal exchange rate published in *International Financial Statistics*. The nominal rate is adjusted by dividing by the wholesale price index in the destination market. The rationale for this adjustment is that the optimal export price should be neutral with respect to changes in the nominal rate that correspond to inflation in the destination market. The wholesale price indexes and real GDP data (used for the income series) are annual averages taken from *International Financial Statistics*. The specific industries selected and the data sources for the unit value data are listed in the data appendix.

Estimation and Results

Equation (9.9) is estimated by pooling the data across destination markets for a given export industry in the source country. Thus, each of the 60 German industries and 18 U.S. industries constitutes a separate panel on which pricing behavior across markets is estimated. A Gauss–Newton procedure is used which minimizes the total sum of squared residuals across time and destinations. The method is equivalent to maximum likelihood provided that the errors are assumed to be normally distributed, uncorrelated across equations and over time, and have equal variances. Estimation of an unrestricted covariance matrix is precluded by the presence of a full set of time dummies in estimation.

I will estimate three separate versions of Equation (9.9) for the German industries. Model (1) imposes the constraint that the response of prices to exchange rate innovations is identical for all destinations (i.e., the degree of PTM is independent of destination). Model (2) imposes the same constraint, but drops the U.S. data from the sample of German destinations in each industry. Model (3) relaxes the constraint of identical price adjustment across destination markets and uses data for all destinations. My reasons for considering these different versions of equation (9.9) are to examine the robustness of the findings on PTM and to focus on whether the U.S. data in particular drives the results, either due to the comparatively large fluctuations in the dollar against the DM or because pricing behavior differs.[28]

The results for the German industries are presented in Tables 9–1 through 9–4. I have grouped the industries into four categories: consumer products (Table 9–1), steel and other metal products (Table 9–2), other industrial products (Table 9–3), and chemical products (Table 9–4). The divisions are not always clear, but may nonetheless be useful in organizing the evidence and helping connect the results on PTM to the theories discussed in the first section above. In order to keep the focus on how exchange rates affect pricing, I report only the estimates of β and a couple of diagnostic statistics for each model in each industry. It is impractical to report all of the time and country effects for each industry.

TABLE 9–1
Estimates of PTM Coefficient β: Results for German Exports—Consumer Products

Industry	Model 2 β(s.e.)	Model 1 β(s.e.)	Model 3 β_{us}(s.e.)
Beer	−0.09(0.21)	−0.19(0.21) F=14.03*	−0.57(0.17) DW=0.75
White wine	0.10(0.10)	0.01(0.08) F=7.45*	−0.22(0.02) DW=1.08
Sparkling wine	0.68(0.35)	0.42(0.33) F=2.55	−0.18(0.32) DW=1.77
Olive oil	0.36(0.23)	0.36(0.17) F=4.44*	0.02(0.20) DW=0.93
Cocoa powder	0.46(0.14)	0.15(0.19) F=1.87	−0.21(0.23) DW=1.08
Sandals	−0.48(0.49)	−0.34(0.26) F=6.56*	−0.57(0.15) DW=0.52
Blouses	−0.26(0.31)	−0.20(0.27) F=9.88*	−0.27(0.14) DW=1.87
Record players	0.12(0.35)	−0.06(0.34) F=0.35	−0.02(0.45) DW=1.08
Razor blades	0.72(0.46)	0.60(0.39) F=1.65	0.08(0.27) DW=2.20
Fan belts	−0.76(0.15)	−0.43(0.12) F=7.74*	−0.56(0.12) DW=1.77
Autos under 1 L.	−0.63(0.18)	−1.06(0.21) F=4.30*	−1.00(0.18) DW=2.55
Autos 1.5–2 L.	−0.23(0.21)	−0.56(0.20) F=3.94*	−0.65(0.22) DW=0.85
Autos 2–3 L.	0.12(0.15)	−0.05(0.14) F=9.14*	0.03(0.11) DW=0.97
Autos over 3 L.	0.59(0.17)	0.44(0.18) F=6.97*	0.03(0.13) DW=1.48
Pneumatic tires	−0.33(0.12)	−0.47(0.11) F=1.16	−0.66(0.14) DW=2.29

* Reject constraint at 5% level.
NOTES:
All models are based on estimates of equation (9.9). Model 1 constrains the value of β to be identical across export destinations. The reported F-values test this constraint against the unconstrained Model 3. I report the Durbin-Watson statistic for the U.S. price equation for Model 3. Model 2 is the same as Model 1 except the United States is eliminated as a destination of shipments to explore the sensitivity of PTM to the inclusion of U.S. data. In all models γ is constrained to be the same across markets.

TABLE 9–2

Estimates of PTM Coefficient β: Results for German Exports—Steel and Other Metal Products

Industry	Model 2 β(s.e.)	Model 1 β(s.e.)	Model 3 β_{us}(s.e.)
Semi-gold plate	−0.63(1.60)	−0.43(0.33) F=1.49	−0.77(0.32) DW=2.67
Gas cont., steel	−0.29(0.26)	−0.60(0.09) F=6.75*	−0.49(0.10) DW=1.82
Aluminum rods	0.15(0.12)	0.01(0.11) F=4.86*	−0.03(0.15) DW=2.55
Barbed wire,thin	−0.56(0.17)	−0.80(0.10) F=2.85*	−0.94(0.12) DW=1.96
Barbed wire,med.	−0.42(0.10)	−0.76(0.09) F=6.65*	−0.72(0.09) DW=2.14
Barbed wire,thick	−0.70(0.10)	−0.80(0.25) F=0.27	−0.66(0.21) DW=1.12
Steel containers	−0.21(0.29)	−0.28(0.26) F=4.10*	−0.59(0.21) DW=1.77
Steel rails	−1.14(2.00)	−0.15(0.44) F=1.82	−0.55(0.49) DW=1.21
Iron&steel cans	−0.36(0.11)	−0.59(0.13) F=2.67	−0.72(0.16) DW=0.55
Rivets	−0.26(0.21)	−0.24(0.20) F=5.09*	−0.21(0.18) DW=1.58
Steel wire	0.22(0.20)	0.17(0.22) F=0.19	0.12(0.41) DW=1.87
Platinum plating	0.20(0.13)	0.07(0.14) F=3.91*	−0.12(0.15) DW=0.78
Platinum,semi-fin	−0.11(0.27)	−0.23(0.26) F=0.85	−0.44(0.27) DW=1.03
Nails	0.44(0.57)	0.18(0.42) F=2.80*	−0.39(0.36) DW=2.10

* Reject constraint at 5% level.
NOTES:
All models are based on estimates of equation (9.9). Model 1 constrains the value of β to be identical across export destinations. The reported F-values test this constraint against the unconstrained Model 3. I report the Durbin-Watson statistic for the U.S. price equation for Model 3. Model 2 is the same as Model 1 except the United States is eliminated as a destination of shipments to explore the sensitivity of PTM to the inclusion of U.S. data. In all models γ is constrained to be the same across markets.

TABLE 9–3
Estimates of PTM Coefficient β: Results for German Exports—Other Industrial Products

Industry	Model 2 β(s.e.)	Model 1 β(s.e.)	Model 3 β_{us}(s.e.)
Coated paper	–0.26(0.29)	0.03(0.15) F=3.78*	0.18(0.12) DW=2.81
Wicks, soaked	0.32(0.31)	0.03(0.20) F=14.78*	0.06(0.26) DW=0.47
Glass balls&tubes	–1.10(0.41)	–1.07(0.26) F=8.02*	–1.28(0.22) DW=1.32
Electric heaters	0.87(0.25)	0.51(0.22) F=11.38*	–0.02(0.14) DW=1.69
Ceramic tiles	–0.50(0.06)	–0.46(0.07) F=4.46*	–0.20(0.12) DW=2.20
Cer. tile, glazed	–0.62(0.16)	–0.36(0.13) F=3.08*	–0.15(0.15) DW=1.78
Glass panels	0.11(0.50)	0.10(0.37) F=2.67*	0.26(0.20) DW=1.54
Fireproof tiles	–0.18(0.13)	–0.13(0.15) F=3.92*	0.06(0.18) DW=0.73
Ornam. ceramics	–0.48(0.46)	–0.48(0.38) F=1.01	–0.57(0.29) DW=1.44
Induct. furnaces	–0.12(0.20)	–0.08(0.18) F=0.55	–0.17(0.17) DW=1.10

* Reject constraint at 5% level.
NOTES:
 All models are based on estimates of equation (9.9). Model 1 constrains the value of β to be identical across export destinations. The reported F-values test this constraint against the unconstrained Model 3. I report the Durbin-Watson statistic for the U.S. price equation for Model 3. Model 2 is the same as Model 1 except the United States is eliminated as a destination of shipments. In all models γ is constrained to be the same across markets.

TABLE 9–4
Estimates of PTM Coefficient β: Results for German Exports—Chemical Products

Industry	Model 2 $\beta(s.e.)$	Model 1 $\beta(s.e.)$	Model 3 $\beta_{us}(s.e.)$
Organic compds.	−0.22(.25)	−0.36(0.19) F=1.11	−0.22(0.16) DW=2.21
Aluminum hyd.	−0.16(0.31)	−0.42(0.18) F=1.49	−0.41(0.27) DW=1.17
Titanium pigmt.	−0.55(0.14)	−0.69(0.12) F=1.40	−0.85(0.17) DW=1.14
Titanium diox.	−0.40(0.18)	−0.67(0.18) F=1.87	−0.96(0.15) DW=2.25
Vitamin A	−0.40(0.58)	−0.37(0.38) F=3.24*	−0.02(.30) DW=1.34
Vitamin C	−0.11(0.04)	−0.12(0.05) F=0.72	−0.15(0.07) DW=2.01
Synthetic dyes	−0.39(0.15)	−0.33(0.09) F=16.07*	−0.30(0.07) DW=1.90
Special dyes	−0.48(0.17)	−0.39(0.26) F=1.01	−0.18(0.32) DW=2.15
Aluminum ox.	−0.56(1.06)	−0.89(0.68) F=1.03	−0.48(0.50 DW=1.65
Aldehyde deriv.	1.10(0.52)	0.65(0.27) F=0.29	0.45(0.24 DW=2.08
Manganese ox.	0.55(0.24)	0.47(0.25) F=1.55	0.03(0.39) DW=1.36
Aromatic ketones	−0.26(0.27)	−0.35(0.22) F=2.20	−0.38(0.24) DW=1.85
Hydrocarbons	0.27(0.19)	−0.67(0.16) F=7.14*	−0.82(0.14) DW=2.08
Hydrogen	1.12(0.21)	−0.37(0.15) F=8.95*	−0.16(0.19) DW=1.66
Glykocides	0.07(0.17)	0.01(0.14) F=6.63*	0.04(0.12) DW=0.85
Oleic acids	−0.81(0.29)	−0.87(0.24) F=1.27	−0.96(0.26) DW=1.54
Calcium, barium	0.47(0.43)	0.36(0.17) F=4.95*	0.02(0.20) DW=0.50

* Reject constraint at 5% level.
See NOTES of Table 9–3 for full explanation of table entries.

Choosing Between the Models

First, consider the difference in results across the alternative models that are estimated. In comparing the estimates of PTM obtained with and without the U.S. data (i.e., Model 1 vs. Model 2), there do not appear to be important systematic differences between the two. Although the estimated values of β in Model 1 reveal more evidence of PTM, there are only five instances of sign reversals in the four tables, only two of which are of substantial magnitude (two chemicals: hydrocarbons and hydrogen). The inclusion of U.S. data appears to sharpen the finding of PTM for consumer products, steel, and chemicals, but not for other industrial products. Most striking is consumer products, in which, absent the U.S. data, there is hardly any evidence of PTM in the standard sense (i.e., negative βs indicating stabilization of prices in local currency).

To the extent the U.S. data increase measured PTM in steel, it may be due to the fact that trade restrictions on various steel products in the U.S. market during this period caused dollar prices of imports to be more rigid than otherwise, necessitating PTM on the part of German exporters. In chemicals, geographically distinct regions may be a necessary condition for price differentials to arise. Products may be sufficiently homogeneous that without the U.S. market in the sample, correlation between price differentials and exchange rates is weakened.[29] Although trade policy and geography might explain the differences in these categories, in consumer products that seems less likely. The United States is not noted for particularly restrictive quantitative policies on consumer products, nor does the Atlantic Ocean seem necessary to maintain price differentials across countries—as it may be in primary chemical products.

In comparing Model 1 against Model 3, where β can vary by destination, the F-statistic reported beneath the parameter estimate for Model 2 allows a direct test between the two models. In consumer and other industrial products, the data reject the constraint in most cases. In steel products the industries are split evenly across the alternatives, whereas most chemical products accept the restriction.[30] The ramifications of choosing one model over the other are not great, except for consumer goods and steel, where the preponderance of products point toward the unrestricted Model 3, which in turn usually implies more PTM in the U.S. market than the common estimate from Model 1.

Beneath the estimates of β from Model 3, I report the Durbin-Watson statistic from the residuals in the U.S. destination pricing equation. Under the null hypothesis, the autocorrelation pattern should not differ across destinations, but since DW statistics are calculated for each destination in regression output, I report the U.S. DW statistic in all cases.[31] There is fairly strong evidence of positive autocorrelation in the residuals for some consumer and industrial products, but little in steel and chemicals.

There are a number of possible reasons why one might expect autocorrelation of residuals to arise. First, it could result from measurement error in the dependent variable. A sporadic outlier that is correlated with a large exchange rate movement may cause positive autocorrelation. Second, unmodelled dynamics in price adjustment may cause price adjustment to be related to past exchange rate changes. This might be particularly important in products like autos with infrequent price adjustment.[32] Since positive autocorrelation does not seem to be a pervasive problem, I have not attempted to correct for it in this work. The appropriate response is likely to vary by industry, so that a serious pursuit of this issue would detract from discussion of pricing policies in the large. The DW stats are not so low as to raise concern that the regressions are spurious.

Evidence on Pricing to Market

Let me now consider what the data seem to show about the pattern of pricing to market across industries. I will begin with the parameter estimates for the German data. For Germany, I will concentrate most of my discussion on the parameter estimates for the constrained model, with the caution that in some cases that model is rejected by the data.[33] Recall that negative values of b imply that markup adjustment is associated with stabilization of local currency prices. For example, a value of $-.5$ means that in response to a 10 percent depreciation (appreciation) of the buyer's currency, the exporter would reduce (increase) his markup by 5 percent relative to the markup charged to other destination markets. Positive values of β imply that destination-specific markup adjustment amplifies the effect of exchange rate changes on the local currency price.

The evidence for conventional PTM is remarkably weak in consumer goods industries for German exports. By "conventional PTM" I mean markup adjustment that would stabilize prices in the local currency relative to a constant markup policy. Notice that for large autos, markup adjustment has a destabilizing effect on price. This is also true for several other products, although we should note that the U.S. βs in Model 3 for alcoholic beverages tend to show more PTM than those in the constrained model.

Let me offer three reasons why we might observe positive βs. First, measurement error may bias β upward. If product categories include many varieties and more expensive varieties have less elastic demand, βs will be biased upward by measurement error that is correlated with exchange rates. When the exporter's currency is weak, cheaper varieties make up a larger share of export quantities, by assumption of more elastic demand. Unit values would give the appearance of destabilizing markup adjustment even if all varieties have constant elastic demand and therefore constant DM prices. Second, if market share matters and much of the movement in exchange rates is temporary, then interest rate effects dominate cost effects, and we may observe positive βs. Third, under some demand conditions an "opportunistic" pricing strategy is optimal. Suppose there are "Beck's drinkers" and "beer drinkers," the former with inelastic demand for Beck's and the latter who view it as having close substitutes. When the DM is weak, Beck's lowers its markup to sell to beer drinkers. When the DM is dear, they sell only to Beck's drinkers at a high price.

Regarding the results for German consumer products, the possibility of bias must be taken seriously, especially in autos where product heterogeneity is greatest. Even so, other evidence on prices and sales in the U.S. auto market confirm a basic qualitative finding of the table. Market shares of German producers have fallen much more in the large, high-quality end of the auto market (e.g., Porsche) with the fall in the dollar since 1985. This is consistent with the estimated degree of PTM near zero in Table 9–1 combined with the entry of new Japanese producers in that segment of the market. German cars in the smaller end of the market have not lost as much market share, again consistent with the markedly higher degree of PTM in those categories.[34]

There is robust evidence of PTM in two auto accessory categories: tires and fan belts. PTM in sandals and blouses seems to be a robust finding across specifications as well. The positive estimates of PTM in cocoa, olive oil, and razor blades are puzzling. The correlations are robust across specifications for the most part and it is not obvious that the explanations for positive bs are relevant. Generally speaking, this evidence is weaker than the evidence of PTM in Japanese consumer goods exports that is presented in Marston (1990) or Knetter (1992). Since the market constraints are likely to be similar, this may be a sign of different pricing strategies across Japanese and German consumer goods exporters.[35] Perhaps Japanese consumer goods exporters take a longer view than their German counterparts, using pricing strategies that stabilize local currency prices. On the other hand, they may simply face (or fear) more trade restrictions.

Moving to Table 9–2, there is rather strong evidence of PTM in steel products. Products are more narrowly defined in these cases, so measurement error is much less of an issue. Parameter estimates appear to exhibit more stability across the models, with the exception that PTM to the U.S. market may be more pronounced. Nonetheless, for a large share of the industries, price adjustment offsets 50 percent or more of the effect of exchange rate changes on prices. In 13 of 14 cases, the estimated value of β for the U.S. is negative, while β is negative in 10 of 14 industries in Model 1. As noted earlier, the disparity across those specifications may be a consequence of trade restrictions that were prevalent in the U.S. steel market beginning in the 1970s and continuing into the 80s.

The results in Table 9–3 show less evidence of PTM. Ceramic tile, glazed and unglazed, ornamental ceramics, and unprocessed glass balls and tubes all have robust estimates of PTM in the neighborhood of 50 percent or more. The estimates for most other products are indistinguishable from zero.

Table 9–4 reports PTM for 17 chemical products. The evidence clearly indicates that PTM is an important phenomenon. This is surprising, since we think of many of these products as relatively homogeneous and easy to transport. The observation that price differentials can vary with exchange rates as much as the data suggest signals market segmentation. Those skeptical of this evidence need only consult issues of *Chemical Marketing Reporter* or other trade publications during the mid-1980s. Reports of price differentials between the European and North American markets were numerous and usually attributed to exchange rates. These findings are probably no more surprising than Giovannini's estimates of price discrimination in Japanese ball bearings, nuts and bolts, and so on.

Table 9–5 presents the estimated values of β for 18 U.S. export products. Two raw commodities, yellow corn and raw cotton, are included in part as a check on the method. We would be skeptical of the data or method if these industries revealed large price differentials on average or strong evidence of PTM. In fact, the estimated country effects for these products reveal average price differentials across destinations of no more than 5 percent. The estimates of PTM are virtually zero, as reported in the table. This is the answer one would expect for a homogeneous agricultural commodity.

Both the consumer and chemical/industrial products categories tell a very similar story. There is almost no evidence of PTM in the data. The exceptions are photographic film, industrial lacquers, and two types of paper. For nearly all other categories, the estimated values of β are positive or

TABLE 9–5
Estimates of PTM Coefficient β: Results for U.S. Exports

Industry	Model 1 β(s.e.)
RAW COMMODITIES	
Yellow corn	–0.01(0.05)
Raw cotton	0.07(0.10)
CONSUMER PRODUCTS	
Cigarettes	0.32(0.15)
Bourbon whiskey	0.07(0.20)
Aluminum foil	0.10(0.49)
Photographic film	–0.33(0.38)
Autos over 8 cyl.	–0.06(0.19)
Autos under 8 cyl.	0.00(0.10)
CHEMICAL/INDUSTRIAL PRODUCTS	
Aluminum oxide	1.53(0.32)
Titanium dioxide	1.07(0.50)
Nitrile rubber	0.21(0.23)
Industial lacquers	–0.36(0.42)
Putty	–0.09(0.44)
Kraft linerboard paper	–0.24(0.11)
Photocopier paper	–0.40(0.44)
Primary cell batteries	0.22(0.63)
Integrated circuits	0.81(0.53)
Snap-action switches	1.99(0.64)

NOTES:
Model (1) is based on equation (9.9), but constrains the value of β to be identical across export destinations.

virtually zero. This is consistent with Mann's work (1986) and subsequent work of my own on U.S. exporter behavior. I have argued elsewhere that although nearly all studies are in agreement on this basic fact, there is very little evidence that U.S. firms behave differently than foreign firms in the same industry. Formal statistical tests in Knetter (1992) cannot reject identical price adjustment to exchange rate changes across source countries within an industry.

Exact industry matches are rare when comparing the U.S. and German data presented here, although a few comparisons are possible. U.S. price adjustment behavior in bourbon is similar to what I find in alcoholic beverages generally for Germany. The estimated behavior in autos is also indistinguishable from what we find for large German autos. Aluminum oxide and titanium oxide price adjustment in the U.S. does differ markedly from the estimated behavior for German exports.

While it may be tempting at first glance to conclude that the evidence confirms the view that U.S. export pricing policies validate the thesis of "short-term" behavior of American industry, that is not a legitimate conclusion. These results do not say anything very conclusive about *country-specific* differences in pricing strategies across U.S. and German exporters. It is clear, however, that pricing behavior in the U.S. industries studied here is quite different from what we observe in the German export industries. PTM does not appear to be commonplace in U.S. manufacturing exports.[36] That may only suggest that U.S. manufacturing exports are concentrated in industries in which little PTM is possible. Industry-mix effects may explain low pass-through on U.S. imports and relatively high pass-through on U.S. exports.

CONCLUSION

In summary, the data show that PTM is a strategy that is widely adopted in manufacturing exports in a sample of German export industries, but far less common in U.S. export industries. Within the German export industry sample, PTM was lower than expected in consumer goods industries and relatively high in steel and chemicals. Given that price discrimination can be maintained in the latter categories, it is quite possible that measurement error due to quality change that is correlated with exchange rate fluctuations may bias the unit value data against the finding of PTM in consumer goods. Within the sample of U.S. export industries, only 4 of 18 showed any indication of PTM. Whether there is any country-specific relationship is not clear, since there is wide variation in behavior across industries and little overlap of industries across countries in the data sample.

The mapping between theoretical models of PTM and empirical estimates is very difficult. At present, the literatures are far apart. Empirical work has primarily assembled facts that can be compared with implications of various theories, without providing conclusive tests of them. While this is useful, future empirical research on PTM and pass-through should take the form of detailed studies of individual industries that attempt to account for trade restrictions and other factors that have been largely ignored in the literature to date.

NOTES

1. See for example Richard Meese's (1990) recent survey or the monograph by Paul Krugman (1989).
2. Indeed, the notion of "pricing strategies" is only sensible if firms operate in an imperfectly competitive environment. In perfect competition, market constraints dictate that the firm's only decisions are whether and how much to produce—the environment is neutral. In imperfect competition, firms must assess the likely response of competitors and foreign governments to their range of possible actions. The first discussion of the concept of PTM appears in Krugman (1987).
3. Third-degree price discrimination occurs when different buyers face different, but constant, prices for each unit of the product. It is possible that PTM involves some second-degree discrimination as well (i.e., buyers facing a nonlinear pricing schedule).
4. I will present some evidence on the sensitivity of costs to exchange rate changes, but that is a secondary issue for this paper.
5. I will use the term "local currency" to refer to price in the market of final sale. "Import price" is the price of a tradable good in the buyer's currency. "Export price" is price in units of the seller's currency.
6. This question is of particular interest given the increasingly widespread popular belief that U.S. managers suffer from "short-termism" [see, for example the study by the MIT Productivity Commission (1990)]. If that were true, then we might expect to observe U.S. exporter behavior that is relatively less oriented toward preserving foreign market shares by adjusting markups to stabilize foreign currency prices of exports.
7. Factors other than own price that may affect the elasticity of demand are suppressed for current purposes. They will be considered in empirical implementation of the model.
8. This point is analogous to that made in Bulow and Pfleiderer's critique (1983) of Sumner's investigation (1981) of the cigarette industry.
9. This result is related to Brander and Spencer's analysis (1984) of the effect of tariff changes on import prices.
10. Klein and Murphy (1988) explore the ramifications of nonconstant marginal cost for exchange rate pass-through in more detail.
11. Sensitivity of pass-through to capacity utilization might provide an alternative explanation for structural breaks in the pass-through relationship that have been

documented by Baldwin (1988) for U.S. imports in the 1980s. His preferred interpretation is that large exchange rate swings change market structure by affecting entry and exit in markets.

12. This section borrows extensively from Knetter (1992).
13. This maximization could easily be recast in terms of real prices and profits without affecting any of the main results or empirical implications.
14. Econometric research on pass-through has always introduced cost measures in addition to exchange rates in regression equations. Nonetheless, considering relative export price behavior instead of single bilateral pass-through relationships may provide a superior method of controlling for the effect of cost changes on prices.
15. While these results are for the given linear market demand schedule, Dornbusch shows how general functional forms of demand will alter the basic relationship. For any given market demand, the qualitative relationships between pass-through (or PTM) and market structure described here still hold.
16. With temporary appreciations, one can imagine that a certain volume of shipments must be maintained in order to keep distributors either in business or carrying the product line.
17. See Reboul (1987) and Jozzo (1987).
18. This impact of anti-dumping law on PTM was first suggested in Marston (1990).
19. If anything, the data suggested markup adjustment on U.S. exports amplified the effect of exchange rate changes on prices measured in the buyer's currency.
20. Varian (1989) identifies cement in Belgium and plasterboard in the United Kingdom as examples.
21. The issue of whether PTM is temporary or permanent arises when error correction models are estimated. Kasa (1992) explicitly assumes the law of one price holds in the long run. Gagnon and Knetter (1991) consider both possibilities. Tests cannot determine which assumption is more appropriate.
22. Adjusting the nominal exchange rate for changes in the price level in the destination market imposes the condition that export prices are unaffected by changes in currency values that leave the relative price in units of foreign currency unchanged. Both the exchange rate and income series for each destination is normalized around its mean before taking logs. Thus, at the average values for these series, the (log of) price charged to any destination is given by the sum of the time and country effects.
23. In estimation, one of the time or destination effects must be dropped to avoid singularity. In this case, the destination effect for the U.S. will be dropped, thus the magnitude of the time effects will be normalized around the level of unit values of shipments to the United States. The country effects for other destinations will indicate the difference in unit values relative to the United States at average levels of the exchange rate and income.
24. The model is linear in the parameters, whereas the equation (9.8) derived in the first section suggests an interaction between the time effects used to control for cost and the elasticity of price with respect to exchange rate changes. I have evaluated the nonlinear version of equation (9.9) in Knetter (1991) and found the results to be similar to those obtained with the linear model. There were instances of convergence problems and implausible parameter estimates with the nonlinear model, which may be attributable to the relatively high frequency of outliers in the unit-value data used

in estimation. Thus, I will concentrate on the linear model in this chapter.

25. Gagnon and Knetter (1991) have estimated an error correction version of equation (9.9) for the auto industry and found the short run and long run estimates of PTM to be similar.

26. The only important exceptions are U.S. exports of photographic film and switches, which are for the period 1978–87. Changes in product categories precluded a longer sample.

27. For German exports the destination markets always include the United States. Other common destinations are France, the United Kingdom, Japan, Canada, Sweden, and Italy. For U.S. exports the most common destinations are Canada, United Kingdom, Germany, Japan, Australia, and Sweden.

28. The results of previous research by Mann (1986), Giovannini (1988), Knetter (1989), Marston (1990), and Ohno (1989) taken together suggested much more PTM by non-U.S. exporters than by U.S. exporters. While this may suggest different behavior, it may also be due to a U.S. "destination effect." Knetter (1992) finds no real evidence of a U.S. effect on a smaller data set than that considered here.

29. Note, however, that the evidence of PTM remains quite strong even without U.S. data.

30. These results differ from Knetter (1992), in which the constraint of a common β was nearly always accepted by the data. Those tests were based on data in first-differences. Part of the change in results may be due to a weaker relationship in the differenced data, since there is more noise in the short-run than the long-run response to exchange rate changes.

31. I have used a small sample correction factor of $(t/(t-1))$ to the d-statistic since there are only 13 time series observations.

32. The observation of positive autocorrelation for auto pricing equations across a number of source countries was the motivation for Gagnon and Knetter's (1991) error correction estimation.

33. Even in cases of rejection, the coefficient still captures a rough average of the degree of PTM across destinations, with the country-specific estimates being somewhat more dispersed around the average in those cases.

34. Since people often associate PTM with German auto pricing due to an anecdote by Krugman (1987) regarding gray markets, I feel compelled to point out that these estimates only imply that price differentials between the U.S. and *other export markets* do not appear to be sensitive to exchange rates. It is entirely possible that (1) differentials between the U.S. and German domestic price fluctuate with exchange rates (the domestic market is not part of my comparisons here) and/or (2) differentials exist that are not related to exchange rates. The fact that one can still find advertising for "chop shops" to modify autos produced for sale in Europe suggests that the gray markets of the mid-1980s may have been more than an exchange rate-induced phenomenon.

35. I should note that Marston's evidence comes from price indexes in which the upward bias described for unit values could not apply.

36. Regrettably, the unit value data are at a severe comparative disadvantage vis-à-vis price indexes for examining PTM in high technology industries. The quality change and product innovation in those fields makes unit values poor measures of price. As a result, such industries are not considered in the data set.

REFERENCES

Aussenhandel nach Waren und Laendern, Fachserie 7, Reihe 2, Wiesbaden: Statistisches Bundesamt, various issues.

Baldwin, R. (1988). "Hysteresis in Import Prices: The Beachhead Effect." *American Economic Review*. September, pp. 773–85.

Baldwin, R., and H. Foster. (1986). "Marketing Bottlenecks and the Relationship Between Exchange Rates and Prices." MIT mimeo, October.

Baron, D. (1976). "Fluctuating Exchange Rates and the Pricing of Exports." *Economic Inquiry*. 14, pp. 425–38.

Bulow, J., and P. Pfleiderer. (1983). "A Note on the Effect of Cost Changes on Prices." *Journal of Political Economy*. 91, pp. 182–85.

Dixit, A. (1989). "Hysteresis, Import Penetration, and Exchange Rate Pass-Through." *Quarterly Journal of Economics*. May, pp. 205–28.

Dornbusch, R. (1987). "Exchange Rates and Prices." *American Economic Review*. 77, March, pp. 93–106.

Dunn, R. (1970). "Flexible Exchange Rates and Oligopoly Pricing: A Study of Canadian Markets." *Journal of Political Economy*. 78, January, pp. 140–51.

Feenstra, R. (1989). "Symmetric Pass-Through of Tariffs and Exchange Rates Under Imperfect Competition: An Empirical Test." *Journal of International Economics*. 27, February, pp. 25–45.

Feenstra, R. (1988). "Quality Change under Trade Restraints in Japanese Autos." *Quarterly Journal of Economics*. February, pp. 131–46.

Froot, K., and P. Klemperer. (1989). "Exchange Rate Pass-Through When Market Share Matters." *American Economic Review*. 79, September, pp. 637–54.

Gagnon, J., and M. Knetter. (1991). "Markup Adjustment and Exchange Rate Fluctuations: Evidence from Panel Data on Automobiles and Total Manufacturing." Federal Reserve Board, IFDP #389, October, revised March 1991.

Giovannini, A. (1988). "Exchange Rates and Traded Goods Prices." *Journal of International Economics*. 24, February, pp. 45–68.

Goldstein, M., and M. Kahn. (1985). "Income and Price Effects in Foreign Trade." *Handbook of International Economics*. Jones and Kenen, eds. pp. 1041–1105.

Hooper, P., and C. Mann. (1989). "Exchange Rate Pass-Through in the 1980s: The Case of U.S. Imports of Manufactures." *Brookings Papers on Economics Activity*. 1, pp. 297–329.

Isard, P. (1977). "How Far Can We Push the Law of One Price?" *American Economic Review*. 67, pp. 942–48.

Japan Exports and Imports. Tokyo: Japan Tariff Association, various issues.

Jozzo, A. (1987). "Invoicing with the ECU," *The European Currency Unit*. Levich, ed. London: Euromoney Publications.

Kasa, K. (1992). "Adjustment Costs and Pricing-to-Market: Theory and Evidence." *Journal of International Economics*. February, pp. 1–30.

Klein, M., and R. Murphy. (1988). "Exchange Rate Interdependence and Import Price Pass-Through." Boston College WP#166. June.

Klemperer, P. (1987). "Markets with Consumer Switching Costs." *Quarterly Journal of Economics*. May, pp. 375–94.

Knetter, M. (1989). "Price Discrimination by U.S. and German Exporters." *American Economic Review*. 79, March, pp. 198–210.

Knetter, M. (1991a). "Pricing to Market in Response to Unobservable and Observable Shocks." Dartmouth College working paper 89-16, revised March 1991.

Knetter, M. (1991b). "Is Price Adjustment Asymmetric?: Evaluating the Market Share and Marketing Bottlenecks Hypotheses." Dartmouth College working paper 91-10, July.

Knetter, M. (1991c). "Did the Strong Dollar Increase Competition in U.S. Product Markets?" Dartmouth College working paper 91-15, September.

Knetter, M. (1992). "International Comparisons of Pricing-to-Market Behavior." *American Economic Review*, forthcoming.

Kravis, I., and R. Lipsey. (1977). "Export Prices and the Transmission of Inflation." *American Economic Review*. February, pp. 155–63.

Krugman, P. (1987). "Pricing to Market When the Exchange Rate Changes." *Real-Financial Linkages Among Open Economies*. S. Arndt and J. Richardson, eds. Cambridge: MIT Press.

Krugman, P. (1989). *Exchange Rate Instability*. Lionel Robbins Lecture monograph, Cambridge University Press.

Mann, C. (1986). "Prices, Profit Margins, and Exchange Rates." *Federal Reserve Bulletin*. 72, June, pp. 366–79.

Marston, R. (1990). "Pricing to Market in Japanese Manufacturing." *Journal of International Economics*. 29, December, pp. 217–36.

Meese, R. (1990). "Currency Fluctuations in the Post-Bretton Woods Era." *Journal of Economic Perspectives*. 4, Winter, pp. 117–34.

MIT Commission on Industrial Productivity. (1990). *Made in America*. MIT Press.

Ohno, K. (1989). "Export Pricing Behavior of Manufacturing: A U.S.-Japan Comparison." *International Monetary Fund Staff Papers*. 36, September, pp. 550–79.

Parsley, D. (1991). "Pricing in Foreign Markets: An Examination of Exchange Rate Pass-Through at the Commodity Level." Owen Graduate School of Management mimeo.

Reboul, J. (1987). "Gaz de France and the ECU." *The European Currency Unit*. Levich, ed. London: Euromoney Publications.

Richardson, J. (1978). "Commodity Arbitrage and the Law of One Price." *Journal of International Economics*.

Schedule E: U.S. Exports. Washington, DC: Commerce Department, various issues.

Sumner, D. (1981). "Measurement of Monopoly Behvior: An Application to the

Cigarette Industry." *Journal of Political Economy*. October, pp. 1010–19.

Varian, H. (1989). "Price Discrimination."*Handbook of Industrial Organization*. Schmalensee and Willig, eds. Amsterdam: North-Holland.

Whitaker, M. (1993). "Strategic Management of Foreign Exchange Exposure in an International Firm." chapter 11 this volume.

CHAPTER 10

MANAGING ECONOMIC EXPOSURE TO FOREIGN EXCHANGE RISK: A CASE STUDY OF AMERICAN AIRLINES

John F. O. Bilson

INTRODUCTION

A recent survey awarded American Airlines (AMR) the title of the best-run airline in the United States. Over the past decade, the airline has expanded rapidly in both the domestic and international markets and has developed a reputation for reliable and quality service. AMR has survived and grown in an industry in which many of the major participants have failed. Through this difficult period, AMR, along with United and Delta, have emerged as industry leaders competing effectively on a global scale. While the operational excellence of AMR is widely recognized, it has not resulted in superior returns for investors. AMR stock has underperformed in the general market and has been characterized by substantial volatility. The stock declined by 45 percent between July and December 1987, and it also fell by 50 percent between September 1989 and September 1990. The stock has also been volatile on the upside. It rose 145 percent between December

The factual statements herein have been taken from sources that we believe to be reliable but such statements are made without any representation as to accuracy, completeness or otherwise. The opinions expressed are solely the responsibility of the author.

1987 and September 1989, 132 percent between September 1984 and July 1987, and 56 percent between September 1990 and May 1991. Typically, these movements in equity values were not associated with variations in operational factors like strikes, safety issues, competitive pressure, loss of market share, or over-indulgence in debt. Rather they were the result of factors external to the regular operation of the company: the 1987 stock market collapse, the United Airlines takeover attempt, the Gulf War, and the problems in Eastern Europe. These external events have their immediate impact on market prices: stock prices, interest rates, energy prices, and exchange rates. As these prices change, they alter the perceived profitability of the airline and the changing expectations are compounded into the stock price.

The main question that I would like to address in this chapter is the feasibility of managing these external risk factors. While it is clearly impossible to predict the events that will influence the market in the future, it is possible to examine the relationship between the risk factors and the return on the stock. For example, it is difficult to predict the future direction of energy prices, but it is reasonable to predict that higher energy prices will cause AMR equity to depreciate relative to the market, because energy prices directly increase airline operating expenses and they may also reduce load factors.

If the risk factors can be identified, they can be hedged through the use of derivatives. For example, the airline could purchase crude oil futures to offset the market exposure to energy prices. At some level of participation, the stock should not be affected by movements in energy prices, because the gain on the futures position would offset the markets perceived anticipated loss in profitability. The questions that arise in this regard concern the estimation of the size of the required hedge position and the costs of engaging in the hedge.

Foreign exchange exposure is of increasing importance in the airline industry as the large carriers expand into foreign markets. Net foreign currency cash flows at American Airlines have grown from $119 million in 1986 to $393 million in 1990. International revenue has grown from 19.3 percent of the system total in 1986 to an estimated 26.7 percent in 1990. While the bulk of this expansion has been in the European market, service to the Far East is expected to grow rapidly in the near future. It is consequently important to know how the profitability of the airline will be influenced by the inevitable fluctuations in the price of foreign currencies against the dollar. In the first section of this chapter, I will examine a traditional accounting approach to this issue and then propose an alternative measure of economic exposure to foreign exchange risk. In the second section of this chapter, I will address the issue of active management of foreign exchange exposure. In the final section, I will combine the two approaches and examine the impact of the strategy on the performance of AMR equity.

ESTIMATING EXPOSURE TO FOREIGN EXCHANGE RISK

In developing the ideas for this section, I have benefitted from access to an internal study at American Airlines on the topic [AMR (1991)]. The AMR study is primarily concerned with the effects of exchange rates on the dollar value of foreign currency denominated cash flows. Excess cash flows from international operations in 1990 are predicted to be $393 million dollars. These cash flows are allocated on a global basis as follows:

	Cash Flow ($ Millions)	Per Cent
Canada	80	20%
Europe	197	50%
Pacific	63	16%
Other	54	14%
TOTAL	394	

Approximately 40 percent of these cash flows are denominated in foreign currency. There are two primary sources of currency exposure. The largest source arises from the timing lag between the sale of a ticket in a foreign currency and the receipt of the revenue in dollars. This delay averages 15 to 45 days in the major markets. After a ticket is sold in a foreign currency, a delay will occur before AMR receives the revenue (denominated in foreign currency) from the sale. If the foreign currency should depreciate between the time the ticket is sold and the time the revenues are repatriated, a loss will be recognized on the transaction. Since AMR has positive excess cash flows in its foreign markets, this analysis suggests that AMR is net long in foreign currencies and that hedge activities should involve short positions in foreign currencies.

The second source of exposure results from the impact of exchange rates on anticipated future cash flows. Since it is impractical to reset ticket prices at short intervals, a depreciation of a foreign currency will reduce the dollar value of future cash flows if the foreign currency price and the load factors are stable. This consideration also suggests that

AMR is naturally net long in the foreign currencies where it is operationally involved.

If this approach is correct, an appreciation of foreign currencies should be associated with increased profitability and a rise in the value of AMR stock. However, the effect of the exchange rate on the profitability of an airline is considerably more complex than its effect on cash flows and contemporaneous load factors. For the American consumer of international air travel services, appreciation in foreign currencies increases the total costs of international travel. While the airline ticket cost, which is denominated in dollars, is typically not affected immediately, all other travel costs should increase in proportion to the change in the exchange rate. It is therefore reasonable to assume that American overseas travel will be adversely effected by the appreciation of foreign currencies. It is true that a depreciation of the dollar should make travel to the United States by foreigners less expensive, but if foreign travellers have a preference for their national airline, U.S. carriers could be still be adversely effected. This effect would not be immediately apparent in load factors since international travel typically is planned in advance. However, if the market efficiently forecasts anticipated future revenues, the decline in profitability should be immediately reflected in the stock price.

Movements in exchange rates also reflect underlying economic conditions. The prospect of a recession in the United States will decrease the demand for the U.S. currency and lead to a depreciation of the dollar. Since airline travel is cyclical, anticipated future revenue from both domestic and international travel is likely to decline with a prospective recession. While this decline is unlikely to be reflected in current revenues, it should be reflected in the stock price. Finally, the exchange rate could also have an indirect effect on energy prices. When the dollar depreciates, U.S. energy prices have to rise in order to maintain parity with world prices. If the industry cannot offset the cost increases with higher prices, anticipated future profitability will be adversely effected.

I intend to explore this issue by returning to the analysis of stock returns. Consider the regression equation:

$$R_{AMR} = B0 + B1\, R_{SP} + B2\, R_{CR} + B3\, R_{DM} + U, \qquad (10.1)$$

where R_{AMR} is the rate of return on AMR, and R_{SP}, R_{CR}, and R_{DM} are the rates of return on the S&P500, Crude Oil Futures, and the DM, respectively. The regression coefficients can be interpreted as hedge ratios. For example, if $B3$ is estimated to be .2, then the influence of this risk factor on AMR returns could be eliminated by taking a short position in DMs equal to 20 percent of the dollar value of AMR equity. If foreign currency appreciation benefits AMR, then the $B3$ coefficient should be positive. In essence, the regression approach relies on the foresight of market professionals to discount any changes in the present discounted cash flow of the corporation.

Equation (10.1) was estimated using monthly data over the period from January 1985 to December 1991. The following results were obtained:

$$R_{AMR} = -.0059 + 1.2389\, R_{SP} - 0.1469\, R_{CR} - 0.2077\, R_{DM} + U$$
$$\phantom{R_{AMR} =} (0.0086) \quad (0.1572) \quad\;\; (0.0775) \quad\;\; (0.2232) \tag{10.2}$$

$$\text{R–SQ} = .50 \quad \text{S.D.} = .07 \quad F(3,80) = 26.73 \quad N = 84$$
(Standard Deviations in parentheses beneath the coefficients)

As expected, the S&P500 and crude oil are significant determinants of the return on American Airlines equity. For the currency component, we concentrate on the DM because over 75 percent of AMR non-North American revenues are from Europe. The estimated exposure to the DM is equal to approximately 20 percent of the value of AMR equity. Based upon an estimated market value of $5 billion at the end of 1991, this exposure could be hedged by swapping a $1 billion dollar denominated loan into a DM-denominated asset. It is also important to note that the regression suggests that the market perceives that AMR is hurt by a depreciation of the dollar. It should be noted that the coefficient is only one standard deviation from zero and consequently does not pass conventional tests of statistical significance.

In part, the lack of statistical significance may reflect the fact that market analysts do not immediately discount exchange rate changes into the price of AMR equity. In order to explore this possibility, a lagged value of the return on the DM was added to the regression. (Preliminary data analysis demonstrated that market and energy factors were incorporated immediately). The extended model produced the following results.

$$R_{AMR} = -0.0039 + 1.2362\, R_{SP} - 0.1529\, R_{CR} - 0.2269\, R_{DM} - 0.2361\, R_{DM}(-1) + U$$
$$\phantom{R_{AMR} =} (0.0088) \quad (0.1570) \quad\;\; (0.0776) \quad\;\; (0.2237) \quad\;\; (0.2217) \tag{10.3}$$

$$\text{R–SQ} = 0.50 \quad \text{S.D.} = 0.074 \quad F(4,79) = 20.36 \quad N = 83$$
(Standard Errors in Parentheses beneath the Coefficients)

Once again, the two currency exposure coefficients are not statistically significant. However, the combined values total approximately 45 percent of AMR equity. Using these estimates, the required hedge is a $2,250 billion swap.

Our final attempt to estimate the exposure of AMR relies on the natural logarithms of the levels of the prices. In order to reduce the serial correlation in the residuals of this regression, the Cochran-Orcutt transformation was employed.

$$L_{AMR} = -3.5396 + 0.9829 \, L_{SP} - 0.1793 \, L_{CR} - 0.7753 \, L_{DM} + U$$
$$\quad\quad\quad (0.9471) \quad (0.1107) \quad (0.0716) \quad\quad (0.1617) \quad\quad\quad\quad (10.4)$$

$$R\text{–}SQ = 0.53 \quad S.D. = 0.076 \quad F(3,79) = 175$$
$$RHO = 0.72 \quad D.W. = 1.81$$
(Standard Errors in Parentheses)

In this case, the exposure to the mark is estimated to be 77 percent of the market value of AMR and the hedge ratio does pass standard tests of statistical significance. This suggests that the airline does face a significant exposure to currency risk but that the timing of the effect is not coincident. Since AMR does have the ability to hedge foreign exchange exposures, it could be that analysts wait for the quarterly earnings estimates before revising their projections of future earnings growth. While the relationship may not be coincidental, the analysis does suggest that AMR exposure to foreign currencies is of the same order of magnitude as its exposure to the general stock market and is of considerably greater importance than its exposure to energy prices. This exposure could currently be hedged by borrowing $3.85 billion in the United States and investing the funds in Deutsche Mark denominated assets. It is important to note that this strategy assumes that AMR is hurt by dollar depreciation even though the corporation is net long foreign currencies on a transactional basis.

To guage the importance of the DM exposure of AMR, I have related the peak-to-valley performance of AMR equity to the total return on a one-month EuroMark deposit, funded by a one-month Eurodollar borrowing.

Period	Return on AMR	Return on DM Deposit
12/84 – 7/87	76%	55%
7/87 –11/87	–53%	12%
11/87 – 8/89	188%	–22%
8/89 – 9/90	–51%	24%
9/90 – 5/91	56%	–7%
5/91 –12/91	7%	15%

The relative performance of the two investments is graphically presented in Figure 10–1. In the first period, from December 1984 to July 1987, the two investments were positively correlated. It is important to note that during this period, the business exposure of AMR to European currency rates was relatively minimal. Before 1987, AMR's European routes linked New York with London and Frankfurt. New York/Tokyo and New York/Geneva/Zurich were added in 1987. In 1987, European routes accounted for only 7 percent of system traffic. It is consequently not entirely unexpected to find a lack of correlation between AMR returns and the DM in the period prior to 1987.

The picture changes dramatically with the rapid growth in AMR's crossatlantic presence after 1987. During the market collapse of 1987, the 53 percent decline in the value of AMR equity was partially offset by a 12 percent increase in the value of the DM deposit. During the 1987–89 recovery in the American market, AMR rose by 188 percent and the associated strength in the dollar caused a 22 percent decline in the value of a DM deposit. A similar pattern of negative correlation emerges in the 1989 mini-crash and the 1990–91 recovery.

These estimates suggest a far higher hedge ratio in the 1987–91 period. A time weighted estimate of the delta from the above figures suggest that the hedge ratio should be around 4.40. In other words, the DM investment, funded by U.S. dollar borrowing, should be equal to 4.40 times the market value of AMR. Combining this hedge with an investment in AMR would have resulted in a considerable reduction in the volatility of AMR returns.

Period	AMR	DM	Combined
7/87 –11/87	–53%	+53%	0%
11/87 – 8/89	+188%	–97%	+91%
8/89 – 9/90	–51%	+105%	+56%
9/90 – 5/91	+56%	–30%	+26%
5/91 –12/91	+7%	+66%	+73%
Average	29%	+19%	+48%
Std. Dev.	93%	+72%	+28%

FIGURE 10–1
DM Hedge—Value of $1,000 Initial Investment

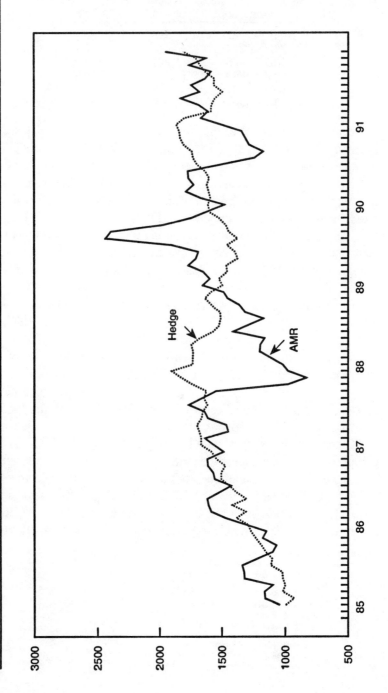

The 4.4 hedge ratio offers an extreme example of the ability of mark deposits to diversify the investment risks of AMR equity. However, such an extreme strategy embodies the risk that the historical correlation between the returns could break down and that losses on both the stock and the currency could occur at the sime time. In practical terms, it is always prudent to assume that the future hedge ratios are less than the historical. This approach may be justified in terms of Bayesian procedures with the prior assumption that the true hedge ratio is zero. In any case, these results do demonstrate that a DM hedge would have had a dramatic influence on the volatility of AMR equity holdings during the period under study.

For an American investor in AMR, this analysis suggests that each $100 investment in the stock should be supplemented by borrowing $440 in dollars and investing the proceeds from the borrowing in DMs. While this recommendation may appear to be extreme from a U.S. perspective, it would probably appear less so from the perspective of either a European or a Japanese corporation. Because of the multicurrency environment in Europe, foreign exchange activities play a major role in the treasury activities of most large European corporations. A similar situation exists in Japan because of the export orientation of the manufacturing sector. In all of the discussion of the decline in U.S. competitiveness in the 1980s, the importance of trading in currencies has not been sufficiently stressed. Many Japanese exporters to the United States were able to maintain their U.S. markets despite the appreciation of the yen because they had already locked in favourable exchange rates.

In the next section, I shall supplement the basic hedge strategy with a discretionary component. As stated above, the risk of the hedge strategy is that a real, negative shock in Europe—the collapse of the CIS, Eastern Europe, Eastern Germany, France, England, Italy, and so on—could cause a depreciation of the mark and a decline in crossatlantic travel. While historically these events have been associated with an appreciation of the U.S. market as a safe haven, there can be no presumption that this correlation will continue into the future. It is consequently necessary to modify the hedge model with a discretionary portfolio which should benefit from sustained currency movements.

MODELS OF DISCRETIONARY CURRENCY TRADING

Discretionary trading models may be considered as a combination of a forecasting methodology and an asset allocation methodology. The forecasting methodology posits a relationship between a set of indicator variables and the rate of return on the asset. The output from this process is a vector of expected returns and an estimate of the covariance matrix of returns. The asset allocation methodology uses this information to determine a set of positions in each instrument which maximizes an objective function.

The indicator variables may be divided into three classes: value, yield, and trend. Most models attempt to buy undervalued, high-yielding and up-ward-trending currencies, while selling overvalued, low-yielding and down-ward-trending currencies. Value investing in the stock market typically concentrates on the fundamental value of the underlying revenue flows relative to the purchase price. In the currency markets, value most often refers to the value of the exchange rate relative to its purchasing power. Numerous studies have demonstrated that exchange rates have diverged widely from purchasing power parities during the floating rate period and that these divergences have subsequently been corrected in part through stabilizing movements in exchange rates. In Bilson (1984), I demonstrated that deviations from purchasing power parity could be used to forecast the returns on foreign currency forward contracts. However, in order for PPP deviations to have a significant influence on expected returns, the deviations must be very large (i.e., over- or undervaluations in the 40 percent range) and that a trading program based upon PPP could be subject to large negative equity swings before the corrective process asserted itself. At present, the major currencies do not appear to be greatly over- or undervalued relative to their purchasing power. For this reason, we will ignore value-based trading models in this presentation.

Figure 10–2 plots the one-month Eurocurrency deposit rates for the major currencies. The floating rate period has witnessed some extreme movements in interest rate differentials. In the early literature, these interest rate differentials were considered to reflect the market's anticipated rate of depreciation of the exchange rate. Thus a high-yielding currency was expected to depreciate against a low-yielding currency. If this view of the market is correct, and if market expectations are rational, then interest rate differentials should represent an unbiased forecast of the subsequently observed actual rate of depreciation. Numerous tests of this hypothesis have been undertaken in the 1980s. [See Hodrick (1987) for an excellent review.] All of the statistical studies have found that, at best, the subsequent rate of appreciation of the exchange rate is unrelated to the interest rate differential or, at worst, high-yielding currencies tend to appreciate against low-yielding currencies.

These findings have given rise to a small industry which engages in

FIGURE 10–2
Short-Term Interest Rates

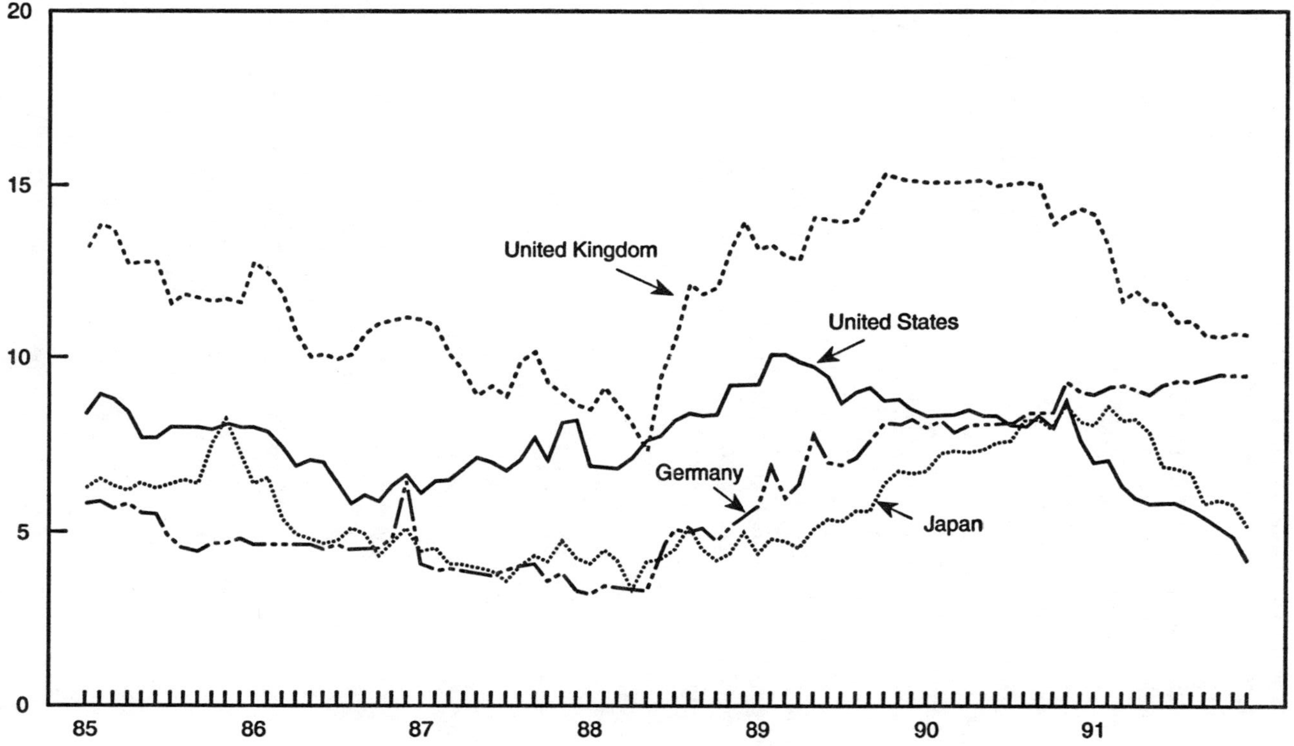

currency speculation based upon interest rate differentials. Under the assumption that the change in the exchange rate is random, the interest rate differential becomes a forecast of the expected return on a forward contract. Using estimates of the correlations between currencies, the financial programs create portfolios of positions which maximize the expected return for a given level of risk. I shall develop a variant of this type of program below.

The third indicator variable that we shall use to forecast currency returns is trend. The question of whether exchange rates trend is one of the more controversial topics in modern international finance. On the one hand, traditional econometric methods based on regression methodology fail to find any predictable pattern of autocorrelation in monthly changes in exchange rates. On the other hand, studies using filter rules [Levich and Thomas (1990), Alexander (1961), and Sweeney (1988)] have found that simple rules generate predictable profits from foreign exchange speculation.

In two previous papers [Bilson (1990, 1992)] I have proposed a resolution to this conflict based on a nonlinear autoregressive model. This model begins by specifying that the trend in the exchange rate is equal to the rate of appreciation or depreciation over the past three months. We begin by regressing the ex-post return on a forward contract in this measure of trend. The equations were estimated over the period from April 1975 to April 1991.

$$\text{BP} \quad \text{Return} = .0012 + .0352 \times \text{Trend} + u$$
$$\qquad\qquad\quad (0.49)\quad (0.86)$$

$$R^2 = .003 \quad \text{S.E.} = .035 \quad N = 192$$

$$\text{DM} \quad \text{Return} = -.0007 + .0384 \times \text{Trend} + u$$
$$\qquad\qquad\quad (0.29)\quad (0.91)$$

$$R^2 = .004 \quad \text{S.E.} = .035 \quad N = 192$$

$$\text{JY} \quad \text{Return} = .0013 + .0521 \times \text{Trend} + u$$
$$\qquad\qquad\quad (0.51)\quad (1.29)$$

$$R^2 = .008 \quad \text{S.E.} = .036 \quad N = 192$$

(T-Statistics in parentheses beneath the coefficients)

The dismal R^2 and T-statistics from these regressions would certainly lead a regression analyst to the conclusion that exchange rates evolve as a random walk.

The problem with the regression analysis is that it posits a linear relationship between the past trend and the future expected return. This is very different from the implicit predicted returns from the filter rule models. The filter rules generate buy/sell signals as a function of trend. They consequently imply that the expected return generating function is a step function. When the market is trending up, the system generates a buy signal. The strength of the buy signal is not influenced by the size of the trend.

In order to understand the importance of the nonlinearity, we begin by dividing the trend into standard deviation blocks. The regressions above indicate that the monthly standard deviation of the return is approximately 3.5 percent. The standard deviation of the three-month change is consequently approximately 6 per cent [3.5 × sqrt(3)]. We define the standardized trend as the actual trend divided by the standard deviation. In the next step, we create dummy variables for blocks centering on .5, 1, 1.5, and 2 standard deviations and examine the average ex-post return for each block. The system of equations was estimated using Zellner's seeming unrelated regression technique with the coefficients constrained to be the same for each currency. The estimation period was April 1975 to April 1991. The following estimates were obtained.

TREND (T)	Coefficient	T-Statistic
−2.0	1.16	1.62
−1.5	−0.31	0.64
−1.0	−0.69	1.80
−0.5	−0.80	2.50
0	−0.14	0.42
+0.5	+0.97	3.08
+1.0	+0.81	2.19
+1.5	+0.95	2.07
+2.0	−0.26	0.52

Notes: −2.0: T<−1.75
$\quad\quad$ −1.5: −1.75<T<−1.25
$\quad\quad$ −1.0: −1.25<T<−0.75
$\quad\quad$ −0.5: −0.75<T<−0.25
$\quad\quad\quad$ 0: −0.25<T<+0.25
$\quad\quad$ +0.5: +0.25<T<+0.75
$\quad\quad$ +1.0: +0.75<T<+1.25
$\quad\quad$ +1.5: +1.25<T<+1.75
$\quad\quad$ +2.0: +1.75<T

The estimated coefficients are plotted in Figure 10–3. It is clear from these results that there is a clear pattern of positive autocorrelation in the .5 to 1.5 standard deviation range on both the positive and negative side. On the other hand, the extreme observations (those greater than 1.75 standard deviations in absolute value) tend to be negatively correlated with subsequent returns. Since the regression models minimize the sum of squared residuals, these extreme observations have a large influence on the determination of the slope of the regression line. For this reason, the linear regression fails to find the positive serial correlation in the normal trend range.

These results can be used to formulate a simple filter rule regression model. Let Z1 equal 1 when the trend is between +.25 and +.75 standard deviations and let Z1 = –1 when the trend is between –.25 and –1.75 standard deviations. We next add an over-bought/sold overlay. Let Z2 = +1 when the trend is greater than 1.75 and –1 when the trend is less than –1.75. Estimation of this model provides the following results.

$$\text{Return} = .0976 + 0.8156 \, Z1 - .5427 \, Z2$$
$$(0.45) \quad (5.54) \qquad (1.36) \qquad\qquad (10.5)$$

(T-Statistics in parentheses)

These results clearly indicate the presence of trends in foreign exchange rates. They support the idea that the reason why linear autoregressive models have failed to find autocorrelation is the linearity of the functional form.

While the dummy variable approach is a useful technique for resolving the conflict between regression and filter rule studies of the foreign exchange market, it is an imperfect foundation for the development of a trading strategy. Buy/sell systems have the feature that they require large discrete changes in position based upon small changes in price. Large losses can be incurred as the price moves back and forth over the swing price. We therefore restate the previous results in the form of a continuous trend following model.

Our final forecasting equation has the following form:

$$\text{Return} = b1 \times X1 + b2 \times X2 + b3 \times X3 + u \qquad (10.6)$$

where:

$$\text{Return} = [S(t+1) - F(t)] / F(t),$$

FIGURE 10–3
Trends and Currency Returns

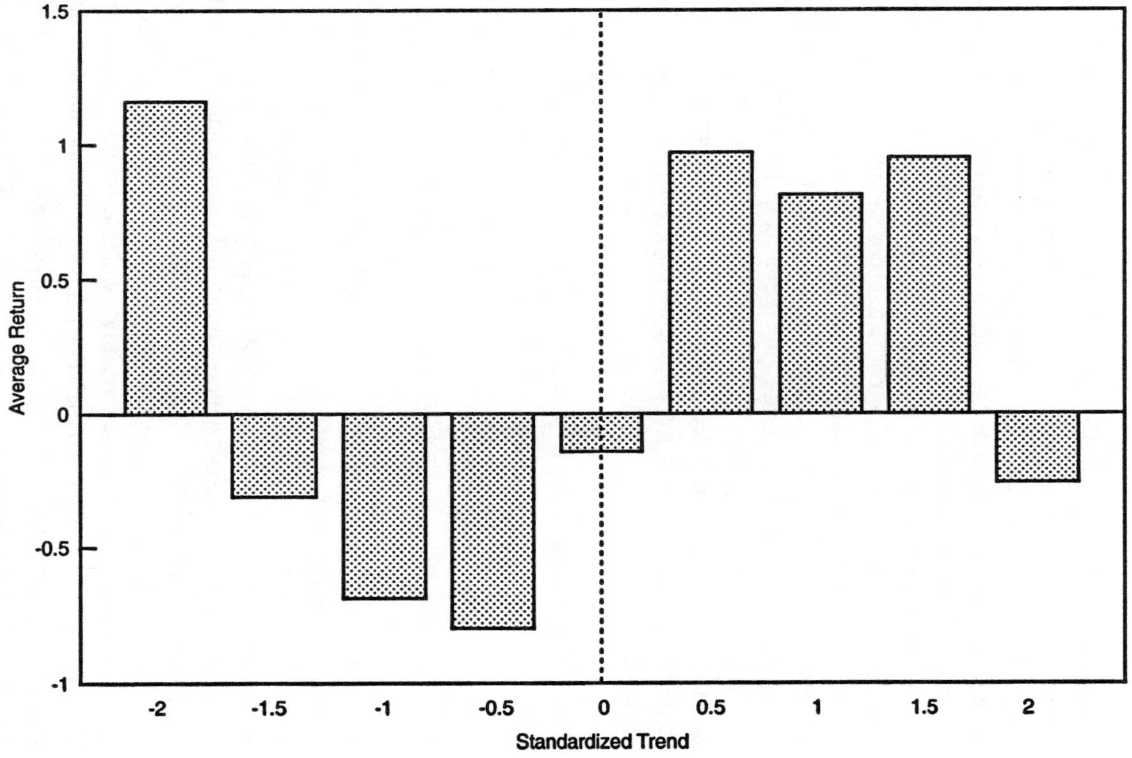

$X1 = [F(t) - S(t)] / S(t)$, the yield indicator,
$X2 = [F(t) - F(t-3)] / F(t-3)$, the trend indicator, and
$X3 = X2 \exp[-abs(X2) / std(x2)]$.

The third variable, which we shall refer to as the 'discounted' trend, accounts for the nonlinear pattern of serial correlation by discounting large trend values. As we shall see below, incorporating the discounted trend allows the model to capture the pattern of nonlinearity described in the dummy variable regressions.

There is always a concern that a regression model will over-fit the sample data and fail to provide consistent postsample forecasts. We therefore restrict the estimation sample to the period from April 1975 to December 1984. We will then examine the out-of-sample performance of the model over the time period used in the previous section of the chapter.

As in the dummy variable regression, the model was estimated by Zellner's seemingly unrelated regression procedure with the coefficients restricted to be the same for each currency. The following results were obtained.

$$\text{Return} = -1.1606 \times X1 - 0.1278 \times X2 + 0.6999 \times X3 + u \qquad (10.7)$$
$$\phantom{\text{Return} = } (2.84) \qquad\quad (2.56) \qquad\quad (4.44)$$

(T-Statistics in parentheses)

All of the coefficients are statistically significant at the 1 per cent level. The coefficient on the interest rate differential is not significantly different from unity. The shape of the trend-following component of the model is plotted in Figure 10–4 along with the results of the dummy variable model. It is clear from this Figure that the continuous function does an adequate job of capturing the pattern of serial correlation in the data.

We now have the first component of the discretionary trading strategy. The forecasting equation uses readily available information to predict an expected return on each currency in each period. In addition, the estimation procedure provides an estimate of the covariance matrix of the residuals, which is assumed to be constant through time, and which is also estimated over the April 1975 to December 1984 period. The assumption that the covariance matrix is static is extreme, and much recent work has been done on estimating dynamic models of volatility and correlation [See Hsieh

FIGURE 10–4
Nonlinear Trend Following

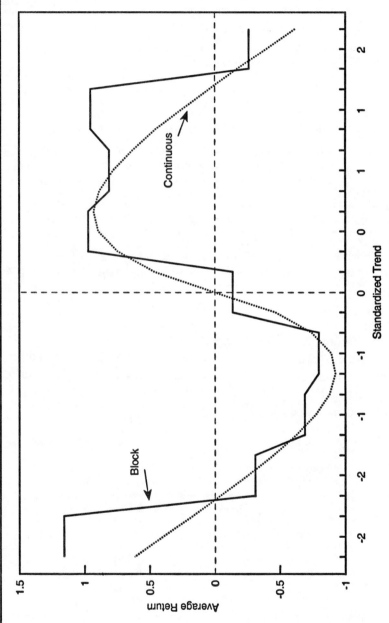

(1992), for example]. While it is unrealistic to assume that a practitioner would not update estimates of the coefficients and covariance matrix, this assumption does provide a strong postsample test of the model.

In the next step, we use the output from the forecasting model to create a mean-variance optimal portfolio of positions. The investor's objective function is assumed to be of the form:

$$E(U) = q' \, E(y) - (\tfrac{1}{2}g) \, q'Vq \,, \tag{10.8}$$

where q is an $(n \times 1)$ vector whose typical element is the dollar value of the position taken in a particular currency, V is the $(n \times n)$ covariance matrix of forecast errors, $E(y)$ is an $(n \times 1)$ vector of expected returns, and g is a scaler representing the investor's degree of risk aversion. Setting g equal to 10 percent of the investor's capital results in a risk return tradeoff which is similar to that of the S&P 500. $q'E(y)$ is the expected profit on the position, and $q'Vq$ is the anticipated variance of profit.

Maximizing $E(U)$ with respect to q, and setting the resulting first-order conditions equal to zero, leads to the following expression for the positions:

$$q = g \; VI \, E(y), \tag{10.9}$$

where VI represents the inverse of the covariance matrix.

In the following analysis, we estimate the position vectors for the three major currencies against the U.S. dollar and then evaluate the performance of the simulated currency strategy. We will begin by evaluating the absolute performance of the strategy and then consider its contribution to the AMR hedge model.

The annual returns in the postsample period are calculated to be:

Year	Return
1985	28.37%
1986	-2.52%
1987	22.15%
1988	26.77%
1989	12.88%
1990	54.68%
1991	-7.04%

In evaluating these returns, it is important to remember that a forward contract is not an investment requiring the placement of capital. Consequently, the returns are scaled by an arbitrary risk aversion factor. A corporation implementing this strategy in a independent profit center would typically be required to place between 10 percent and 25 percent of the face value of the positions as good faith, or margin, deposit. Hence the return on margin could be 4 to 10 times the returns reported above.

The mean-variance model predicts that the standard deviation of the return from the strategy is equal to:

$$STD= SQRT[g\ E(y)]. \qquad (10.10)$$

This result can be used to test whether the postsample results are significantly different from (a) the expected results and (b) zero. For the entire monthly sample, the mean return is .74 standard deviations below the expected return, a result that could be attributed to sampling variation. The mean return is 3.74 standard deviations from zero, which suggests that it is highly unlikely that the postsample profitability was due to chance.

We also calculate the t-statistics on an annual basis:

Year	From Expected	From Zero
1985	0.85	2.07
1986	−1.81	−0.20
1987	0.39	1.75
1988	−0.05	1.53
1989	−0.84	0.71
1990	0.89	2.60
1991	−0.80	0.71
Mean	−0.26	1.31
Std.Dev.	0.35	0.35
t-Statistic	−0.74	3.74

These statistics also suggest that the departures from the expected returns are due to sampling variation, while the mean of the "from zero" series is significantly different from zero.

DISCRETIONARY TRADING AND AMR EXPOSURE MANAGEMENT

In this section, I will combine the hedge program with the discretionary trading approach. While a totally risk-averse investor might not be interested in the discretionary program, I would argue that a totally risk-averse investor would not be interested in holding AMR equity. We shall see that the discretionary approach adds value to the strategy by increasing the average return on the currency position and by preventing large losses on the passive hedge portfolio. The hedge analysis demonstrated that a hedge of AMR's economic exposure would require a substantial swap of dollars into Deutsche Marks. The risk of this strategy is that the mark would depreciate strongly against the dollar. Historically, a depreciating mark has been associated with unfavorable mark-dollar interest rate differentials and a prior downward trend in the mark. If the discretionary trading model is correct, then it can be used to hedge the hedge position against strongly adverse movements. The discretionary program may be considered as an alternative version of the hedge program. Instead of implementing a static hedge, the corporation could use the discretionary program to dynamically hedge its exposure. Which approach is of the most value is the topic of this section.

We begin by examining the annual returns on the two strategies relative to the performance of AMR equity.

Year	AMR Equity	Dynamic Trading Rule	Static Hedge	Minimum Variance Portfolio
1985	+10%	+30%	+24%	+54%
1986	+26%	–3%	+22%	+49%
1987	–46%	+24%	+18%	–12%
1988	+45%	+28%	–15%	+45%
1989	0%	+12%	+1%	+8%
1990	–21%	+69%	+13%	+33%
1991	+39%	–8%	–2%	33%
Average	+7%	+22%	+9%	30%
Std.Dev.	33%	+26%	+14%	24%

These results demonstrate the benefits of currency hedging for an investor in AMR. Both the trading and hedge strategies were profitable in the down markets of 1987 and 1990. In the 1988 rally in the dollar, the trading strategy effectively offset the loss on the hedge strategy.

In the final column, we compute the returns on a minimum variance portfolio of the three returns. Since forward contracts do not require the placement of capital except for margin purposes, we assume that the implementation of the currency strategies does not require capital to be taken away from the capital of AMR. Thus the combined return is assumed to be equal to:

$$R(\text{Total}) = R(\text{AMR}) + w1 \times R(\text{Trade}) + w2 \times R(\text{Hedge})$$

The minimum variance values of the weights are $w1 = .57$ for the trading strategy and $w2 = 1.10\%$ for the hedging strategy. Based upon the current market value of AMR of approximately \$5 billion, these values suggest a nominal investment of \$2.85 billion in the trading strategy and \$5.5 billion in the hedge strategy. With a 10 percent margin assumption, the actual capital requirement for these positions would be approximately \$835 million dollars. The "return" on this investment during the sample period would have been an increase in the average annual return from 8 percent to 30 percent and a reduction in the annual standard deviation from 33 percent to 24 percent.

The relative performance of the strategies is plotted in Figure 10–5. In reviewing this chart, it is also useful to compare the performance during the main cycles in AMR returns.

Period	AMR	Trade	Hedge	Min. Var.
12/84 – 7/87	76%	50%	55%	181%
7/87 –11/87	–53%	0%	12%	–41%
11/87 – 8/89	188%	48%	–23%	213%
8/89 – 9/90	–51%	50%	24%	23%
9/90 – 5/91	56%	7%	–7%	56%
5/91 –12/91	7%	–3%	15%	19%

While the currency strategy was unable to prevent a substantial loss during the 1987 crash, the return in the preceding period from the strategy was over twice the return on the underlying stock.

Up to this point, we have been primarily concerned with the relationship between equity and currency returns. We now turn to the cash flow implications of the hedge strategy. In each period, we calculate the market value of AMR as the product of the beginning of period stock price and the total common shares outstanding. We scale the trading program at 57 percent of this value and the hedge program at 110 percent. We then calculate the profit or loss on the programs and compare these with the change in the market value of AMR and the total earnings of the corporation, which we calculate as the product of the end of period earnings per share and the end of period total common shares outstanding.

FIGURE 10–5
Currency Hedging Strategy—Value of $1,000 Initial Investment

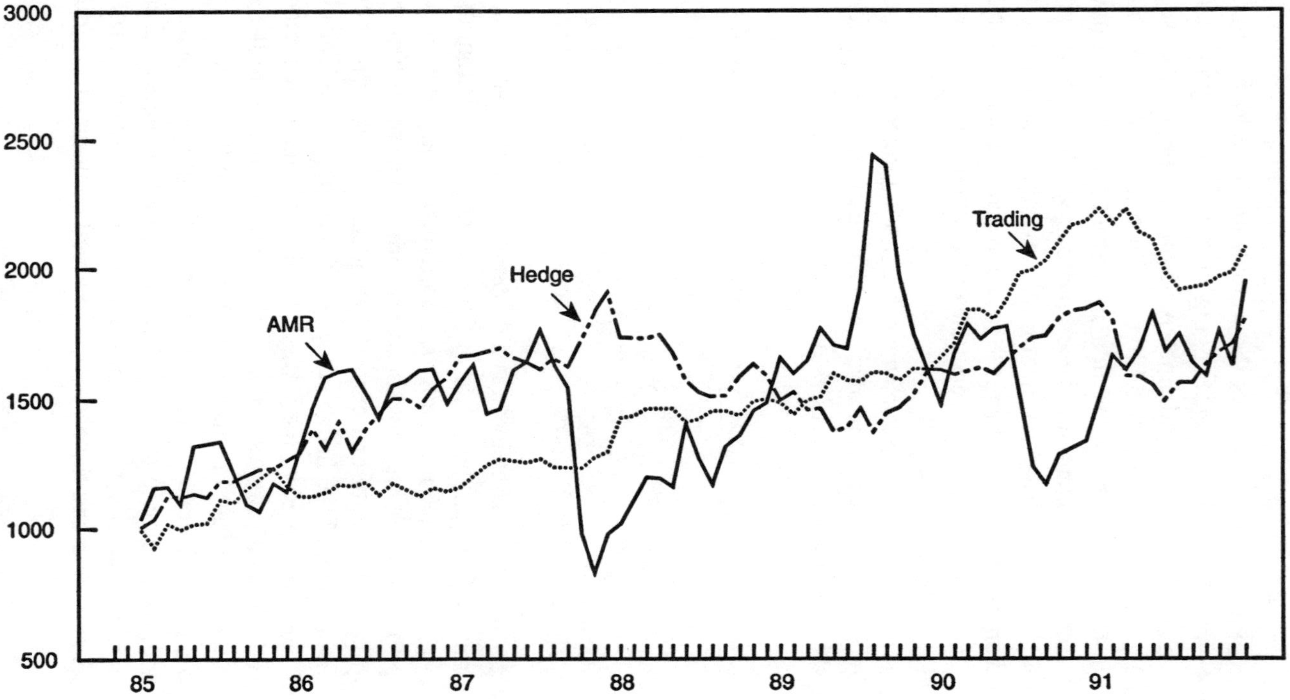

Year	AMR	Trade	Hedge	Earnings
1985	677	343	639	348
1986	721	-22	730	271
1987	-1076	342	499	192
1988	1081	361	-400	465
1989	454	267	218	445
1990	-595	1080	473	-39
1991	1802	-200	-24	-241
Average	437	310	305	205
Std.Dev.	980	402	402	260

(All figures are $ million)

Using the minimum variance weights, the cash flows from the currency strategies are, on average, three times the size of conventional earnings and larger, in aggregate, than the average change in market value. The only year in which the currency strategy had serious cash flow implication was in 1991, when total losses of $224 million exacerbated losses from conventional earnings. However, AMR market value did increase by $1,802 million in 1991. Overall, the hedge strategy was successful in generating revenue when the market value of AMR declined.

These estimates are in-sample in the sense that the hedge ratios were estimated from contemporaneous data. (However, the parameters of the trading strategy were estimated from prior data.) The lag between the initial presentation of these results in May 1992 and their final publication does permit a true postsample evaluation of the strategy. The period from January 1992 to September 1992 provides a solid test of the strategy because of the sharp movement in the dollar–DM exchange rate during this period. The mark appreciated against the dollar by 13 percent from the end of December 1991 to the end of August 1992. During the same period, the price of AMR equity fell by 21 percent from $70.5 to $55.5. The decline in AMR equity was attributed to the continuing sluggishness of the U.S. economy and to fare wars both domestically and internationally. In October 1992, AMR announced that it was laying off 500 to 1,000 midlevel managers in an effort to reduce costs by $300 million. Chairman Robert Crandall commented "A decision to lay off employees is both difficult and painful. We are loath to take this step. However, our actions reflect the dismal financial condition of the entire airline industry and the absolute need to find a better match between costs and revenues." (*Wall Street Journal,* October 16, 1992) AMR also intends to reduce capital spending through 1995 by $8 billion by deferring orders and options for new jets. AMR lost $48 million in the second quarter of 1992 and is expected to post a larger loss in the third quarter.

If the approach taken in this chapter is correct, these problems could have been avoided by the adoption of an appropriate hedging strategy. To illustrate the point, I have mechanically extrapolated the trading and hedge models for the first nine months of 1992. I will first present the returns on AMR relative to the returns on the two strategies.

Date	AMR	Trade	Hedge
Jan	0.35%	0.08%	–1.17%
Feb	7.96%	2.81%	0.19%
Mar	–3.44%	4.68%	0.17%
Apr	–9.99%	2.72%	2.87%
May	–4.72%	4.58%	6.05%
Jun	2.18%	–3.10%	3.85%
Jul	2.32%	–2.16%	5.62%
Aug	–16.07%	17.61%	–0.14%
Sep	2.93%	–0.78%	–3.98%

Somewhat surprisingly, the discretionary trading strategy actually provides a higher degree of negative covariance with the AMR returns during this period. Of the four months in which AMR returns were negative, the trading strategy generated positive returns with a similar order of magnitude. In particular, the 16 percent loss in August was offset with a 17 percent gain from the trading strategy, while the hedge position did not provide any offset.

We now consider the minimum variance weighting defined above. The currency return is defined as 57 percent of the trading return and 110 percent of the hedge return. The combined return is equal to the return on AMR plus the return on the currency program.

Date	AMR	Currency	Combined
Jan	0.35%	–1.23%	–0.88%
Feb	7.96%	1.81%	9.77%
Mar	–3.44%	2.86%	–0.58%
Apr	–9.99%	4.71%	–5.28%
May	–4.72%	9.27%	4.55%
Jun	2.18%	2.47%	4.65%
Jul	2.32%	4.95%	7.27%
Aug	–16.07%	9.88%	–6.19%
Sep	2.93%	–4.82%	–1.89%
Average	–2.05%	3.32%	1.27%
Std.Dev.	7.39%	4.65%	5.56%

On average, an investor in AMR lost 2 percent per month in the first six months of 1992. The returns were also fairly volatile. The monthly standard deviation of 7.39 percent translates into an annualized standard deviation of approximately 25 percent per annum. Currently, the implied volatility on AMR is trading around 30 percent. The addition of the currency trade increased the average monthly return from –2.05 percent to +1.27 percent and reduced the standard deviation from 7.39 percent to 5.56 percent.

In Figure 10–6, the value of an initial $1,000 investment in AMR and the currency program are plotted. Over the period from the end of December to the end of September, $1,000 invested in AMR would have declined to $810, a loss of 19 percent. Over the same period, $1,000 invested in the currency program would have increased to $1,331, an appreciation of 33 percent. The combined return would have increased by 10 percent over this period. In terms of dollar magnitude, a $5 billion dollar allocation to the currency program would have returned $1,650 million dollars over the period. This sum would have been sufficient to compensate AMR investors for their loss of market value and would have been approximately 10 times as large as the losses from conventional operations.

In the quote given above, Mr. Crandall speaks of the absolute necessity of acheiving a better balance between costs and revenues. The point of this

FIGURE 10–6
Postsample Performance Review—Value of $1,000 Initial Investment

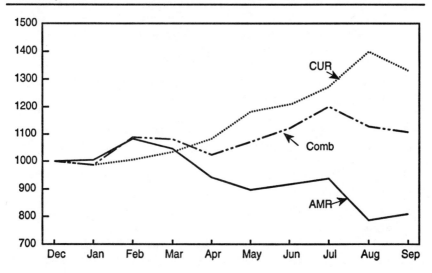

chapter is to suggest that this balance is strongly effected by developments in the foreign exchange market. If the corporation had effectively managed its external risk factors, then it would not have had to revise its operations to bring costs and revenues into balance. Instead, revenue from hedging activity would have permitted the airline to expand operationally and to reduce debt at a time when its competitors were experiencing difficult conditions. While some would suggest that the strategy discussed here is best left to the investor, rather than the corporate treasurer, this suggestion does not provide much benefit to the 500 to 1,000 managers who are destined to lose their jobs because of the corporations neglect of risk management.

REFERENCES

AMR Corporation. (1990). "Foreign Exchange Exposure." September.

Alexander, S. (1961). "Price Movements in Speculative Markets: Trends or Random Walks?" *Industrial Management Review*. 2, pp. 7–26.

Adler, M., and D. Simon. (1986). "Exchange Risk Surprises in International Portfolios." *Journal of Portfolio Management*. 4, pp. 44–53.

Bilson, J. (1981). "The 'Speculative Efficiency' Hypothesis." *Journal of Business*. 54, pp. 435–52.

Bilson, J. (1984). "Purchasing Power Parity as a Trading Strategy." *Journal of Finance*. July, pp. 715–25.

Bilson, J. (1990). "'Technical' Currency Trading." *The Currency Hedging Debate*. L. Thomas, ed. London: IFR.

Bilson, J. (1992). "Hedging Currency Risk." *Handbook of Global Investing*. S. Levine, ed. New York: Harper Collins.

Dooley, M., and J. Schafer. "Analysis of Short Run Exchange Rate Behavior: March, 1973 - November, 1981."*Exchange Rates and Trade Instability*. D. Bigman and T. Taya, eds. Cambridge: Ballinger.

Hodrick, R. (1987). *The Empirical Evidence on the Efficiency of Forward and Futures Foreign Exchange Markets*. Harwood Academic Publishers.

Hsieh, D. (1992). "The Implications of Nonlinear Dynamics for Financial Risk Management." Duke University monograph. January.

Sweeney, R. (1986). "Beating the Foreign Exchange Market." *Journal of Finance*. 41, pp. 163–82.

Sweeney, R. (1988). "Some New Filter Rule Tests: Methods and Results." *Journal of Financial and Quantitative Analysis*. 23, pp. 285–300.

Taylor, S. (1990). "Profitable Currency Futures Trading: A Comparison of Technical and Time Series Trading Rules." *The Currency Hedging Debate*. L. Thomas, ed. London: IFR. pp. 203–40.

CHAPTER 11

STRATEGIC MANAGEMENT OF FOREIGN EXCHANGE EXPOSURE IN AN INTERNATIONAL FIRM

Marcia B. Whitaker

General Electric (GE) is a global company, with 13 key business operations all over the world, dealing in dozens of currencies. International activities include export sales, international sourcing, manufacturing and sales affiliates abroad, and joint ventures, and other business associations. For some years now, GE managers have been challenged to "think globally" in all aspects of their business, and this mindset permeates our organization.

Management of currency risk goes hand-in-hand with the globalization of today's business environment. GE's philosophy of foreign exchange exposure management is consistent with what we refer to as "Work-Out!"— GE shorthand for empowerment of those closest to the action, and the consequent elimination of layers of staff review and bureaucracy. Thus, at GE, foreign exchange is not a staff responsibility, but an integral part of managing a global business. It is one of a number of external factors that a business must manage.

Businesses are empowered to do it themselves, not only by the company's philosophy, but by the reality of the situation. They are closet to the strategic and tactical decisions which are most relevant to FX exposure management. They must decide such things as how and where to source materials and components; where to locate manufacturing facilities, and how to manage their working capital. Treasury's job is to work with the businesses as they go through their analysis and come up with a comprehensive currency management plan, but the business itself is responsible for implementation and results.

Our major objectives for foreign exchange management are earnings and cash flow. The strength of our balance sheet and the relatively small size of GE's exposed assets give us the luxury of placing less emphasis on our Cumulative Translation Account. The CTA has ranged from $133 million to $417 million in the last five years, and has represented, at most, less than 2 percent of shareowners' equity. Since almost all of our affiliates use their local currency as their functional currency, very little balance sheet exposure actually affects earnings.

Ultimately, we must deliver earnings in dollars to our shareholders. As such, the businesses are responsible for dollar net income, and therefore for management of their income-related currency exposures. The objective is to neutralize exposure, not to take views on the markets. Hedging is encouraged, as a short-term tactical solution, to stabilize near-term net income. It is not seen as a substitute for a long-term, strategic mindset. Nor is it seen as a profit center, either within the business or in treasury.

The exposure management techniques we use reflect our business objectives, and really fall out of the analysis of particular exposure situations. I would like to take you through the analysis of several such situations which we have looked at recently, to give you an idea of our issues, solutions and outcomes.

MAJOR APPLIANCES' GLOBAL FOCUS

Our major appliance (white goods) business had a mainly domestic focus for many years. In the mid-1980s, appliances decided to enter the North American gas range business through a Mexican joint venture with a local partner. They built a plant in Mexico to serve both the export market and eventually, what they foresaw (correctly, as it turns out) as a growing Mexican market for modern domestic appliances. Their initial foreign exchange concern was a 1982-style devaluation and de facto confiscation of dollar-denominated financial assets. The solution had two principal elements: one was an offshore sales company, to minimize locally-held dollar assets to the extent possible, the other was careful management of working capital and cash flow exposure to maintain a balanced position. These are classic strategies in devaluation-prone currencies where hedging instruments are either unavailable or prohibitively expensive.

The strategy worked well throughout the 1980s, but within the last two years, the environment has changed. First of all, the local Mexican market for major appliances (including refrigeration and home laundry products, which the joint venture also supplies) has expanded, and GE Appliances is well-positioned to take advantage of the increased local demand. The result, of course, is that we now have more peso assets on the books. Also, financing these assets by borrowing in local currency—a classic hedging technique—remains stubbornly expensive. The business did a lot of homework on the Mexican economic situation and on forecasting cash flows and income statements by currency. Their assessment of the former and their analysis of cash flows and expected returns in the business led them to a greater degree of comfort with an increased level of Mexican asset exposure. The strategy is working well, and appliances is very enthusiastic about the second stage, as it were, of their Mexican investment.

Appliances also began rethinking the currency aspect of their sourcing strategy. The impetus was an acquisition in Japan, which led them to examine possible "natural hedges" stemming from Japanese souring contracts. These contracts had traditionally been denominated in dollars, but are now being renegotiated into yen to take advantage of yen inflows from the acquisition. This also inspired the formation of a cross-functional "Sourcing Currency Team" to look for similar opportunities, including managing currency risk in house rather than having it done (often at a premium) by the vendor through a dollar pricing mechanism.

It is important to note that while treasury and appliances' finance operation worked on setting up the team, most of the ideas and implementation have come from the team members themselves—those people with day-to-day responsibility for purchasing contracts, payables administration. that a corporate staff person in a large, decentralized company can never know as well as those who are actually on the line.

MANAGEMENT OF CROSS-BORDER FLOWS

Our plastics business is a veteran of globalization, having been active in Europe, among other places, for many years. With a large plant in Bergen op Zoom (the Netherlands supplying marketing affiliates all over Europe), the business's currency exposure was centralized at the manufacturing site.

All intercompany sales were denominated in the marketing affiliate's local currency, which was also the currency of third party sales. This system worked well until we acquired Borg Warner's chemical business, which included several European manufacturing sites. To enable multisite centralized administration, a netting system was installed, which has proven very effective, with concomitant benefits in the areas of short-term debt, cash management, and currency exposure forecasting. Other GE European business have joined the netting system as well. I should also mention that, while netting systems do not actually change the composition of affiliate currency exposures, ours has turned out to have at least one hidden benefit for exposure management. By automating the timely payment of intercompany invoices, we have avoided payment delays (or worse) due to independent currency views on the part of local management.

GE Medical Systems inherited an even more complex set of cross-border transactions with its acquisition of the Thomson CGR medical business in 1988. With multiple-site manufacturing, cross-border sourcing, and exports to the Americas and Asia as well as other European countries, joining the netting system was an essential first step. However, even the smaller sales affiliates were left with six or eight European currencies to manage. Also, currency positions were difficult to forecast since product could come from one of a number of different manufacturing sites. The solution here was to denominate all intercompany sales in ECU (the European Currency Unit), which greatly simplified exposure management, operations, and forecasting.

You will have noticed by now that I am describing is remarkably everyday and ordinary tactical foreign exchange management. I have yet to discuss long-term strategic currency issues, and I have not even mentioned any of the exotic currency derivatives which everyone seems to be talking about these days. I have saved them for last because they really don't occupy an important position in GE's currency management operations. It is not that we don't think strategically—we do! But we are not about to take long-term views on where currencies are going. As I mentioned earlier, currency is an element of risk which businesses must deal with along with a whole host of others, such as inflation, political issues, the direction of economies and markets, actions by competitors, and so forth. We assess risk, we plan, we make decisions, we maintain flexibility wherever possible. And we believe that these are good ways to deal with currency risk as well.

Regarding derivatives, our tendency is not to let the tail wag the dog, using exotic instruments when other solutions suffice. Where we have known, relatively short-term exposures, we almost always use forward contracts for coverage. The businesses are, in most cases, reluctant to pay for the privilege of possibly doing a little better on rates via an option, especially when the forward rate gives them a satisfactory margin. Obviously, in bidding or similar situations, where forwards are inappropriate, options would be used for coverage. The businesses also use them occasionally when margins allow—often when the current rate is very favorable *versus* their plan. "Range forward" type strategies are also popular, particularly since no up-front payment is required.

I hope I haven't disappointed you by not discussing leading-edge-of-technology sorts of things. As you can see, foreign exchange exposure management at GE relies more on thorough knowledge of our own exposures, risks, and resources than on exotic new instruments. Many of our most successful outcomes were initiated by ideas from the field—not by grand schemes from corporate staff. And they worked, enabling businesses to compete more effectively in the global arena.

DISCUSSION

COMMENTS ON EXCHANGE RATES AND CORPORATE STRATEGIC MANAGEMENT

Kenneth A. Froot

I want to pick up on a topic that has been discussed by a number of authors in this volume: corporate hedging of exchange rate risks. In doing so, I want to ask—if only rhetorically—why corporations should hedge against exchange rate fluctuations? What are (or ought to be) the goals of such hedging programs? This question comes logically prior to any discussion of hedging performance or implementation, yet we have discussed only the latter topics thus far.

We have seen how companies can estimate a "beta" for their exchange rate exposure, just as they do a beta against the S&P500 (or other market aggregate). All that needs to be done is to regress a company's stock return on the contemporaneous exchange rate change and on other factors. John Bilson did just this in his paper; he regressed the return on American Airline's stock on market returns, oil price changes, and exchange rate movements.

Now the coefficients that result from this type of regression have already been critiqued. We know that the underlying risk exposures are complex and change over time, so that the regression is (at least slightly) misspecified. We know that the coefficients often turn out to be surprisingly small and statistically insignificant. We have debated whether these small coefficients are due to a lack of corporate exchange-rate exposure, the presence of market imperfections and frictions, and/or measurement errors. But in all cases, we have implicitly assumed that these betas could somehow inform us about appropriate hedging strategy. That is, that we could smooth out a firm's stock price with respect to exchange rate changes by undertaking a hedge dictated by the exchange-rate beta.

What I want to argue is that these methods—whether good or bad as measures of exposure—cannot and should not be used to formulate hedging strategies. In particular, the extent to which we allow a firm's stock price to respond to exchange rate changes ought to depend on a very different set of considerations.

To see why betas are useless for designing hedging strategies, let us think further about American Airlines. Like many other firms, AMR has a large and statistically very powerful exposure to the market, and a smaller and weaker exposure to currencies. Surely, if the objective of a hedging strategy is to smooth out the stock price (for shareholders), then American should try to offset its stock's market risk by *shorting* a market aggregate, like the S&P. Given American's high beta, it would need to hold a very large short position to smooth its value in the face of market fluctuations.

Of course, I know of no firm that undertakes such a hedge. And the very idea that companies should go short S&P futures sounds ludicrous. Why, then, do so many practitioners suggest hedging our exchange rate exposures? One answer is that foreign exchange exposures are less observable than are market exposures. This cannot be right. Investors can easily determine how sensitive their portfolios are to exchange rates and undertake adjustments in risk exposures themselves (they do this all the time for S&P exposures).

To answer this question correctly, let us go back to why we think it inappropriate for firms to hedge out their market risks. The reason is presumably that a firm that *did* hedge out its market risks might get into trouble. When the market goes up, business is good and investment spending picks up. Firms spend money on expansion. But just at this point, a hedge position losses money and siphons off cash. Firms don't want to undertake this hedge because it drains cash just when it is needed. Implicitly, firms in these circumstances must find it costly to go to the capital market for funds. This suggests that firms' no-hedging policy on S&P is driven by considerations of state-by-state cash availability. Firms wish to match sources and uses of cash on a contingency basis, and shorting S&P futures would typically interfere with this.[1]

The same logic ought to apply to exchange rate hedging. Hedging should only be undertaken to the extent that it aids (and does not interfere) with companies' attempts to match their sources and uses of cash across different values of the risk variable (i.e., the exchange rate). Since uses of cash—and not just its sources—matter, hedging policy therefore should have little to do with overall exposure as measured by beta. Firms must investigate their exposure in cash flows *and investment opportunities* internally. They should then determine their hedging policy in a way that insures these fluctuate together. There is little point in trying to eliminate all fluctuations in firm value due to price fluctuations. If the economy goes sour or the domestic currency appreciates and raises costs, there may be little a company would do with money from a hedging position, except to return it to shareholders. If hedging cannot raise the value of a firm (by letting it undertake valuable additional investment opportunities), then hedging should not be pursued.

NOTES

1. See Kenneth A. Froot, David Scharfstein, and Jeremy Stein, "Risk Management: Coordinating Corporate Investment and Financing Policies," *Journal of Finance*, December 1993, for an elucidation of this argument.